Across the Wounded Galaxies

Interviews with
Contemporary American
Science Fiction Writers

Across the
Wounded Galaxies

Conducted and Edited by
Larry McCaffery

UNIVERSITY OF ILLINOIS PRESS
Urbana and Chicago

© 1990 by the Board of Trustees of the University of Illinois
Manufactured in the United States of America
C 5 4 3 2 1

This book is printed on acid-free paper.

Library of Congress Cataloging-in-Publication Data

McCaffery, Larry, 1946-
    Across the wounded galaxies : interviews with contemporary
American science fiction writers / conducted and edited by Larry
McCaffery.
        p.   cm.
    Contents: Introduction—Gregory Benford—William S. Burroughs
—Octavia E. Butler—Samuel R. Delany—Thomas M. Disch—
William Gibson—Ursula K. Le Guin—Joanna Russ—Bruce Sterling
—Gene Wolfe.
    ISBN 0-252-01692-0 (cloth : alk. paper)
    1. Science fiction, American—History and criticism. 2. Authors.
American—20th century—Interviews. 3. Science fiction—Authorship.
I. Title.
PS374.S35M39 1990
813'.0876209—dc20
                                                    89-20488
                                                    CIP

—cross the wounded galaxies we intersect, poison of dead sun in your brain slowly fading—Migrants of ape in gasoline crack of history, explosive bio-advance out of space to neon—

—William S. Burroughs, *The Soft Machine*

For all my friends.

And for Sinda.

Contents

Acknowledgments

My thanks first to the authors, for their willingness to talk seriously with me about their works and their lives. Several of these interviews were done in collaboration with Sinda Gregory (my wife and a literature professor at San Diego State University), my friend Jim McMenamin, and cyberpunk scholar extraordinaire Brooks Landon (who teaches literature at the University of Iowa). Thanks to all three for their valuable input. I also received specific and valuable suggestions from John Shirley, Ann Weir, George Slusser, Harriet Speye, Samuel R. Delany, and Neil Barron; Neil also supplied essential bibliographical information and sent me copies of difficult-to-locate books on a moment's notice. Jim McMenamin assisted me by transcribing interviews, handling correspondence, and providing me with occasional beers and plenty of fine experimental jazz and rock tapes that helped me maintain my sanity during some trying times. This manuscript would not have been completed without his assistance. Thanks also go to Mark Urton, Mort and Shirley Shagrin, Elise Miller, Edie Jarolim and Kathy Sagan (twin Manhattan accomplices and friends), my brother Michael, Dan McLeod, Jerry Farber, Nick Nichols, Jerry Griswold, Elsie Adams and other members of the English department at San Diego State University, and to other friends and acquaintances who, if you are reading these words, know how much I appreciate your support and encouragement.

San Diego State University's English department and the College of Arts and Letters supplied mini-grants, travel money, and released time to work on this project. I thank, too, the editors of the journals where some of the interviews, or parts thereof, first appeared: *Fiction International, Mississippi Review, Missouri Review,* and *Science Fiction Studies.* Versions of the interviews with Samuel R. Delany and Ursula K. Le Guin appeared in *Alive and Writing: Interviews with American Authors of the 1980s,* conducted and edited by Larry McCaffery and Sinda J. Gregory (Urbana: University of Illinois Press, 1987).

Introduction

Big Science. Hallelujah. Big Science. Yodellayheehoo.

    —Laurie Anderson, "Big Science"

A new world
is only a new mind.

    —William Carlos Williams, "To Daphne and Virginia"

Surely, it's apparent by now that science fiction writers are producing some of the most significant art of our times. Equally apparent is the pervasive influence of science fiction (henceforth, SF) on other fictional forms as well as on television, the cinema, advertising (television advertising in particular), rock and electronic music, and numerous hybrid forms. We see its influence in the clothes we wear and the architectural features of the shopping malls we walk through. We hear its effect in the slang we use and in the white noise hovering constantly in the airwaves just beneath perceptibility. In short, we are already living out the existences predicted by earlier generations of SF authors.

    Much of the artistic energy apparent in contemporary American SF is obviously the same energy that is rapidly transforming American lfe today into the materials of an SF novel. Still, it's difficult to account for American SF's rapid transformation from its despised, ghettoized subgrenre into an art form of considerable sophistication. Critics specializing in SF have already begun extensively exploring the subgenre's literary history, the political and cultural contexts that produced so many disruptive and decisive changes within and outside SF during the '60s, and SF's relationship to popular culture and "serious art." (For a good overview of these studies, see Neil Barron's exhaustive annotated bibliographical guide to SF, *Anatomy of Wonder*.) Equally significant are recent speculations about SF and its relationship to culture and art (such as in Robert E. Scholes's *Structural Fabulation* or Brian McHale's *Postmodernist Fiction*). Some critics acknowledge the centrality of SF more indirectly as they examine the chief issues of postmodernism, twentieth-century history and politics, and the history of ideas. For example, Fredric Jameson's various discussions of modernism and postmodernism (notably in *The Political Unconscious* and "Postmodernism, or the Cultural Logic of Late Capitalism") have been widely used to account for specific SF themes and stylistic tendencies; the poststructuralist analyses of Jean-François Lyotard, Arthur Kroker, and Jean Baudrillard are central to the current cyberpunk controversy; Thomas Kuhn's *Structure of Scientific Revolutions,* Alvin Toffler's *Third Wave,* and the anthropological investigations of Claude Lévi-Strauss and Margaret Mead are now regularly cited in serious discussions of SF. If nothing else, the conversations contained in *Across the Wounded Galaxies* confirm that these diverse and eclectic approaches are justified by the diverse and eclectic nature of contemporary SF—a genre that draws its inspiration from Lou Reed and Karl Marx, Dada and Derrida, Wrestlemania and Heisenberg, Pac-Man and punk, as well as Asimov and Heinlein.

As was the case with my two earlier collections—*Anything Can Happen: Interviews with Contemporary American Novelists* (with Tom LeClair) and *Alive and Writing: Interviews with American Authors of the 1980s* (with Sinda Gregory)—my aim in *Across the Wounded Galaxies* has been to create a context that would allow authors to discuss in some depth their works, their backgrounds, and their aesthetic impulses. A natural dialogue emerges as these writers discuss common or divergent goals, formal methods, thematic treatments, views about their genre. The main focus here is not on personality issues—the numerous SF specialty magazines and fanzines provide plenty of that. Nor am I trying to convince people of SF's cultural and artistic significance, or to draw converts. The time for defensive posturing about SF has passed, just as similar arguments concerning the cinema became superfluous in the early '60s, and just as parallel discussions about rock music will eventually seem anachronistic. *Across the Wounded Galaxies* takes it for granted that SF deserves our serious attention, that the issues being examined by contemporary SF authors are absolutely central to late twentieth-century life and art. My premise is that SF's formal and thematic concerns are intimately related to characteristics of other post-modern art forms, that SF has been influencing and influenced by these forms. Science fiction can, in fact, be seen as representing an exemplar of postmodernism because it is the art form that most directly reflects back to us the cultural logic that has produced postmodernism.

What has been occurring within SF is also important because it has had the effect of promoting an active engagement between science and the arts—an interaction that has been badly (and sadly) undernourished, especially in the United States. While SF has long been a "respectable" and perfectly "legitimate" endeavor in Europe—witness the tradition of H. G. Wells, Karel Capek, Olaf Stapledon, Aldous Huxley, and George Orwell, right up through Vladimir Nabokov, Italo Calvino, and Stanislaw Lem—American SF has, almost since its inception, been stigmatized as low-brow, adolescent fare. Ironically, the country that first placed a man on the moon, that has probably contributed most to the development of this century's technological wonders (and horrors), is also a country where SF has only recently begun to attract the attention of major artists. Clearly this wedding of science and the arts is a welcome development. Science needs our most active and wide-ranging imaginations. It needs humanistic insights, perspectives that derive from our hearts and our ethical sensibilities as much as from logic and calculation. It needs science fiction.

Americans have grown accustomed to our fabulous world of satellite dishes, organ transplants, laptop computers, answering machines, and instant replays. Significantly, our world eerily blends the most extreme utopian and dystopian features of earlier science fiction. We scan the morning newspapers, hardly blinking as we skim past news of Chernobyl and of Uranus or Neptune flybys, of gene-splicing and computer viruses, of Michael Jackson and Ronald Reagan (exemplary heroes of a cyberpunk era), of the "harvesting" of organs from brain-damaged babies. Technology has so profoundly entered our collective consiousness that most Americans have grown equally blasé about both apocalypse and utopia. Nuclear annihilation and immortality; a manned mission to Mars and the permanent destruction of the ozone layer; the creation of artificial life (and artificial intelligence) and the cynical manipulation of our imaginations by politicians and the media; the development of basketball-sized tomatoes or cholesterol-free eggs and the ravaging of Amazon rain forests—these mind-boggling possibilities have merged with the banal particularities of our daily lives. Most Americans (and most American artists) haven't examined how such developments are affecting the physical, moral, emotional, and intellectual dimensions of our lives. One of the greatest strengths of SF, then, is its capacity to *defamiliarize* our science fictional lives and thereby force us to temporarily inhabit worlds whose cognitive distortions and poetic figurations of our own social relations—as these are constructed and altered by new technologies—make us suddenly see our own world in sharper relief.

It's now possible for people *physically* to inhabit their lives without *imaginatively* or *ethically* inhabiting them, but dramatically increased intellectual skills are required if we are to fully grasp the underlying scientific principles producing the transformations around us. While railroads, steel mills, and assembly lines were fundamentally altering America's landscape and mind-set, it was still possible for the average person to grasp the principles underlying such changes. Today, the specialization required to understand developments in the computer and defense industries, or in biology, physics, astronomy, and chemistry, is simply too great. However, people do need some form of imaginative access that will allow them to judge the changes occurring today. Without this access there can only be passive, uninformed acquiescence—always dangerous, especially when we realize that scientists and businessmen may employ decision-making processes that are either amoral (the abstract logic of corporate capitalism) or even actively immoral (the personal or nationalistic exercise of power and greed).

What is at stake here is not merely how close technology can bring us to the perfect simulation of sounds and images, or if we can finally produce razor blades that don't wear out, tires that don't go flat, weather forecasts that are reliable, or a transportation system that doesn't pollute the atmosphere and relies on renewable resources. Even more significant than the material changes are the concurrent shifts that technology produces in our systems of evaluation and judgment, our sense of inner space, and our relationship to subjective memory, desire, and sensory stimulation. The basic paradigms and distinctions that we've relied upon to understand ourselves and our relationship to the universe—the categorical oppositions, for example, of organic/inorganic, male/female, originality/duplication (image/reality, artifice/nature), human/nonhuman—are themselves undergoing startling transformations and reconsiderations. Accompanying these changes, and intimately related to them, are other, equally crucial shifts: in the ways that political, national, and personal control has increasingly merged with economic control; in the ways that the control of information becomes coexistent with the control of production and distribution of goods. "Culture" suddenly becomes a "commodity," entertainment becomes advertising or propaganda, and simulation becomes reality. Underlying all of this is the redefinition of the terms involved in a set of even more fundamental issues related to what it means to be "human" (or to be "alive" at all)—questions about what is admirable and significant about human behavior, what qualities we value (and reward) in human beings and what no longer seems important in assessing what we do, what we *are*.

The following interviews supply ample evidence that contemporary American SF has not only been reflecting these issues and concerns directly and compellingly but has also produced a body of work that assesses and analyzes these new technological modes of "being in the world." In choosing interviewees, I was guided principally by intuition and matters of personal taste, though I was particularly anxious to talk with writers whose works have had a significant impact on the evolution of American SF during the past twenty-five years. I was more interested in originality and quality than in sheer output or popularity. I was also drawn to authors whose thematic preoccupations overlapped those of their postmodernist contemporaries. By focusing on writers who seemed to be grappling with issues of form and content, I necessarily omitted from consideration many fine SF authors of a more conservative aesthetic orientation. This focus, however, has the benefit of creating a ready-made subtext having to do with the interaction between SF, the pop underground, and postmodernism. Implicit in postmodern aesthetics has been the sense, common to every artistic movement, that specific changes in historical, cultural, and philosophical/scientific outlooks require new aesthetic orientations. Life in America has changed very dramatically, in both crucial and trivial ways. The postmodernist fiction of Donald Barthelme, Thomas Pynchon, Robert Coover, Don DeLillo, Ronald Sukenick, Raymond Federman, and others has energetically sought a formal means more suitable than traditional realism to describe our world today. The same can be said of the science fiction created by the writers interviewed here.

This is not to say that specific aesthetic tendencies and thematic concerns of SF authors are identical to those of their postmodernist cousins—or derived from (or even specifically influenced by) postmodernist art. The nature of and motivations for stylistic innovation in SF are dauntingly complex and frequently misunderstood by readers who bring to SF the assumptions of mainstream fiction. Samuel Delany, Joanna Russ, and Gregory Benford all emphasize that SF cannot be analyzed and evaluated as if its governing assumptions were those of "mundane fiction" (as Delany refers to mimetically oriented fiction). Details, metaphors, narrative conventions, and characters in an SF work do not function as they would in a work that is attempting to render a believable illusion of our world. Occasionally we find an SF author who aims to achieve the same psychological depth and social verisimilitude found in great realistic novels—Tom Disch's *334,* for example, can be seen as an "experimental" novel in the sense that Zola's fiction was experimental; the same can be said of Ursula Le Guin's *Always Coming Home* or Gene Wolfe's massive Book of the New Sun tetralogy. All of these works project worlds of such elaborate (though often fabulous) specificity that we sense we're encountering people and places every bit as "substantial" as those found in the great realist texts.

Even this substantiality is of a different sort, however, because SF always deals with an "extrapolated world" rather than with the "real world." Its illusionary basis is always foregrounded rather than disguised by formal methods designed to generate a readerly sense of what Darko Suvin has termed (in *The Metamorphoses of Science Fiction*) "cognitive estrangement." Although SF always returns us to this planet, the return is usually via "detours" involving alien experiences, cultural and metaphysical assumptions, and mind-sets. Just as the experience of living abroad often provides travelers with new insights into their own society, the differences—the "estrangements" produced by the interaction of the familiar and unfamiliar—most typically establish the freshness of vision that we associate with the best SF.

I have attempted to create a framework of discussion that recognizes SF's relationship to the traditions of other established literary forms (satire, fantasy, the romance, the fabulous voyage, and the gothic novel, as well as realistic fiction) while paying particular attention to SF's distinctive features. I solicited information about personal backgrounds and aesthetic and intellectual inclinations that had drawn these authors to SF. It also seemed important to probe their perceptions about specific trends and debates within SF—the significance (or irrelevance) of the New Wave movement during the '60s and of the cyberpunk controversy of the '80s, the relative merits of hard versus soft SF, the viability of SF as a means of suggesting political, racial, or sexual agendas. Not surprisingly, many of these writers acknowledge a certain kinship with postmodernist authors (Pynchon, Burroughs, and Barthelme being probably the most frequently cited). The key social and political events of the past generation—including the Vietnam War, the rise of feminist and gay rights activism, racial tensions, the spectre of nuclear and ecological disasters, U.S. foreign policy in Central America and the Middle East—all regularly appear in transmuted forms in their fiction.

SF writers share with their postmodernist cousins a sense of urgency about the need to re-examine central narrative assumptions and metaphorical frameworks. This focus has produced a greater emphasis on reflexive, metafictional approaches, as is evident in Tom Disch's *Puppies of Terra,* Joanna Russ's *Extra(Ordinary) People,* and numerous works by Samuel Delany. Just as important have been less overtly self-conscious attempts to reinvigorate a number of the specific myths, metaphors, and motifs that had grown to dominate SF narratives. The "mad scientist," the benevolent (or monstrous) robot, the galactic empire and alien encounter motif, apocalypse, the dystopian political system — these have all emerged naturally as vehicles for expressing our society's collective fears and desires about technology, death, and isolation and the related search for personal and collective transcendence, peace, and community. The imagery and metaphors used to express these universal longings and fears quickly become stale, mere formulaic clichés. One particularly interesting example of such a reinvestigation can be seen in the recent reworkings of perhaps the most familiar SF motif of them all: the alien encounter. Nearly all of the authors interviewed here have had a go at this metaphor, just as any actor worth his salt tries his hand at Hamlet or Lear. Listening to Ursula Le Guin discuss *The Left Hand of Darkness,* Joanna Russ her *Extra(Ordinary) People,* Octavia Butler her Patternist series, or Bruce Sterling his *Schismatrix,* it becomes obvious how vital and resonant this particular metaphor remains as a vehicle for examining a remarkable range of epistemological, anthropological, racial, sexual, and political issues.

While SF authors have been sifting through familiar SF elements and discovering new complexities and syntheses, they have also been boldly exploring literary terrain where no authors have gone before. Despite its enduring symbolic and thematic preoccupations, by its very nature SF is preeminently concerned with "the new," and with finding lingoes and metaphors capable of rendering a sense of the new. Black holes, digital and analog computers, relativity, information and chaos theory, the Big Bang, video games, and a proliferating array of recently developed technologies all provide potentially rich, highly individualized terminologies and metaphors that are only now being tapped by contemporary SF authors. And because SF owes its allegiance not only to the actual but also to the possible, it is especially receptive to the creation of new myths whose implications openly challenge earlier ones. Joanna Russ and Octavia Butler, for example, have developed mythic alternatives to stereotypical sexual and racial myths and have demonstrated that things could indeed be different from the "natural" way they are now. In a different way, Samuel Delany, Bruce Sterling, William Burroughs, and Ursula Le Guin construct vivid and intricate cultural and linguistic alternatives to demonstrate the ideological and provisional nature of our current sexual, political, and philosophical systems.

While my questions to these authors imply a certain kinship between the aesthetic aims and thematic preoccupations of SF and postmodern fiction, there is an area where the two forms clearly differ: namely, SF, unlike most other serious or experimental fiction, is created by full-time writers. Although several of the authors interviewed here have had some academic affiliation at one time or another, only Joanna Russ has consistently supported herself primarily as a university teacher. It seemed useful to explore this difference in professional orientation. Certainly, the fact that SF authors must work within the insular, fiercely competitive SF publishing industry presents practical, personal, and aesthetic challenges that are less relevant to the literary avant-garde. To what extent, for example, do SF authors feel constrained by writing for a mass market traditionally consisting of teenagers? How do they circumvent these constraints, consciously subverting their audience's genre expectations? What formal problems result from working with certain structures (such as the multivolume series format) that have evolved primarily due to commercial considerations? How do they respond when they see certain "mainstream" authors like Don DeLillo, Doris Lessing, Marge Piercy, Denis Johnson, and Ted Mooney moving into their own territory?

Finally, a personal note. When I embarked on this series of interviews, I did so partly as a means of re-exploring and re-evaluating my own past—a past in which SF played a very important role. I discovered SF as an eleven-year-old growing up in what seems, in retrospect, an almost parodically alienating environment: I was living with alcoholic parents in the hyper-repressive military setting of Okinawa during the '50s. SF, together with rock 'n' roll, provided me with the first inkling that others shared some of my intuitions about society's physical, imaginative, and sensual limitations. Robert Sheckley and Elvis Presley, Chuck Berry and Philip K. Dick, Jerry Lee Lewis and Ray Bradbury, Theodore Sturgeon and Little Richard were all equally important; they linked me up with a world totally alien from the one I had grown up with, yet utterly exhilarating, exotic, and alive. Having the opportunity to reconnect with that sense of a community of intensely imaginative, often intensely idealistic writers—who typically also shared a common bond of feeling personally and intellectually turned off by what was happening around us—has been one of the great pleasures of preparing this book of interviews. *Across the Wounded Galaxies* allows me to share this experience of visiting a personal past that is also part of what I feel certain is our collective future.

An Interview with
Gregory Benford

As a man and as a writer, Gregory Benford exhibits a fascinating set
of oppositions: practicing physicist and fiction writer; rural Southerner
and international traveler; a major practitioner and eloquent defender
of hard SF (which insists on rigid adherence to scientific plausibility);
and an author whose work is perhaps most notable for its emotional
resonances, its emphasis on the mysteries of human psychology and
sexuality, its moving presentations of human uncertainty and fear of
death. Part mystic, part Huck Finn, part steely-eyed physicist, Benford
possesses the expansive intelligence and literary imagination that permit
these seeming contradictions to interact, producing fiction that successfully embraces the ying of rationality and the yang of human emo-
tion.

If we can speak of the "postmodernism" of cyberpunk authors such
as William Gibson and Bruce Sterling—for instance, their work's impulse toward collage, reflexiveness, a flaunting of artifice, and a recycling
of popular literary formulas in order to undermine those formulas or
expand their assumptions—then Benford's work can probably best be
understood as a particularly successful example of the "modernist"
branch of contemporary SF. Indeed, what may initially strike readers
about his meticulously crafted, psychologically convincing, and verbally
graceful fiction is the skillful manner in which he has appropriated a
number of key modernist experimental devices and applied them to a
succession of familiar SF motifs and plot structures. Beginning with *In
the Ocean of Night* (1977)—a pivotal work marking the end of his

extended apprenticeship—and continuing through a series of major works written in the late '70s and '80s (including *Across the Sea of Suns* [1984], a sequel to *In the Ocean of Night*), Benford successfully infuses his work with various narrative features usually associated with modernist realism: stream-of-consciousness techniques and other poetic, associational narrative voices; multiple, contradictory, and otherwise prismatic storytelling methods; the development of complex interactions of settings in time and space that result in startling juxtapositions and discontinuities; and a concern with "deep psychology," including an evocative exploration of human sexuality that is unusual in SF for its subtlety and perceptiveness.

As the following interview indicates, Benford's employment of modernist devices has been self-conscious and systematic. Equally apparent is that his particular application of these methods differs in certain ways from those of his modernist ancestors. Having first come to SF writing as a teenager, he has gradually but steadily matured as a writer and thinker. This maturity began to find its literary expression as Benford (who says he avoided literature classes in college) began to read widely as an adult. His discovery of William Faulkner, for example, had an especially direct impact on *Against Infinity* (1983). There Benford recasts many of the familiar elements of "The Bear" by setting his novel on a new version of Faulkner's frontier (the Jovian moon Ganymede) and having an aging hunter guide an idealistic youth on a search for a strange alien creature. Such a recasting not only allows Benford to re-examine the validity of Faulkner's original motifs (the place of the frontier in our collective imagination; humankind's defilement of the natural world) but to extend the implications of Faulkner's frontier mythology by questioning whether these concepts of the frontier and the alien encounter are inevitable aspects of any human conception of the world around us.

Benford's best-known work is *Timescape* (1980), a novel that perfectly illustrates his ability to simultaneously develop convincing psychological portraits and meticulously work out treatments of scientific principles. *Timescape* contains probably the most realistic and convincing depiction ever presented in an SF novel of the daily lives of actual working scientists. Benford vividly shows us that the lives and work of these men and women are affected by—even grounded in—the same sorts of jealousies, passions, and loneliness in which we all partake. *Timescape* is equally notable for its careful handling of plot—scientists working in a 1999 world hurtling toward ecological disaster attempt to transmit a warning message to Earth in 1962 by means of tachyons—which allows Benford to present fascinating, mind-boggling implications about the nature of time as conceived by contemporary physicists. Perhaps most remarkable, however, is that for all of his meticulous attention to scientific and psychological realism, he manages to evoke a powerful sense of wonder and awe at the universe's inhuman immensity and aesthetic perfection—and of mystery and longing involved in human efforts to bridge the gap between ourselves and what lies outside our imaginations.

I interviewed Gregory Benford in October 1988 on one of those warm, perfect San Diego mornings that are the source of so much irrational jealousy on the part of nonresidents. He was attending a physics conference at San Diego's Town and Country Convention Center. Now in his forties, he is a personally engaging, outgoing man whose replies to my questions (delivered in an accent that retained a Southern twang) were both carefully measured and full of boyish enthusiasm. Our poolside conversation was once interrupted by what I initially took to be a visitor from one of his alternate universes; it turned out to be his twin brother and fellow physicist, Jim Benford. Gregory Benford genuinely enjoys not only the abstract processes involved in examining issues and abstractions but also the heat, humor, and excitement generated by intellectual confrontations. It's an enjoyment that's evident in his fiction as well.

Larry McCaffery: You've developed successful careers both as a research scientist and as a fiction writer. Have you found these activities to be fundamentally different, or do they share underlying affinities?

Gregory Benford: I get a similar feeling from scientific and literary labors, the unconscious set free. I got used to writing in high school, where I must have written a half-million words. At first I just liked the idea of storytelling, so while I was in graduate school, I wrote some stories and started publishing. Only very slowly, as I read more widely and thought about things, did I come to see that storytelling would let me deal with crucial issues that the narrow mechanisms of science and academic philosophy wouldn't allow me to handle. I deplore the reductionism of specialists. The atomization of experience by science, the inducing of artificial relationships with icons—these are cultural crimes we should offset with integrative arts and sciences. As a research scientist I feel particularly charged with the task of talking clearly, humanly to others. I sense this time as a great adventure fraught with peril, and I'd like to shake awake the slumbering culture that isn't paying much attention to its runaway and self-devouring parts. Science stands for truth in the minds of most people, while fiction lies. So SF is either the truth about lies or lies about the truth. I like being part of a renegade art, the rats in the walls of the critical establishment. The bland promises of bourgeois realism are lies, too—but ignorant lies.

LM: You deal with some of the interactions between imagination and science in your novel *Timescape*. What started you writing that book?

GB: *Timescape*'s evolution has a fairly ornate history. I had written a paper on tachyons with two other physicists. (It was eventually published in 1970.) That paper gave me some ideas for stories, and I wrote a couple of them—one called "Oxford 3:02 A.M." and the other called "Cambridge 1:58 P.M." The latter already contained the characters from *Timescape*. I then had a notion about writing a book that would deal only with the Cambridge side of *Timescape*. I started with that narrower notion, but then it occurred to me that I needed to include the people on the receiving end of this time experiment. I ended up working on that novel for over a decade, slowly accumulating all the details I wanted to use for the characters. Only in the last year did I begin to see all the interconnections and the metaphors—and know what to do with them.

LM: *Timescape* gives me a real sense of how scientists work together and how their psychological makeups affect their work. Was creating this comprehensive sense of actual science something you were consciously aiming for, or did it just evolve with the rest of the book?

GB: That realism evolved slowly. I wanted to ground the book as much as possible—to enlist the devices of realism in the service of the fantastic. The fantastic premises give us perspectives on ourselves. Our revelation that we live in a vast canvas of space and time calls us to respond with images of travel in space (the rocket icon) and time (time travel and alternative worlds fiction), to grapple with these staggering truths. Do they truly diminish the importance of being human? SF struggles with that question better than any art I know. At any rate, the obvious way for me to develop my own premise about time travel was to tell as much of the truth as possible about how scientists actually work. This, in turn, dictated a lot of how the book evolved. I wanted to be relentless in sticking to the facts of the world, to the way people actually are—the program of hard SF, in other words—and yet admit the possibility of the fantastic elements that underlie the logic of the way the book progressed. I accepted something that Kafka and the magic realists had realized: If you're going to tell a fantastic story, you had better ramify it with as much realism as you can provide. So in a sense the main factor generating the book was simply my wanting to tell the truth.

LM: You've said in an essay that describing how real scientists actually work would normally be boring—which is why most SF presents such a glamorized, distorted view. The only way around this, you suggest, is to get deeply inside these people, to show how their minds and passions are engaged.

GB: It's important to recognize that scientists' habits of mind are different from other people's. Science is also predicated on the personalities of those who somehow wind up going into science. Scientists really aren't like show salesmen or bureaucrats or anybody else. These differences help explain why scientists are becoming more powerful in the world; they emerge as a truly international class whose fidelity to scrupulous truth gives them a kind of moral authority.

LM: The scientific habit of mind must show up somehow when a scientist, like you, is writing a novel. Some of the new people entering SF today—William Gibson, for instance—don't necessarily have extensive scientific backgrounds. Probably this gives their work a different "feel."

GB: But most SF is written by nonscientists. You must be a good observer, though. What rings false in a lot of SF, now and always, is the lack of observation. Take J. G. Ballard's remark: The crucial problem of SF is that it is not a literature won from experience. To write within SF already requires *so much* suspension of disbelief. To do the job, the author must truly know the deep-level operations of science and technology, and rigidly apply these to the fictional context. You *can't* just sit at home and make it all up. Working within these restrictions is analogous to a poet working within the constraints of, say, a sonnet; those restrictions impose a gossamer possibility of excellence that isn't there when you're working with free verse. In a sonnet or in a hard SF work, in other words, you have the possibility of greater success. You can't just use the popular imagery or lingoes of science. I don't think Bill Gibson, for example, really knows or thinks much about artificial intelligence. Repairing hot rods in your garage doesn't teach you much about rocket ships. It's a start, maybe—but only that.

LM: Gibson, Bruce Sterling, and other cyberpunk writers created quite a furor within SF during the mid-1980s. You've spoken out against the principles that seem to underlie cyberpunk—your argument centering, as I read it, on the failure of cyberpunk writers to explore the scientific implications of their fictional premises with much sense of what these implications actually involve. Could you talk a bit about the hard versus soft approach to SF, and how it relates to cyberpunk in particular?

GB: In a long review a while back ["Hard? Science? Fiction?" *Amazing,* July 1987], I treated about a half-dozen books and suggested that at least some portions of cyberpunk are indeed hard SF. But what's different about most cyberpunk authors—particularly about Gibson and Sterling—is that they have been preoccupied by the *surfaces* of

the future. That's where they make contact, say, with J. G. Ballard—
who has always been interested in the fiction of surfaces or appearances,
what you might call the psychic domain. This is not too crazily different
from, for example, the stylistic mannerisms of Arthur C. Clarke, who
is not often thought of as a stylist. But in fact, Clarke has a style, in
part a style of striking images which was best visualized literally in *2001*.
Stanley Kubrick really understood Clarke, in that he gave you the
austere, silent beauty of surfaces. Yet that movie is really hard SF *in
context*. Hardness in SF has always been double edged: it's about sticking
to facts in the physical world, as we understand it theoretically; but it's
also about being remorseless about your implications, following these
through to the end. That's what keeps genuine hard SF away from
becoming either the wish-fulfillment fantasy or those endless techno-
empire games of replaying World War II in a "hard" context.

LM: Gibson's *Neuromancer* has been attacked along those lines. He
doesn't systematically pursue the implications of the science he's em-
ploying there; he's more interested in the psychic domain.

GB: A concern with the aesthetics of technology is a legitimate variant
of hard SF. But the downfall of Gibson and some other cyberpunks is
that they really don't *know* that much. Their implications are all, deep
down, superficial. And those superficial aspects of technological change
are not the whole story, or even the most *interesting* story. For example,
artificial intelligence is going to change the bulk of humanity's views
of something as basic as what it means to be human. Aristotle's definition
of an intelligent person who was useful and capable of significantly
participating in society was someone who had the ability to do sums—
a capacity you can buy in any market these days for three dollars. The
definition of human beings (and therefore the entire program of humanism) is obviously time dependent. There are no eternal verities in
such definitions. Nor is there such a thing as *the* human condition.
When hard SF is at its best, it's more aware of this revisionism than
any other field. Thinking out the future of computerization, for example,
means you must look at its effects in new ways. It's not enough to
present these effects the way the cyberpunks do, by saying, "Well, there's
going to be an underclass of computer criminals." That's not the main
thing that's going to happen. So the program of cyberpunk is worthwhile
to some extent, but so far it's been inadequately done. Which isn't to
say it won't be better done. My feelings about cyberpunk aren't completely negative—I've learned from it, enjoyed a lot of it.

LM: A lot of other postmodernist art seems similary fascinated with
surfaces. Wouldn't you agree that a focus on surfaces—particularly the
wildly proliferating images and reproductions of the media—can be
used to suggest a lot of deeper implications about the characters in-

habiting these worlds? For instance, a work like Marc Laidlaw's *Dad's Nuke* or Bruce Sterling's *Schismatrix* explores the bizarre (and often grotesquely funny) results of capitalism's growing efficiency at manufacturing pop cultural images and then projecting these into people's consciousnesses. These images may be surfaces, but they affect our values and sense of identity in ways fundamentally different from the surface features of life fifty or a hundred years ago.

GB: This incursion of the media into people's consciousness is indeed different today. It's much more ferocious, more slickly and efficiently handled, and exploits a shorter attention span. The cyberpunks may well be doing ground-breaking work in this area, though I haven't seen much yet. Recycled Raymond Chandler ain't electrifying. A lot depends, of course, on what you mean by pop culture. The religion of the Egyptian pharaohs was a pop culture: it permeated ancient Egypt and held the state together. It was full of imagery. If you want to look at pop icons, you can simply look at the pyramids. The boundary between pop and high culture is itself a modern invention; what was once pop will later be high, and sometimes vice versa. The epic poem as a literary mode, for example, is dead. It's not high culture anymore, it's fossil culture.

LM: One difference between how people today exist versus fifty years ago or two thousand years ago is that technology's ability to bombard us with images, meanings, and alleged projections of what is real makes it difficult to establish any relationship with a stable reality.

GB: Right. Consider the "relation space" of a typical person thousands of years ago. He or she had real relationships with perhaps a hundred other villagers and knew *of* the gods and figures from myths. Artificial relationships. Now we know a few dozen close friends and have hundreds of artificial relationships with media creations. These fictive relationships have great influence on our perceptions of reality, inducing us to define ourselves in terms of Bogart's toughness, Cosby's affability, Monroe's sexiness, Einstein's saintliness. But we know these increasingly as disembodied images, no deeper than advertising clichés. MTV has, for example, chopped the soul of rock 'n' roll into strobed icons. Some SF writers have copied this effect from media culture without realizing that SF, with its great weight of sustained discourse, needs more than that. I found George Alec Effinger's *When Gravity Fails* interesting because it takes a rather more plausible computer-dominated landscape (Arabic) and consciously plays with Chandlerian modes. Gibson mostly just copies them. Neither, though, truly confronts this profound issue in current popular literature: how to retain classic narrative unity while incorporating the centrifugal effects of technology. The job of SF is not to be hip or to be with it. We should be *ahead* of it.

LM: What are likely to be the most significant things ahead of us?

GB: Obviously, computers will supplant whole areas of human activity. Forty years ago there was a well-known job called routing. Someone designed the daily or weekly program for truck drivers to optimize their deliveries over a large area. The router would find the minimum route and timing for all of them. That job is totally done by computers now; somebody wrote an algorithm for it in the '50s, and it became commonly used in the '60s. There will come a time, I expect, when truck drivers will have computer programs on line in their cabs to deal with variations. Lots of jobs we're familiar with are going to cease to exist.

LM: Near the opening of *Across the Sea of Suns* there is a description of how the humans and the spaceship are interfacing. It's followed by the quote, "We are machines," which suggests that the crew is losing its humanity. Yet throughout that book—and indeed, this is a central notion throughout your work—you contrast this descent into the animate with the sexuality of your characters. You present sex as one of those irreducible elements of our spirit, of life itself.

GB: Sexuality *is* one of the ways we define our humanity. That's why we instinctively think of people who are perceived as being unsexy or asexual as lesser human beings—they aren't playing with all the colors on their palettes. The glib thing to say is that sex is the consolation prize for death. Sex is nature's way of saying, "You know, we're going to be needing another one of you," and the orgasm is nature's way of telling us when to stop. It's just as important for SF to try to understand how technology is affecting our sexuality—to examine where these biological and genetic advances are taking us sexually—as it is to see how it's changing our economic system or our long-range military planning. Ultimately, it may be *more* important.

LM: Your focus on developing contexts in which to study this sort of thing seems unusual in hard SF.

GB: Actually, my experience is that scientists are more highly sexed than most people.

LM: Your scientists in *Timescape* certainly demonstrate that—even the "bad" characters.

GB: Are there bad characters in that book?

LM: Sure—Ian Paterson.

GB: But since readers all seem fascinated by him, how "bad" can he be? He's the character people can't forget, and unforgettability is in my definition of a good character—Macbeth is a character you remember, but he's not a great guy. In terms of hard SF dealing with sexuality and semimystical or spiritual issues, I'd say it's becoming increasingly difficult to categorize what any given group of SF writers are going to be dealing with. This is a good thing, of course. The dialogue and the perceived area of discussion in hard SF has been narrow in the past, but it's broadening, probably because hard SF almost inevitably calls up deep philosophical questions. The best hard SF writers almost necessarily have deep mystical underpinnings because *science* has considerable mystical content.

LM: Certainly your own work often has a strong mystical element.

GB: Science confronts our deepest concerns more readily now than does, say, religion, or academic philosophy, or even the humanities, which keep trying to replay the glory days of Athens without noticing that the definition of human beings has changed. Every mathematician/physicist down deep is a Platonist. You shake us awake at night and we'll agree that, when we look around us at the universe, we're seeing a rude, crude image of an underlying beautiful symmetry—the old shadow on the cave wall. What this view calls into question, of course, is, What's the *nature of, the knowability of* this Platonic perfectibility?

LM: It's interesting how close that question is to what medieval theologians, as well as Dante and Milton, were asking.

GB: It's the same question, but we look to a different discipline for answers. Science today is telling us about the questions human beings will always ask. In the last forty years, radio astronomy has told us more about the origin, nature, and destiny of the universe than did the previous two thousand years of philosophy. Nobody seriously looks up what Aquinas said on these issues when they can see the existence of the three-degree microwave background radiation left over from the Big Bang. One piece of data can get you an unspooling cloth of speculation that never ends. Similarly, every piece of data closes doors. We no longer believe in the steady-state universe. It's hard to believe that God intended us to deduce everything that is moral and right in this world without referring to the way the world was made. One great clue about what the world means is *how it was put together,* whether you regard it as a found artifact or not.

LM: Yet your fiction continually emphasizes the *ambiguity* of human perception at least as much as the truth-function of scientific systems. In fact, in *In the Ocean of Night* and *Across the Sea of Suns* you question the whole notion of objectivity—you point to the coded, metaphorical nature of language and scientific laws, and to the human subjectivity implicit in these systems. At first glance, that seems like a peculiar issue for a hard SF author to be stressing—but then, an acceptance of the interaction of mind and matter seems to be something modern science has had to acknowledge.

GB: And being aware of that acknowledgment is crucial to understanding what hard SF is—and isn't. People who regard my handling of this general area as antithetical to my hard SF stance simply aren't very sophisticated. You can no longer believe in that life of serene Newtonian separation between us and the mechanical universe; that view truly has no philosophical content today. Our paradigm of modern cosmology is that everything started with the Big Bang and has been running ever since in a self-organizing manner that arises from natural laws. While that certainly seems true, with this premise comes the question: Is this evolution totally disconnected from the advent of intelligence? I'm not so sure that it is. Intelligence may be functioning at very high, but imperceptible, levels in the universe.

LM: That suggests an almost mystical sense that intelligence and the operations of the universe may be enmeshed.

GB: I don't accept orthodox skepticism's view about our inability to comprehend the world. Quantum mechanics is a perfect paradigm of the intuitive expansion of categories. So is relativity. We can make progress in comprehending the alien, in other words. And the universe is quite alien. That's where I part company with Stanislaw Lem, who is essentially an unreconstructed follower of David Hume. But it's been a century and a half since Hume, and in the interim we've learned more about human capacity to encounter strange phenomena, not just to evolve new categories, but to realize the impermanence and the provisional nature of categories. In quantum mechanics the wave/particle duality is really saying, Here's this thing that sometimes looks like a wave, sometimes looks like a particle, but it's neither. It's fundamentally unknowable in the sense that you don't have a simple picture. This unknowability arises because we evolved in an African veld where you threw stones and swung from tree branches and saw waves in the lakes. Those were your fundamental categories. There's no guarantee that these categories will work when you go down by ten orders of magnitude. Today we understand this, so we can find ways of describing a phenomenon such as light, and of feeling intuitively comfortable with it; but these are ways in which we can't even verbalize the experience any longer. Newtonian mechanics can verbalize its pictures. That's what was clean about it—it could still use the metaphors of the African veld. Quantum mechanics can't.

LM: The kinds of truly bizarre realities that quantum mechanics is dealing with (black holes, subatomic particles) seem to require a mathematical language in order to be described—they're literally unimaginable from any ordinary standpoint.

GB: Quantum mechanics indeed requires this sort of abstract reasoning in order to describe these mind-bending, nonveld realities. It also demands an intuitive feel, not easily conveyed in words. A particle physicist would probably say that words are just things we now put between the equations. Words don't convey, truly, what the equation is doing. We're using different categories of knowledge beyond that verbal experience, categories traditionally used by philosophers. But whereas traditional philosophy is immersed in language, physics now transcends some elements of language. Obviously, a nonverbal perception of the universe is very difficult to convey, particularly in literature—which makes it such an exciting challenge.

LM: How have you dealt with the challenge of inventing a context?

GB: I've tried to deal with this in *Against Infinity,* which is about the fundamental unknowability of the world and the fact that the infinite is our ultimate concern. That's why I gave it that typical '50s title— *Against Infinity*—which calls up images of tough guys in hard spacesuits confronting the bitter vacuum of the frontier. I wanted to show that there's a difference between "frontier" and "wilderness." In American literature, the frontier is represented by the West (Robert Heinlein uses a version of the Western frontier, and in many ways the Western mythos has largely dominated American SF). But another set of motifs in American literature centers around the wilderness and the South, as in Thoreau and Faulkner. These two distinctly different strains in American fiction are also strongly present in SF. The frontier metaphor is the one that's really common, but since I'm from the South, I wanted to see if the Southern wilderness mythos could be applied.

LM: Faulkner's use of the wilderness motif in "The Bear" has to do with a set of values, an almost intuitive, mystical—or specifically tran- scendental—world view.

GB: This transcendental element in SF goes far back. There's more similarity between Arthur C. Clarke and Thoreau than there is between Clarke and Heinlein. Having come from the South, I've always been immersed in a more intuitive perception of literature, and certainly I have never been a great fan of the frontier per se. I grew up in a place that was strange, alien, and also a part of the underculture of America. Not on the frontier—a different experience. *Against Infinity* is, as you just noted, a deliberate rediscussion of "The Bear." I attempted, within an SF form, to bring in all the implications of the wilderness motif, to suggest the idea of confronting the unknown as a fundamentally un- knowable category against which you always batter yourself.

LM: The way you present Manuel Lopez's series of encounters with the Aleph seems designed to link "wilderness" with the basic concept of our evolving ways of understanding an ever-changing unknown. (I'm thinking of the passage where you describe the Aleph as "like something restlessly remaking itself, forever discontented.") You embrace the skep- tic's view that we will never fully understand the unknown, but you also seem to believe that we can develop ways of understanding (like our modern view of light, which you mentioned earlier) that put us closer in touch with an evolving universe.

GB: One of my main intentions in *Against Infinity* is to suggest that you can make some progress. In the last century we really have made progress in confronting the deeply strange, and part of this progress lies in our recognition of our limitations. That's enormously reassuring to my way of thinking, because it means we're never going to solve these problems—and that's great news to the human race. We're never going to achieve a sense of finality because of the fundamentally provisional nature of all knowledge, including science. The only people who know things for sure are the theologians—or rather, let's say the pulpit powers. Barth (Karl, not John) would not say that he knew things for sure. I wrote *Against Infinity* to talk about the process of growing up and understanding the fundamental strangeness of the world, and of embracing that strangeness. Most people obviously don't embrace it. They run away from it and watch "Monday Night Football," or join the Republican party. I've always been attracted to science because of its provisional nature, not for its assurances.

LM: That's the opposite of what most people would assume.

GB: That assumption derives from this fundamental misunderstanding of the history of science that I was alluding to earlier. If science *weren't* provisional, it wouldn't be believable. We have simply ceased to believe people who are dead certain. What the average person doesn't recognize is that the whole scientific method is just a way of discovering things with increasing reliability, and *always* checking. That's the only category of human endeavor in which checking your answer is perpetual, therefore underlining its provisional nature. Most people still want to rely on the pharaohs. They want certainty, and science is the reigning source of that. It's what you use in advertisements to reassure people that your product is better than others, the lab smock metaphor. SF can gently say, No, this is not the complete answer by any means. It's important to realize that science tells you things that are a lot more believable than the ideas that people are hawking on the streets, but there will always be new issues tomorrow.

LM: In "Running Out of Speculative Niches," David Brin argues that hard SF may be facing a crisis: "The knowable universe may be finite and we [hard SF writers] may be filling in the gap faster than we think." That kind of attitude seems directly at odds with your point that there will be new issues tomorrow.

GB: I understand David's point; I simply don't agree with it. If anything, the flourishing of hard SF in the '80s speaks to the fact that, if this tunnel has an end, you sure as hell can't see it now. The better

metaphor is the expanding balloon. There's more space inside, sure—
but there's more surface area all the time.

LM: Could you talk a bit more about your original intentions in
creating *Against Infinity?*

GB: My choice of Faulkner's story as a jumping-off point came from
my desire to clearly make the point about the frontier versus the wilderness. I wanted to break with the whole Heinlein frontier tradition
that SF writers had used so often and instead find a means to present
the wilderness motif. I began to read Thoreau and Hawthorne, and
eventually Faulkner. My other central motive was to write an SF novel
that would self-consciously be about my growing up in the South.

LM: In essays and interviews, you've alluded to the personal significance of your background. Did it have any permanent effect on your
literary sensibility?

GB: Its effects have filtered through in my writing in all sorts of ways,
most obviously in *Against Infinity* but also in other, more subtle ways
that probably wouldn't be obvious. I grew up in a small town in southern
Alabama, around Fairhope, where my parents now live. I lived the true
Huck Finn existence, spending a lot of time down on the river on my
grandmother's farm, taking the skiff upriver to islands, exploring them.
I had everything but Indian Joe, and Jim was present in the form of
lots of blacks. Even my brother is named Jim! (I didn't read *Huck Finn,*
though, until I was living in Japan.) As I was growing up I felt I was
living in this almost mythical wilderness environment that was full of
strangeness—and full of stories, too, presented in those rich, quirky
Southern lingoes. That immersion in storytelling is one of the things
behind the fact that, when I started *Against Infinity,* I knew I wanted
to talk about my ingrained sense that storytelling is primarily a *verbal
art.* A different way to present these ideas about the wilderness was to
use a voice different from what I had used (or what anybody else had
ever used) in SF: the Southern storyteller's voice, which my brother
and I had grown up listening to. Our stepfather used to tell stories in
the farmhouse while we were sitting around the fire after listening to
the "Grand Ole Opry"—stories about hunting and fishing that he told
in the distinctive, rolling manner that Faulkner used. Our step-grandad
would construct his story in his own style, based on the oral tradition
of the South, ripe with a moral and timebound authority. After all, who
is the narrator of Faulkner's novels? Northern critics reading Faulkner
largely missed the fact that his works represent the way you tell stories
in an environment where storytelling is the principal method of trans-
ferring information. A lot of his so-called experimental devices are
simply part of the complex oral traditions he grew up with.

LM: You create remarkably different contexts in the novel—scien-

tific, economic, metaphysical, personal—for the central idea that
"Nothing remains, nothing is held constant." How did these evolve?

GB: I was aware of wanting to build into the text perpetual change
and perpetual renewal. This notion is treated in economics by a deliberately awkward and reductionist discussion, right in the middle of the
book. It comes from a social theoretician who talks about Marxism and
socialism. A socialist system has got to expand into new worlds in order
to maintain efficient production of goods, so capitalism is always going
to be renewed out at the edges of our society. I tried to make this analysis
sound funny and dumb *because* it's reductionist. I put it in the middle
of the novel to show how we cut up the world and miss part of it by
trying to overanalyze it. In that regard it's a specifically American answer
to the European intellectual view of the world; ever since the nineteenth
century, some Europeans have been frantically looking for -isms they
could attach themselves to, giving them a nice reductionist world. That
drive to eliminate complexity, to account for it somehow through a
system of analysis, betrays a deep *fear* about the irreducibility of things.
Europeans have been running away from the sense of strangeness for
a long time. They are, in the worst sense of the word, deeply "civilized."

LM: You began reading SF when you and your brother were kids,
during a period when your family was moving a lot. Your brother has
commented that you got into SF partly because you felt so culturally
estranged. That sense of estrangement seems to be a part of just about
every SF author's background.

GB: It's a classic pattern. The other is to be an only child, and in a
certain sense Jim and I were only children, since we're identical twins.
Indeed, that sense of isolation from the mainstream—literarily and
culturally—is crucial in a lot of us as writers. Jim and I got involved
in reading SF during the early to mid-1950s, when our father (who was
an army officer) was moving from Japan to Atlanta and then to Germany. By the time we were living in Germany we were already heavily
involved in fanzines, which eased our sense of isolation. Jim and I
started the first fanzine in Europe, something called *Void,* and we were
spending time writing for fanzines, rather than reading books.

LM: When I interviewed Joanna Russ, she mentioned that growing
up in the '50s, with all its repressions and reactionary attitudes, led her
to feel perpetually estranged and isolated. She made the interesting
comment that this feeling of estrangement might be one reason why
she is drawn to the alien encounter motif. Of course, being a lesbian,
she is especially attuned to this.

GB: I can see that, although Joanna strikes me as more of a theoretical
lesbian who came to it very late, led by philosophical principles rather
than instinct. Her problem has been that this feeling of isolation has

converted her into a perpetual rage machine, and this has crippled her work enormously. She wrote a really powerful novel — *The Female Man* — and it appears that she's going to be regarded essentially as a one-book author in the genre. But most people have only one idea, which they repeat. There's a Clifford Simak notion, a Ted Sturgeon notion, and so forth.

LM: Your works are remarkably varied, both thematically and stylistically. Have you been consciously working through different styles and SF motifs?

GB: Most of that diversity reflects two facts: first, I'm easily bored; second, I'm still learning about literature. I never took a literature course at a university, which in the long run may have been a big plus. I hated the teaching of English, and I deliberately took all the English courses by examination, rather than by classes. Now I can read literature afresh, as an adult. Usually, you're exposed to it as a kid in a classroom, ready or not. As I begin to understand and recognize things in literature, I tend to use them in my work. I'm also very aware of form/content issues. When I come to a problem, I try to adopt a method that seems right for what I want to say. To me, literature is not composed of a set of mechanical conventions that writers must revere and emulate. It's a grab-bag of techniques that can be adapted for very different purposes.

LM: Has this evolution of your own literary sensibility led you to go back and rewrite new versions of earlier works?

GB: Undoubtedly. As I've matured, I can see the possibilities missed — and the inadequacies. So I've rewritten them to satisfy my sense of the ideals contained in earlier versions. This is an ongoing thing — I regard every text as provisional. And it's not as if I'm ever really expecting to satisfy my sense of any given set of possibilities. As in science, I don't guarantee anything. I somewhat rewrote *Across the Sea of Suns* for the paperback edition, adding a whole new chapter, because by then my sense of the book had changed. Mostly I felt as if I knew more about these people.

LM: This approach allows you to put into practice the very Derridean notion that a text is provisional, not a fixed thing to be finally interpreted.

GB: So is science. My view is that you stop working on a text when you die, but the world doesn't stop. People reread your books, and then they rewrite them for you. Then they rewrite again, and reread. I guess that's one thing about death to look forward to — you can finally be done with your books, once and for all.

LM: Was there a moment in your career when you recognized that you had become a serious writer?

GB: I began to realize some growth while I was writing parts of *If the Stars Are Gods*. I saw I could possibly write a worthwhile novel with *In the Ocean of Night.* When I started out, I thought that novel was going to involve simply taking a few short stories and stitching them together, but as I worked it seemed to grow and get more complicated. When I finished, it was utterly unlike anything I had envisioned—larger, handling themes and characterization with greater assurance. The same expansion occurred when I was writing *Timescape.* I don't know about other writers, but I've never had the experience of sitting down and saying to myself, OK, I'm going to write a major novel about this or that idea. I just start working and discover what it's going to turn into.

LM: You mentioned the different purposes for which you adapt different modes of storytelling and narrative devices. Do you think that your purposes are fundamentally different from those of a realist author?

GB: SF differs from "literary fiction," not in the relative amount of attention paid to certain types of plot or characters, but at deeper philosophical levels. I suspect, for example, that the antagonism between the literary world and the SF community isn't reducible to the effete-intellectual snobs versus the nerdish engineers so much as to a fundamental dispute about the ideals behind humanism and different allegiances to the past versus the future. SF authors simply don't accept the Shakespearean notion that "Man is the measure of all things." Contemporary SF has rejected that concept much more profoundly than did modernism or surrealism. Realism seems to be deeply reactionary in many ways, grounded in beliefs (and in formal structures designed to convey these beliefs) that no longer apply. "Realistic fiction" is remorselessly and inadvertently about the past. It has a heavy debt to a consensual reality that's psychologically false. On the other hand, developing new categories of some complexity and ambiguity is the fundamental SF goal. If a writer is going to bring about a new world, he or she must first imagine it—which requires, among other things, the act of synthesizing categories. This doesn't mean you have to jettison all conventions of narrative and character relationships, or even that SF can't borrow experimental devices from modernism and postmodernism. But when it does so, the results are different. The SF novel may look as though it has a conventional plot (after all, most elements in conventional plots are devices for achieving narrative pace), but it must undermine the philosophical terms of discussion as it goes along. Magic realism does that, too. But even when SF uses experimental styles and approaches developed by the great modernist writers—stream of consciousness, dislocation, broken narrative—it does so for different purposes, to present different "content," as it were. Run-on sentences won't necessarily suggest internal hysteria or some kind of flooding of consciousness; instead, they may point to genuinely different ways of perceiving the world—ways that emerge, not from psychology and sociology, but from evolution, genetics, even physics. These applications of mainstream methods to achieve uniquely SF ends has been greatly misunderstood by nearly all critics who come to SF with a primarily mainstream literary background.

LM: This effort to undermine the philosophical terms of the narrative as you go along is a characteristic feature of the fiction of Robert Coover, Donald Barthelme, and many other postmodern authors.

GB: Yes, but there's a crucial difference. Coover and Barthelme are working in narrower ground. They often simply attempt to undermine the perceived dictatorial privilege of narrative. SF is not about reminding people that this is only a story. (As we all know, this approach is not a great way to win an audience—they want to *forget* that this is a story!) Being very clever and realizing that there are narrative structures and that you can undermine them is one thing; but using a narrative structure to undermine philosophical notions and ways of looking at reality is a much larger game. That's why, in fact, "postmodernism"— that term is a particularly pernicious example of self-decapitating literary jargon—is a small game, very fashionable for a while, but limited. SF (and fantasy literature in general) is far larger. What, for instance, is the meaning of character when you follow a person through repeated encounters with the *same* events—as in Heinlein's "By His Bootstraps"? Or how do you know who you are when experiences can be made wholly synthetic? There are resonances of Philip K. Dick and James Tiptree, Jr., there; Barry Malzberg and Robert Silverberg, too. Magic realism wasn't invented in the United States.

LM: In "Panderings and Evasions" (*Amazing,* January 1988), you make the interesting point that fantasy forms share with traditional realism and appeal to fairly rigid notions of what's possible.

GB: Yes—because vampires, werewolves, gnomes, and unicorns are the inventions of our ancestors. Fundamentally, they aren't nearly as disturbing as the genuinely new and impossible. Fantasy can nearly always be seen as a reactionary movement because it faces the past, harking back to old beliefs and superstitions. It believes with almost heartwarming and sentimental persuasiveness in identifiable good and evil and in the comfortable notion that these forces can be controlled by humanlike powers divorced from the intellect, like witches or wizards. This sort of focus seems both old-fashioned and dangerously escapist. Its spirit runs deeply against what I take to be SF's central obligations: the John Campbell dictum that imaginative literature must deal with the underlying realities of the world as these are revealed by nature's laws. Most fantasy abandons this pursuit of rational behavior, which makes its popularity deeply troubling. It also affirms the centrality of human perspectives—an illusion.

LM: Your work differs from most realist and SF treatments alike in its frequent refusal to "wrap things up" at the end.

GB: It's never justifiable to manipulate things too obviously just to achieve the finality that most readers admittedly want. That's one of my main objections to most of the fantasy that's appearing today: the life presented in fantasyland too often is simplified to the point of caricature, completely divorced from the messy *human* realities of doubt, ambivalence, complexity. You can see this sort of reductionism in something like *Star Wars,* where the presentation of a pattycake Zen mysticism (The Force) really panders to a kind of fascist power-trip sensibility. I'm not saying this is true of all fantasy—Ursula Le Guin, Elizabeth Lynn, and especially Gene Wolfe are doing some interesting work in this area. And certainly most SF is just as guilty of these kinds of manipulations. Even Le Guin's utopian works, which are enormously crafted, turn out to have little to do with the actual political or social realities she claims to be dealing with. In a lot of ways her sensibility shares that nineteenth-century European intellectual tradition I was referring to earlier, that naive confidence in systems and -isms; Le Guin would be very comfortable, I think, if she could be transported back into the last century, where she could speak with confidence about how things need to be changed.

Consider the mixed bags you find in Marion Zimmer Bradley's Darkover series or Anne McCaffery's Dragon series; or the amusing but ultimately limited approach in some of Larry Niven's work or in Philip José Farmer's Riverworld stories, where everything is worked out very thoroughly but the end results don't add up to anything beyond the customary satisfactions of problem solving. In Niven's Ringworld series, at least you have the sense of an author seriously grappling with the possible consequences of real physical laws. The fact that he's imposed these rigid restraints on himself, and seems to test what might actually occur, helps distinguish his work from most of the other soothing, familiar, and aesthetically dishonest works proliferating today. That's why, to my mind, the most persuasive SF rejects dichotomies, achieving not merely *solutions* but a genuine *synthesis* at the end. Even writers of obvious skills, like Le Guin or Joan Vinge, are too often guilty of allowing their political objectives, or the elements of an ordained plot structure, to undermine the scientific or philosophical plausibility of their stories.

LM: It would seem especially difficult for writers who wish to develop a specific ideological or political perspective to create a context that isn't too obviously structured to suit their own agenda.

GB: This mode of presentation is very evident in most of the leftist SF being written today. People have programs and various liberal axes to grind, but their work doesn't ring true because the oppositions they're creating are overly simplistic. Feminist SF offers a perfect example of this. In most of it you don't find a convincing, fully realized future where technology is appropriated into an overall social structure, because the entire work has been conceived on the basis of a simple opposition: the exploitive or brutal man versus the exploited, nurturing woman. The feminist writers even tend to frame their issues by using the standard models of the present (socialism, communism, capitalism, fascism, whatever) rather than working out some new political or social system more appropriate to the future they want to envision. Interestingly enough, right now some of the best efforts to invent a future that displays real ambiquities likely to be present in a diverse, technology-driven world are coming from writers on the far right—Jerry Pournelle and Larry Niven. With a few exceptions—Harry Harrison's work comes to mind—I don't see writers on the left doing this. At any rate, in my own work I always aim consciously to create an organic synthesis of the complex issues I'm trying to deal with, rather than providing easy but ultimately unsatisfying solutions. That approach is a key way to undermine the typical plot structure.

LM: You're talking less about leaving everything open-ended than about trying to find a synthesis that takes into account the ambiquities inherent in the problems.

GB: Leaving things open-ended can be a way to leave it up to somebody else to write the last chapter for you.

LM: I take it that, as you're working on a novel, you're consciously aware of trying to avoid the pitfalls most closely associated with hard SF—creating merely a mechanical working out of a scientific idea. Being aware that this is a problem must be the first step toward dealing with it.

GB: You have to be aware of this if you're going to balance respect for the way things seem actually to operate versus that need to develop new syntheses and categories. If you lack that awareness of how easy it is to get locked inside the logic of your structure, you won't be searching for keys to let you out. You run up against many of the same formal problems that mystery writers encounter. If you're a detective writer and you don't notice that this is a problem, you end up writing locked-room stories that no one will ever reread—that's the limitation of any such work—rather than using the mystery formula to write deep criticisms of society. That's the difference between Raymond Chandler and Agatha Christie, and also, I'd argue, the difference between Chip Delany and most cyberpunk writers. In SF you must relentlessly carry out the program of the genre: to look at the impact of science on society *in all regards*. You look not just at the surface changes that will facilitate your plot—not just the level of "In the near future people are going to be using computers instead of switchblades to steal from each other"— but you find a way to examine how these technological changes affect your feelings about what a human being *is* in the world. The differences between now and three hundred years ago are much more deeply rooted, more philosophical and metaphysical, than the mere entrapments of technology.

LM: Again, one shared concern between SF and the experiments you find in postmodernist fiction has to do with finding a more suitable means than realism to suggest the implications of these shifts in sensibility—aesthetically, psychologically, socially.

GB: We simply don't live in the same world that writers lived in when they were inventing the novel. Take something like religion, which has essentially gone face down in the last three hundred years. That's an immense change, because society was mostly structured around religion. This will affect everything from the symbols in our art to the basic ways we relate to the universe. And this change was largely brought about by science. One reason SF is such an exciting field right now is that we can ask what happens when you redefine the concept of being human—not just because of computers, but because of biotechnology. How much deviation in the human genotype can we venture without the end product no longer being acknowledged as human? Are you no longer human just because somebody goes in to fix up your inheritable diseases, or because somebody changes your eye color? The same issues are relevant to the animal kingdom: When does an animal stop being an animal and become something else? When do you patent an animal?

LM: You deal with these issues throughout *Across the Sea of Suns*. For instance, you present some of the likely sexual confusions that people are going to be facing in the midst of cybernetic changes. Despite all these bizarre (to us, now) alterations, you show people still experiencing the age-old emotions: jealousy, grief, anger.

GB: Nigel Walmsley has this seemingly inexplicable predilection for relationships with two women at once and one man. It happens in both *In the Ocean of Night* and *Across the Sea of Suns*. How come? It's not based autobiographically—three-way sex is something I've never experienced. It's embedded somehow in the way he is and the way society has changed. I've attempted to envision how it would be a natural outcome. Also, the ability to change sexes is a protracted metaphor for the fact that we're creating contexts in our society whereby people can change social roles, ferociously. What do these changes—which are taking place right now—really mean? Where are they going to lead?

LM: Throughout *Across the Sea of Suns* you create a series of incidents in which your characters respond inappropriately—sexually, intellectually, socially. It's as if they have all this technological sophistication but their capacity to *relate* to this new technology is still primitive.

GB: The metaphor of the inappropriate response to new information is something I wanted to develop in as many ways as I could. Cancer is one form of inappropriate response; the way people deal with aliens in the book is another inappropriate response. People are alienated from their own bodies, biologically, and from other new stimuli—the literal aliens here. Aliens and alienation. One of the crucial Achilles' heels of all organic life forms is this inappropriate reaction to new data or situations—biologically, socially, intellectually. It's one thing that machine civilizations see and know and don't have to the extent we do.

LM: Although, as you point out, even with the machines, there is the possibility of minute errors creeping in, which over time—

GB: —result in false evolution, or cancer.

LM: *Across the Sea of Suns* and *Great Sky River* are sequels to *In the Ocean of Night.* What concerns drew you back to that earlier novel? Why did it seem important to have Nigel as your central character again?

GB: When I was finishing *In the Ocean of Night,* I vaguely sensed the immense problems I had opened up, and I knew I would eventually go back to them. When I finally figured out how to explore these problems, I decided to write the book not only as a *thematic sequel* (a lot of my works have interrelated themes, so I guess you could call them sequels to one another in this sense) but also as a *narrative sequel.* I did this first of all because I knew I wasn't really through with Nigel Walmsley. Second, having an aged man as my central character was appropriate for the big theme I wanted to use—the grand coming-of-age novel for the human race, our finding out what the universe is really like. Third, the sequel approach seemed right because to me the whole problem of human beings—their confrontation with the alien and particularly with machine intelligence (a different category)—is such a giant territory that it makes sense to create a large narrative framework. I'm going to write a number of novels over several decades dealing with this territory. It's going to be my own Yoknapatawpha—a familiar territory I can return to, book after book. I've only thought about how I might tie all this in during this past year. I'm aiming to write a series of narratives loosely connected, the way Faulkner's were; the old storytelling stuff. Some of the books will be connected, and some will stand in narrative isolation. Some will dimly perceive the others in the distance; in a way they'll be cousins, even third cousins.

It has only gradually come to me that this is what I want my work to be about—that this issue had so many facets that I should group them in a constellation.

LM: Earlier you said you consider SF to be primarily a verbal art. Why do you think it's produced so few gifted stylists?

GB: Until pretty recently most SF writers had more of a background in science than in literature. As a result, you don't see much verbal art in SF, an enchantment with the word itself and with a sense of atmosphere. A lot of writers, like Hal Clement, and many *Analog* writers, such as Charles Sheffield, had these remarkable imaginations but simply didn't have the verbal or formal skills they needed to express what they wanted. SF writers have been too long dependent on a certain kind of austere air—Pascal's terrifying spaces. One of the things I was trying to suggest in *Against Infinity* was that the wilderness—whether it's Faulkner's wilderness or what we're going to find when we leave this planet—is always overgrown, filled, choked with atmosphere. The human environment is never clean and austere for long; we tend to mess it up with our words. So even cold Ganymede was turned into a lush wilderness, both physically and metaphorically, by its inhabitants. That's what we're going to do to the whole universe eventually.

There's also something messy and ambiguous about ordinary language that may make most scientists uneasy. Mathematical languages have such a wonderful aura of precision and controllability, which is why scientists are intuitively drawn to them; but they lack a quality that I can only describe as a human expressiveness. As a scientist, I admire and respect the beauty and formal clarity of mathematics, but I've always *loved* ordinary language in all of its many guises. I'm not sure I can describe why I feel this way—maybe it's because it offers such a great method of lying. Ah, I love to lie!

An Interview with
William S. Burroughs

Great authors have a way of creating texts that defy categorization and assimilation. Typically, a full literary generation elapses before the true significance of a radically new imagination can be seen in useful critical perspective; usually it's even longer before such an imagination begins to influence other writers. Consider Jorge Luis Borges, Jack Kerouac, Samuel Beckett, and Thomas Pynchon—authors who changed our notion of what fiction can be. William S. Burroughs has played a similar role in post–World War II American fiction. While Burroughs's seminal influence on the Beat generation, particularly Allen Ginsberg and Jack Kerouac, has been widely (though often cursorily) noted, the full extent of his pervasive influence on contemporary art—which extends to experimental cinema, poetry, performance art, jazz and rock music, as well as fiction—is just becoming obvious now, some thirty years after *Naked Lunch* appeared with perhaps more fanfare than any novel since *Ulysses*. Nowhere has the influence of Burroughs's radical approach to style and content been more apparent than in the work of urban-techno-guerrilla artists such as punk and "industrial noise" musicians, Mark Pauline and the Survival Research Laboratory, and cyberpunk SF writers.

Not surprisingly, Burroughs's work has had its biggest influence on the radical fringe of SF—on those authors who are most concerned with formal innovations, and specifically with presenting visions of urban despair and victimization that share some of Burroughs's nightmarish intensity, black humor, and sense of dislocation. Like J. G.

Ballard, Philip K. Dick, and Thomas Pynchon—three other authors
who have had an analogous impact on SF in the '80s and who were
also operating at the intersection of SF, the avant-garde, and "serious"
fiction—Burroughs is a savage, wickedly humorous satirist. Even in
the early works that are grounded most clearly in the imagery and
clichés of SF pulp fiction (including not only *Naked Lunch* but also
his trilogy, *The Soft Machine* [1961], *The Ticket That Exploded* [1962],
and *Nova Express* [1964]), Burroughs displays a literary imagination
that had fully assimilated the implications of an array of avant-garde
artists, ranging from Rimbaud to T. S. Eliot (who lectured at Harvard
while Burroughs was an undergraduate there), James Joyce, Samuel
Beckett, and the surrealists. His most famous stylistic innovation—the
"cut-up" or "fold-in" method of constructing new texts—was developed
by his friend and collaborator, the painter Brion Gysin. His success in
using this device as a means of short-circuiting the usual linguistic
pathways has tended to obscure the fact that Burroughs is also one of
the most skilled and eloquent modern prose stylists, a writer whose
remarkable ear for the full range of colloquial American idioms is
probably unmatched since Mark Twain's.

Burroughs is also a quintessentially postmodernist artist. Indeed, fully
twenty years before the term "postmodernism" achieved critical as-
cendancy, Burroughs was working out implications today associated
with postmodernist aesthetics that remain unsurpassed in their originality and the relentless nature of their application. The postmodernist
quality of his work derives principally from the formal methods he has
devised to assert that the central threat facing modern humanity involves
the control of individuals through an increasingly sophisticated system
of technologically produced words, images, and other dangerously addictive substances (with drug addiction being an all-pervasive metaphor
throughout his work). Burroughs seeks to willfully subvert such power-
wielding in part through an "innoculation program" in which readers
are presented with montages of pop cultural images, fragmented texts
culled from a bewildering variety of sources (Shakespeare, Kafka, scientific textbooks, '30s pulp SF authors, T. S. Eliot, Denton Welch, etc.),
snippets of Burroughs's daily journals, and other materials. All these
are transformed into texts whose progress is tied less to narrative continuity than to principles of poetic association.

Burroughs's fiction is utterly contemporary in its formal emphasis
on fragmentation, its blending of pop and serious forms, its emphasis
on the transformative process of experience, and its insistence that
"meanings" are always provisional, that even the most sacred texts can
be (and *must* be) continually deconstructed and reconstituted. Equally
contemporary—and of particular relevance to Burroughs's role in the

evolution of SF—has been his thematic preoccupation with reality-as-film, drug addiction, information control, and the technological/biological/psychological manipulation of people who have grown addicted to words, images, sex, and other thanatological substances.

Despite being firmly embedded in postmodernism's dystopian present and near future, Burroughs's work is equally significant in its exploration of universal issues. The human tendency to control and destroy others for greed and sexual gratification; the ongoing human need to resist the destructive impulses of others and themselves; a common search for some means by which to transcend our personal, biological extinction—these and many other timeless issues are examined in a body of work that is "science fictional" in the tradition of Jonathan Swift.

Jim McMenamin and I interviewed William Burroughs in July 1987 in Boulder, Colorado. Several years earlier, he had moved from "The Bunker" (his Manhattan residence) to Lawrence, Kansas, but each summer he has been a regular participant at the Naropa Institute, where he gives readings, addresses the audience, and assists young writers. The previous evening he had delivered one of his patented readings, full of playfulness and discomforting obscenities, pointed social and political commentary, and tall tales. We met Burroughs in the sparsely furnished apartment where he was staying during the conference; the only visible reading material was the *National Enquirer*. At seventy-three, Burroughs appeared healthily cadaverous, and he was spry enough to sprint up and down the stairs several times when he needed to check a reference. Later, when we glanced back at him standing on his apartment balcony, we felt certain we were experiencing something of the same exhilaration that Kerouac must have felt forty-five years ago in Manhattan, when he had just left Burroughs's apartment for the first time.

Jim McMenamin: You've just completed *The Western Lands*. Did writing this novel become a way for you to explore your own views about death and a possible afterlife?

William Burroughs: Naturally. All my books express what I actually believe in, or I wouldn't be writing them. *The Western Lands* also goes into the possibility of hybridization, the crossing of man and animals. This goes against one of the basic taboos: that the species must remain separate. But there must have been a time in the past when hybridization was rampant. Otherwise why would we now have this terrific variety of species? This means there must have been some factors operating then that are not in operation at the present time—some radiation affecting things, or who knows what. This is, of course, related to various theories of evolution. There's the virus theory of evolution, which is one I've always been interested in. If you have a virus producing biological changes that are then conveyed genetically, you can have an entirely new species in a couple of generations instead of it taking millions of years. There's also the punctuational view of evolution, which says that if you take a species of fish from one place and put them in a completely foreign environment, they will mutate very rapidly. Alterations occur in response to drastic alterations in equilibrium in small, isolated groups. So that's another possibility. It's interesting because the evolutionary trend toward standardization will tend to rule this out. There aren't any isolated groups in which such changes could occur. The only thing is that no virus we know of right now acts in that way. Of course, this idea is a version of the Lamarckian heresy of the inheritance of acquired characteristics.

Larry McCaffery: It sounds almost like the biological equivalent of entropy—the idea that things would spread out in a random way so there could be no interaction, the end result being total chaos or death.

WB: Or total lethargy.

JM: What have you been reading recently?

WB: I read a lot of doctor books and spy books. Not much that you would call serious fiction—for that I usually go back a ways. Right now I'm rereading all of Conrad. He's the greatest novelist who ever lived, far and away. You can see a lot of Conrad in my recent work. And Graham Greene, too.

LM: After spending all that time in places like London, New York, Paris, and Tangier, what made you decide to move to Lawrence, Kansas?

WB: Out of all the questions in the world, I've been asked that one so many times recently that I'm sick of it. People act as if there must be something very portentous behind moving to Lawrence. Well, things just don't work that way. James Grauerholz was living in Lawrence, and I had visited there several times. I wanted to get out of New York anyway, for a number of reasons. I'd looked at Boulder as a possibility, and I decided I didn't want to live there. Lawrence just worked out. It's a university town—nothing very special—it's all right.

JM: Do you miss the sensory bombardment that you had in New York, or is it something you don't need anymore?

WB: I didn't have it in New York. My working habits are about the same in Lawrence as they were in New York. I didn't go to parties or discotheques. I've never been to Studio 54. I didn't go to various celebrity in-spots. I didn't do any of those things. So, there wasn't any bombardment. Only in Lawrence I can get out of doors and row, and shoot, and keep cats, and things that I can't do in New York.

LM: Have you been watching the Oliver North testimony and other aspects of the Iran-Contra hearings?

WB: I've watched about five minutes of it, just enough to get a vague idea of what's going on. I'm not interested in all the intricacies. It's clear that the '80s will go down in history as the Lie Decade. Ferdinand Marcos, of course, gets the undoubted prize as the most flagrant and outrageous liar of the Lie Decade. But he's got some competition.

JM: I heard you had met with David Cronenberg to discuss a movie version of *Naked Lunch*. How did that come about—were you already familiar with his work?

WB: No, although when the possibility of doing *Naked Lunch* came up, I made a point of seeing some of his films, and I liked them. I saw *The Dead Zone*—that's the one he did from the Stephen King book— and a few others. I haven't seen *The Fly*, which was apparently very successful. Cronenberg approached us about doing the film, so we met in Tangier. That was two or three years ago, and nothing definite has occurred. Nothing happens until it happens in the film world. Actually, I haven't been paying much attention to films recently. I go very occasionally. About the last film I saw was *Brazil*.

LM: Do you think the media's willingness to offer the public all this excessive violence—on the news, in films, on MTV—will eventually desensitize people to violence?

WB: To some extent, naturally. It's bound to happen. Like the first time you go on a roller coaster, it scares you; the second time, not so much; the third time, not at all.

JM: There seems to be an ambiguity in your presentation of violence—a combination of horror, black humor, grim fascination, maybe even sympathy. Do you see your portrayal of brutality and violence as being primarily an exorcism or a celebration?

WB: Neither. There's a lot of violence in my work because violence is obviously necessary in certain circumstances. I'm often talking in a revolutionary, guerrilla context where violence is the only recourse. I feel a degree of ambivalence with regard to any use of violence. There are certainly circumstances where it seems to be indicated. How can you protect people without weapons? If you're interested in protecting, you can't. I was very much a fan of the Guardian Angels. That's the answer to violent crime, right there. They should have regular patrols in all cities, and that would eliminate the whole crime situation. But nobody—particularly no politician—wants to eliminate any problems. Problems are what keep them in there. Anyway, some system of organized patrols is the obvious answer to that problem.

JM: Obviously, an outfit like that would need to be formed locally.

WB: It would have to be local. But, of course, the last people who would want to see something like this come into operation would be the police. They would become redundant. All these big problems we suffer from are so absurdly simple. Like the drug problem: maintenance for those who can't or won't stop, and effective treatment for those who want to stop. There isn't any effective treatment at the present time, and the government is putting no money into researching the basic mechanisms of addiction. None of the endorphin research is funded with government money. Endorphin is one of the keys to addiction, and it could lead to really effective treatment.

JM: You used to say that apomorphine could be a major breakthrough for treating heroin addicts. Do you still feel that way?

WB: It's been more or less confirmed now that apomorphine stimulates the production of endorphins, just as acupuncture stimulates the body's natural pain killer(s) under certain circumstances. I've got a file like the Manhattan telephone book of inquiries from probation officers and prison officials about apomorphine research. But when I write them back, the first thing you know they're being threatened with the loss of their jobs.

JM: What's behind the lack of governmental research into this area—Drug Enforcement Administration repression?

WB: Certainly. The DEA doesn't want to see an effective treatment for narcotics. My God, where would they be if there weren't any drug addicts?

LM: The public's negative attitude about drugs today seems dangerously simplistic. There was a period back in the '60s when it seemed as if a genuinely enlightened attitude might be evolving.

WB: Yes, it seems like all the ground gained in the '60s—in all sorts of areas—is now being lost.

LM: Is this rightward swing an inevitable reaction?

WB: No swing is inevitable. I'm not even convinced that what we're seeing is necessarily a swing. What we're seeing with drug attitudes is certainly engineered by the administration. They're the ones orchestrating this whole antidrug nonsense, and this hysteria could turn the whole planet into a police state. Hell, probably the biggest danger we face today is a fascist takeover under the guise of this colossal red herring of the drug pretense. Narcs roaming around free from all restraint.

LM: How might things develop if the governments (and whatever multinationals are calling the shots behind the scenes) can maintain the current hysteria level?

WB: My God, it's appalling. Urine tests. What bullshit. Our pioneer ancestors would be pissing in their collective graves at the idea that urine tests should decide whether someone is competent to do his job. Or these sobriety checkpoints on the highways. It's performance that should count. When someone told Lincoln that Grant had a drinking problem, Lincoln said, "OK, let's distribute his brand of whiskey to the other generals and maybe they'll get the lead out of their britches and do something about winning this war." We are being bullied by a Moron Majority committed to enforcing their stupid, bestial, bigoted opinions on everybody else—so you've got all this unthinking adherence to these standards that have nothing to do with the survival of the species. These are the guard dogs who will keep the human race in neoteny until this experiment is finally buried. We've even got brats turning in their parents. If things keep going this way, Reagan and Meese will have turned America into a nation of mainstream *rats!* And if this pretense of the war on drugs—which no one really wants to succeed—allows this fascist takeover to go global, there's going to be a real nightmare. Narcs will be kings! You can already see where this is heading. In Malaysia right now they have the death penalty for possession of more than half an ounce of heroin or morphine, and you can be hanged for more than seven ounces of pot! Anyone even *suspected* of trafficking can be held for two years without a charge or a trial. Anybody on the street who even *looks* like a user can be brought in and held until he gives a urine sample, and if it's positive he can be sent to a rehab center for two years.

LM: Do you think there was ever a practical chance back in the '60s to effect real change? Or was that just a lot of hippie nonsense?

WB: Well, you never know. You can look back on what's happened and you can see various points where a wrong turn was made, an opportunity lost. And these wrong turns weren't just taken in America. The same thing was happening in France, for example. It looked like the students were really going to take over, but then they began falling out among themselves. I'm not saying no real progress was made. Prior to the '60s minorities had no rights at all to speak of, and four-letter words could not appear on a printed page. But considering what the opportunities were, where we are now is pretty discouraging.

JM: In *Cities of the Red Night* you use the familiar SF motif of the alternative universe—with the Captain Mission experiment in Madagascar, and so on—to deal with this idea of the "lost turns."

WB: Yes, what happened with Mission in Madagascar was another possibility. Of course, you had just a small colony of three hundred there, but if it had spread it could have been a whole different ball game for people, a new option. But it didn't spread. They were overwhelmed by a native uprising, probably orchestrated by the British.

LM: You could look at what happened after the Revolutionary War as being another one of those turning points.

WB: That's one reason why it's a pity these pirate colonies weren't able to maintain themselves. If you'd had these kind of movements operating on a worldwide scale, people might have seen what the actual practice of freedom meant. That might have forced the American Revolution to stand by its words. The French, too. But everybody came over here looking for money, money, money. Nothing else on their minds. The American Dream has always been money, not freedom. But you must remember that these situations aren't comparable; people were pouring into the United States, while in Madagascar—and in the other pirate colonies that were formed on Tortuga Island and in the West Indies—there was just a small colony of three hundred people.

LM: Once you get more than a few people involved in any idealistic project it's inevitable—

WB: *Nothing* is inevitable, except possibly the speed of light. That's what the scientists say.

LM: Did the idea for developing a "road-not-taken" premise in *Cities of the Red Night* derive from your readings in science fiction?

WB: It came from various sources. A lot of it came from my sense of the actual possibilities of those real colonies at the time. I was familiar with the way SF had used that idea, but certainly I'd say my handling of it comes more from actual materials than from SF. You can see the appeal of going back and rewriting history from certain crucial junctures. One of the things that interested me in *Cities of the Red Night* was seeing what would have happened if you could get rid of the Catholic influence. Even after the Spanish were kicked out of South America by the liberal revolutions of 1848, their whole way of doing things— the bureaucracy, the language, the calendar, the Church—was still in effect. What would have happened if that influence had left with the Spanish? There must have been a number of crucial junctures in the Russian Revolution, too; depending on how you look at it, other paths that could have been fortunate or unfortunate.

LM: Other paths like what—Lenin not dying as soon as he did?

WB: I'm more interested in what would have happened if Stalin hadn't grabbed the whole thing and held it together. Without Stalin, the whole thing might have foundered into a number of separate, warring factions; then they would never have been able to establish a strong central government and set up the phony, so-called communist state. That state was Stalin's doing.

LM: Several recent SF writers, like Gregory Benford, in *Timescape,* and John Varley, in *Millennium,* have developed ingenious novels purporting to present time travel as being feasible based on what we now understand about physics. If so, maybe things really can evolve differently.

WB: Perhaps, but what we know about biological mutations indicates that certain changes can happen only in one direction. This doesn't necessarily apply to time travel, but as far as we know evolution remains a one-way street. You can see this illustrated in the newts. Newts start their life cycles in the water and they have gills. After a certain time they shed the gills and come up onto land and get lungs. Then they go back and live in the water—but they never get their gills back, even though gills might be convenient. And we know that whales and dolphins must have lived on land at one time, which is why they now have lungs. Obviously, it would be very convenient if evolution would allow them to go back and have gills again, but the whole evolutionary process seems to make this impossible. What this means is that a biological mutation, once established, becomes irrevocable. I'm not sure, but maybe this kind of irreversibility applies to time travel in a general sense.

LM: It's interesting to speculate on how we've now developed the capacity to start tinkering with these basic processes. Biological mutations or evolution may be a one-way street in nature, but perhaps we can intervene in this by surgery and cybernetic engineering to biologically alter ourselves in some favorable ways.

WB: Obviously we could do this, but the social and political difficulties are enormous. Alvin Toffler, the fellow who wrote *Future Shock* (which is a great title), has pointed out in a much better book, *The Third Wave,* that a lot of things like this are not two hundred years away but ten or twenty years away. The problem is that these things could not be absorbed by our increasingly creaky and unstable social system. We have all these people who are really unnecessary, and supposedly we're going to be made more biologically efficient and more intelligent. Well, who's going to make the definitions of intelligence and efficiency? Who's going to implement them? As transplant techniques are perfected so that we theoretically have the dream of immortality within our grasp, who's going to decide which applicants get the transplants? There simply aren't enough parts to go around. Is this going to be a sort of rule by scientists? Politically and socially speaking, we don't have any answers.

LM: You've said that our sociological chaos may really reflect a biological crisis—that is, maybe the human species is the end of an evolutionary line; and if we don't find a way to adapt ourselves somehow to conditions in outer space, we're going to die as a species. Are you seriously talking about our living in outer space?

WB: Certainly.

LM: Isn't that going to require basic changes in our bodies?

WB: Of course. Very drastic changes. It might even require eliminating our bodies altogether. This isn't really so farfetched. You can say that the body is automated by an electromagnetic forcefield, and that forcefield possibly can be separated from the body and transported. One of

our big drawbacks is weight—weight and then, on top of that, having
to transport the whole environment around something that's already
fairly heavy (the human body). But the dream or astral body is virtually
weightless (not completely so, but pretty nearly), so that would be the
obvious way to go. Of course, the Russians are doing a lot of work on
adapting to space, trying to overcome the decalcification problem, but
that's just tinkering.

Then, of course, you have another question entirely: the conditions
on another planet, or in a space station. I know some people at the
Ecotechnic Institute, which is based in Forth Worth, Texas, backed by
oil money. They're building an ecosphere near Tucson. It'll cover over
two acres, and it has an artificial ocean (a small one), fish ponds, and
intensive agriculture. Eight people are supposed to live in there for two
years. The system must be a self-perpetuating environment. About $30
million has gone into the thing already, and space people and foreign
scientists are very interested in the results. The idea is to see whether
you can take a unit like that and put it down anywhere—put it down
on the moon, put it down on Mars or any other planet. I don't know
how far along the thing is right now. I've been meaning to go down
there and look at it.

LM: That's like your analogy of the fish inventing an aquarium it
can take up onto land.

WB: Sure, that's exatly what it is—a giant aquarium. And there are
so many technical difficulties involved. They've got a lot to think about:
temperature control and all that, sewage disposal.

JM: As far as you know, is any serious research being done in the
other direction—things like astral projection?

WB: I don't think so. If there is, it's not being done overtly. Of course,
Bob Monroe, who wrote *Journeys out of the Body,* is still experimenting
down in Afton, Virginia; he's got machines to facilitate leaving the body,
I think. But I haven't heard any results from that. He teamed up with
Kübler-Ross for a while. But having Kübler-Ross at your bedside is
about as ominous as having a priest. Or a vulture.

JM: What about government funding for that type of thing?

WB: Not that I know of. There might well be, but if it's being done,
it isn't overt. I should imagine the Russians are more likely to be into
that. They're really much more practical than we are, you know.

LM: Do you think the fact that we're not conducting serious research
into these areas has to do with the empirical biases of thinking over
here?

WB: The scientists may take it seriously enough. But remember:
when it comes time to allocate money for it, politicians are going to
say to themselves, This is fine, but what are our *constituents* going to

think if they find out about this? Jack Anderson brought out that a lot of psychic research has been done by the CIA secretly in the Nevada desert somewhere. They couldn't justify the appropriations to Congress, and Congress couldn't justify them to their constituents. Well, the Russians don't have to worry about their constituents. That's a big advantage in getting anything done.

LM: Were these the CIA experiments involving the use of LSD?

WB: These experiments were more involved with ESP and trying to set up a way to control and contact agents using ESP. Far-seeing was one of the things; the CIA has done a lot of experiments with far-seeing. The idea was that agents could go and see enemy encampments and emplacements. I've read a number of books on the subject. Quite interesting, well documented. I used the idea in *Cities of the Red Night* with the character Yen Lee.

LM: You had your first hallucinatory visions when you were only about four years old. What kind of experiences were these?

WB: I wouldn't call them hallucinatory at all. If you see something, it's a shift of vision, not a hallucination. You shift your vision. What you see is there, but you have to be in a certain place to see it. There were two that I remember. Little gray men playing in my block house, and green reindeer. I didn't dream up the whole concept of the gray men or the small green reindeer subsequently. I think everyone has one or two of these experiences at one time or another. I think an actual shift of vision is involved. I'm doing some pure chance paintings now that seem to produce these perceptual shifts. For example, you take a piece of plywood and a spray-paint can and stand back and shoot the can with a shotgun. The can explodes—it will go thirty feet. Now you look at this thing and there's a shift. You can see all kinds of things in there. Movies, little scenes, streets. Anybody can see it. They're there somewhere. So I wouldn't speak of it as a hallucination.

LM: If you take LSD and look at clouds, or at any other surface that has a lot of information on it, these sorts of images seem to jump out at you.

WB: Sure. But my point is that you don't need acid to experience these things. It's just a question of looking at it. It used to be that people would look at a Cézanne painting and not even recognize the apples or the fish on the canvas. Those things were really there, but people didn't realize they were looking at something seen by the painter from a certain angle, under certain light conditions. They had to be shown how to look. That's one of the main functions of art, or of any creative thought for that matter: make people more aware of what they already perceive but don't yet recognize. Expand awareness. There's someone in Lawrence, a photographer, who's done "cloud pictures." He waits and gets a clear image and takes that. With a lot of patience, you see, you get a number of perfectly clear faces, animals, all kinds of things. You could get the same thing with vistas, particularly lakes and mountains, but you'd have to shoot a lot of footage to get anything. This sort of thing would be very worthwhile as a photographic experiment. Clouds would be best, though. Well, sometimes leaves. I've done this sort of thing very successfully with some of these paintings. Anybody at all can look and see these images, and they often see the same things. And some of them obviously *are* the same. There'll be a perfectly clear cat, or a number of cats, when they've been on my mind.

JM: Do you think your mind in some way influenced the spray of the paint?

WB: Not in any cause-and-effect way. It's a matter of synchronicity. What you're thinking of, you'll encounter. When I became interested in cats, I began to see cats in Brion's paintings. I'm merely following in Brion's footsteps in the introduction of random factors. That sort of thing also goes on in his calligraphy. This notion that what goes on inside somebody can affect something outside goes against the dogma of scientific materialism, which would insist there can't possibly be any relationship between what you see as you walk down the street and what you're thinking. But that's obviously not true. I'm thinking about New Mexico, and I come around a corner and there's a New Mexico license plate. The Land of Enchantment. Well, that's not an example of cause and effect. I didn't put it there by thinking about it. But I was there at the same time. The whole concept of synchronicity is much more in accord with the actual facts of perception.

LM: Have you experimented with the different effects you get from different types of guns and shells?

WB: Oh, yeah, yeah. A shotgun is about the only thing that will work, because it makes interesting patterns on the other side where it emerges. Sometimes you'll get big patches of paint, and some of these are the most interesting. You actually have two sides to these things — they're not two-dimensional like a regular painting, because the plywood can be three-quarters of an inch thick. I've shot a lot of different shells through plywood, but nothing does it like a shotgun.

LM: These synchronistic effects you describe — having cat images emerge in the paint splatterings while you're thinking about cats — seem related to what's happening in cut-ups.

WB: It's the same principle of allowing a random act to produce effects that you don't know you're going to get. Or on some level you may well know and be doing it exactly right. I've had that happen several times. I'll shoot at the plywood with my shotgun and think, Oh

God, I missed. Later on I find out I didn't really miss but had fired at where it really should have gone.

JM: You've said that the cut-up method gives writers an access to the materiality of language that's analogous to painters' access to the elements of their medium.

WB: Yes. By that I mean a painter can mix his colors on his palette, and the writer using cut-ups can do somewhat the same with words. At one time, of course, writing and painting were one—that is, with picture writing. They're still very close in Chinese poetry and calligraphy.

LM: The development of the phonetic alphabet in the West, so that words are connected to objects only through these arbitrary conventions, must affect the way we think. You'd assume it would make us feel separated from the world around us.

WB: Yeah, but you've got to remember that a lot of the relationships established between words and objects in a picture-writing form, like Egyptian hieroglyphs, is just as arbitrary. How do you say all your prepositions like "before," "toward," "under," "over"? You say them in a rather arbitrary way. And the Egyptian hieroglyphs do have an alphabet, so it's not entirely pictographic by any means. But even so, the grammar of a pictorial language is unbelievably complex and confusing. Egyptologists never really agree on the interpretation of a passage.

JM: You've repeatedly attacked the either/or mode of thinking—all those dualities that seem so essential to Western thought and language, whereas in Chinese, for example, there's no inflection for gender.

WB: And that makes sense. Also, in Egyptian hieroglyphs, while they do have a verb "is," it's not used the way we use the "is" of identity. They don't say, "He is my son" or "The sun is in the sky" but "He *as* my son" or "Sun *in* sky." They don't have to say "is"—they make much less use of the "is" of identity which, as Alfred Korzybski said, is one of the big fuck-ups of Western language. Something "is" something, with the implication that there is some sort of eternal status being conveyed.

LM: That helps produce the basic confusion between idea and object.

WB: Yeah, or between word and object. The idea that if you have a word there must be something corresponding to it. Korzybski used to start his lectures by saying, "Whatever this is, it isn't a table." It's not the label.

JM: You've said that when you were writing *The Place of Dead Roads* you felt you were in spiritual contact with Denton Welch. What sort of contact did you mean?

WB: Any writer feels that sort of contact if he's serious. He's in contact—*real* contact—with his characters. As Genet says, a writer takes upon himself the very heavy responsibility for his characters.

JM: What about Welch intrigued you in the first place?

WB: He's a very great writer. I admired his work, and I thought he fitted right into this role I had in mind.

LM: Did the student rebellions taking place in France and the United States in the '60s have anything to do with your conception of *The Wild Boys?*

WB: No, not really, because *The Wild Boys* was pretty removed from any sequences occurring in reality. It was more like a children's story, *Peter Pan* or something like that.

LM: You seem to be in touch with a lot of young people today. What's your sense of them?

WB: I'm not so much in touch. I mean, I do readings and lectures and I talk to a few people, but I don't feel myself in any sense able to evaluate their *Zeitgeist*. From what I have seen, though, they certainly seem less purposeful than they did in the '60s.

LM: And less willing to take risks, perhaps? In that *Rolling Stone* article a few months ago, you describe an encounter where you offered students a chance to use a wish machine.

WB: They didn't believe it. They didn't have any wishes. I wonder if young people today *have* any wishes. No, it's not that they aren't willing to take risks, exactly. There aren't any risks to be taken. Danger is a very rare commodity in these times, monopolized by intelligence agencies and stuntmen.

LM: Maybe this is one reason why everyone seems so fascinated with Ollie North?

WB: That sort of mindless fascination has got to grow out of this general absence of danger. The middle class feels this particularly acutely. Nietzsche said, "Men need play and danger. Civilization gives them work and safety." Danger is not an end in itself, by any means. It is a conflict of purposes, or a conflict of some sort. The danger is a by-product, just as happiness is a by-product of function. You can't hope for happiness in and of itself; that's like seeking victory without war — the flaw in all utopias. Of course, since danger and happiness are by-products of function, we are in shit-shape today because very few people function in our society. There's no place for them to function.

LM: So do people today have to be more creative about inventing these arbitrary functions?

WB: I don't know what you mean by arbitrary.

LM: I was thinking of something like football, where heroism and danger are generated as by-products. Capitalism could be another example — people assess their successes or failures on the basis of definitions invented by the system itself.

WB: There's no question about that. You see, the frontier's gone, and with it disappeared all those opportunities for taking on a role that really means something. Outer space is the only place that's going to create new roles, and that's monopolized by a very, very few people in the military. So you've got millions of people and very few roles for them. That's what functioning really means: enacting a purposeful role.

JM: In the *Retreat Diaries* you include an anecdote about being asked by the Rinpoche not to take the tools of your trade—your typewriter, paper, pens, whatever—with you on a retreat. You refuse, saying you need to be open to the writing experience at any time.

WB: Right. A writer may only get one chance, so he shouldn't ever put himself in a position where he can't write something down if he wants to. That's not true if you're a carpenter, where you've got plenty of time to build something, plenty of chances.

LM: Computers seem potentially very significant for writers in that they allow you to manipulate textual elements more freely. Have you done much work on word processors?

WB: No. I'm very poor with any mechanical contrivances. I don't know how a typewriter works, for example. I can use it, but I don't know how it works. Right now word processors seem just too complicated to get into. I guess they would be helpful, save a great deal of time undoubtedly, but at this point the effort involved in learning how to use them just doesn't seem worthwhile.

LM: Have you talked with Timothy Leary about his work in designing computer software? He says if artists start designing the software, maybe computers could eventually start opening up our consciousness in creative ways.

WB: I've talked with Leary about this, but I dare say I've not seen these programs work this way. I know with some of these things you actually participate and make decisions about the plot and all that— audience participation. But audience participation has never worked very well in my experience. After all, the audience isn't necessarily coming to a work of art to participate. Brecht and the Living Theater did a lot of experimenting with that sort of thing.

LM: Of course, audience participation with computer-generated novels is limited. You can only respond to the artist's prior structures.

WB: In other words, you're only going to have the choices somebody else has given you. The experience will only be as good as the program. And, of course, once you're talking about audience participation, you've got to realize most of the audience just isn't competent.

LM: A lot of recent SF deals with things like people interfacing with machines and computers, and machines that can program themselves so they can really "think."

WB: It's quite possible people could occupy a machine. Why not?

But as far as machines developing thinking capabilities, the basic problem is that nothing happens without *will,* without motivation. How do you motivate a machine? They have not, so far, developed any machine that can process qualitative data. They could simulate this in a very crude way by different charges of electricity which could indicate that, say, here you have mild annoyance, distinct annoyance, anger, homicidal rage. Those obviously are quantitative differences, but at some point all quantitative differences become qualitative. So now you have a different charge for those—homicidal rage will light up half of the machine, whereas these other states are very faint.

LM: Do you think machines may eventually supplant the human "soft machine"?

WB: Machines aren't going to supplant us without a motive. A machine isn't going to do anything unless it's motivated, any more than a person is. People don't think unless they have a reason to think— which we have at all times, of course. I'm not sure a machine can be given this kind of motivation. How can you frighten a machine? It isn't thinking that's important in this respect—machines can think better than we can. But the machine would have to be motivated—by fear, desire, whatever—before it could ever replace us in the evolutionary movement of things. In other words, it would have to be alive.

LM: SF writers have recently been dealing with these issues about machine intelligence and fear and consciousness. I'm thinking of, say, the computer HAL in *2001: A Space Odyssey,* or Philip K. Dick's androids in *Do Androids Dream of Electric Sheep?* (and in *Blade Runner*). I guess this idea was already there in Mary Shelley's *Frankenstein.*

WB: This whole business about the machine becoming alive at some point has certainly been a theme throughout SF. But they're very vague as to just how this could occur. It depends on what is meant by being "alive," or what you mean by "conscious." Consciousness is always a matter of conflict of some sort.

LM: In *2001* it appears that HAL somehow recognizes the implications of being turned off—that he'll die, cease to exist. Couldn't you program a machine so it wouldn't want to be turned off?

WB: How could this be programmed? To *not want*—that's the trouble. Wanting or not wanting are the stumbling blocks.

JM: Your work has used a lot of SF motifs and imagery. Did your interest in SF (and other pulp forms) start out when you were a kid?

WB: Oh, yes, I read all the SF I could get my hands on. As I remember, there were some good stories in *Amazing Stories* and *Weird Tales,* though I can't remember who wrote them. The best of them seem to have disappeared without a trace. You don't find much really good SF because it's very hard to write; there just aren't many writers who have the imagination and know-how to make you believe this or that could actually ever take place. So you're lucky if you find more than a few good sentences in an SF novel. Every now and then you find a whole good paragraph, or even a chapter. I think Eric Frank Russell is pretty good. His *Three to Conquer* is still one of the best virus books I've come across. So is Henry Kuttner's *Fury.* There's some sword and sorcery stuff by Fred Saberhagen that I like. H. G. Wells's best works still seem to hold up. But I read all those adventure stories and Western stories, science fiction, the Little Blue Books, all that stuff.

LM: It's interesting that in the United States, the most technologically advanced nation in the world, SF until recently has not been taken seriously. Up through the '30s it seems pretty much adventure-story oriented, whereas in Europe you already had this tradition of serious SF writing: Wells, Jules Verne, Olaf Stapledon, Karel Capek, Aldous Huxley, Evgenii Zamiatin, and others.

WB: It's not so much a matter of whether you're writing something that's adventure oriented but how you handle what you're doing; how much you're able to use the adventure formula to convince the reader that you're dealing with something important and believable. You look at Wells and he's adventure oriented: *The Time Machine* and *The War of the Worlds* and all that. He was a great influence on SF at its earliest, along with Jules Verne, of course. *The Voyage to the Moon,* where they lived inside the moon, the insect creatures—that's quite a story. But you're right: SF wasn't taken seriously at first in America. We didn't have any name comparable to Wells or Verne when I was growing up. Maybe we still don't. I'm always hearing people talking about how SF is "coming of age" in America, but I don't know. The main problem with SF seems to be that even though we've had a lot of writers who are dealing with these really strange, remarkable ideas—black holes, the business about relativity and quantum mechanics, machine intelligence, the birth and death of the universe—the way they portray these ideas has been pretty old-fashioned. If you're going to treat these really far-out ideas seriously, you've got to be willing to try something different stylistically.

LM: When the SF pulps really got started in the late '20s and '30s, not only were we in the midst of a depression, which a lot of people would want to escape from, but it was also a time when scientific technology was beginning to affect our everyday lives.

WB: I remember when television was thought of as an SF idea. It seems that a lot of SF these days is really science *fact,* that is, dealing with discoveries that are already actually here. Like they actually have these brain implants you see in *The Terminal Man.* It's not future technology but present technology. Michael Crichton's not trying to *predict* anything so much as to build a story around what we already know is possible.

LM: Back in the '60s, when you started developing your SF trilogy (*The Soft Machine, The Ticket That Exploded, Nova Express*), you seemed to be borrowing some of your key motifs directly from the SF pulps—like your use of Venus and Venusians.

WB: I took that right from all those old SF novels where Venus is thought of as this teeming, dangerous jungle, with all these exotic, poisonous plants and animals. That's what Venus would conjure up for most people.

JM: In *Word Cultures,* Robin Lydenberg argues that a lot of your materials that critics have assumed were metaphors aren't metaphors at all but literal things.

WB: That's right, although we'd have to fool around with definitions of metaphor. What is a metaphor? How is it different from a simile? I don't even know. To me, a metaphor is setting up something that is similar to something else. Writers can't function without them. You can't write a single page without metaphor. (It would be interesting to try—that is, to see if you could write a book without a metaphor.)

LM: That was something that Alain Robbe-Grillet and some of the other French New Novelists seemed to be trying to do.

WB: Yeah, the new realists or whatever they call themselves now. Phenomenologists. They just dealt with certainties. But how far did they really get without metaphor?

LM: They seemed to use geometrical images to describe things, but do they really think geometry isn't metaphorical?

WB: Right away they're talking about circles, squares, rectangles, which are themselves metaphors. How would you describe, for example, a table without reference to any measurements? I mean, how big is it? As soon as you say this table is "a round piece of wood," you've already got a metaphor. How about "a piece of wood so shaped that if you walk around it you come back to the same place you started from"— that's a little awkward. That's what some of the prose of that school sounded like to me. Finally, what's the point?

LM: One significant thing that emerged from these sorts of linguistic investigations was a deeper awareness of some of the things you talk about a lot: the falsities that derive from the implications of the language system itself, like the either/or dichotomy that may have nothing to do with reality.

WB: Which is Korzybski's point. That opposition doesn't correspond to what little we know about the physical world and the functioning of the human nervous system. Every act is not either instinctive or intellectual; it's instinctive *and* intellectual, involving the organism's entire body. You may want to eat something, which most people would say is an instinctive reaction; but in order to actually eat that steak, your rational intellect may be doing things like looking at a map, trying to figure out how to read a menu in French, driving a car, or paying a cab fare. Who's to separate these responses?

JM: The virus metaphor is central to your work, and a lot of things you were describing back in the '60s seem very prophetic today. What's your view about AIDS, for example?

WB: Have you seen the flyer from that society, the United Front against Racism and Capitalism? It claims there is evidence that AIDS could have been a laboratory creation. [Burroughs goes upstairs and returns with the flyer, whose headline reads: "RUSSIA HOPES THAT THE SPREAD OF THE DEADLY AIDS VIRUS WILL BRING AMERICA TO ITS KNEES."] This business about the U.S. or the West being brought to its knees, of course, is very unlikely. The whole AIDS scare is mainly a publicity campaign on the part of Ronald Reagan and that whole Moron Majority lunatic fringe. Compared with smallpox or the Black Death, AIDS is just a drop in the bucket. Certainly, the way in which AIDS is spread in this country suggests that it was done deliberately— but probably by us, not by Russia. After all, what's Russia going to gain by killing off gays and blacks and drug users? They wouldn't be hitting at our military, our manpower, at all. On the other hand, the American government has very good reasons. They want scapegoats, for one thing. Diversions. They want a pretext for more governmental control. Addicts form a perfect conduit for introducing any biological or chemical agent. Addicts buy their needles where they buy their junk. Junk dealers have always got them there all sealed up. They sell hundreds of those things a day. Nothing would have been easier than to put a tiny, minuscule drop of infected blood in some of those needles and, *Whamo,* in a couple of days you've got the virus spread all over New York. What I'm saying is that evidence points to contamination at the source. It's inconclusive, but the circumstantial indications point in that direction. Of course, then there's the African and Haitian scene. There's an interesting article in *Life* magazine about AIDS and the Haitian connection—it's about the women and children, just a pandemic right now. So I wouldn't make any definite statements on whether or not it is a laboratory creation. But it certainly *could have been,* and it could have been spread the way I just described. And there's no question that the U.S. government is much more motivated to do something like this than are the Soviets.

LM: Are you pessimistic about the chances for the human race finding a way to avoid exterminating itself with its own technology?

WB: We certainly have a very, very dark picture here today. But I don't consider myself pessimistic, because that word doesn't have any significance; neither does "optimistic." I mean, if the planet is destroying itself and I say it is, does that make me a pessimist? The only person in the political arena with some trace of good intentions at the present time seems to be Mikhail Gorbachev. To what extent these intentions are genuine, I don't know, but they certainly seem more so than the Reagan administration's.

JM: You've suggested that the only hope for Earth to survive will be if we can get rid of nations. But, as you've also pointed out, in order to do that we'll probably have to get rid of the family system as well. There have been some experiments along those lines in China.

WB: Yes, but if there's going to be any real hope for long-term survival, there have to be some very basic biological changes. As I said earlier, maybe our best hope is to get away from this planet, with its abysmal cycles of overpopulation, depletion of resources, pollution, and escalating conflicts. Now that's going to require biological alterations in the human structure that would make us able to exist in space—that, or we go the out-of-body route, which is probably more practical. But if you look at the human organism as some kind of biological artifact created in response to some design or motive we can't fathom—and I'm convinced that nothing in this universe happens without will or intent—you can see how much is wrong with it. In fact, just about everything we know of seems to have been a basic mistake, biologically speaking. The dinosaurs were a mistake; maybe the way we've evolved sexually is a mistake; maybe the development of the human species is a mistake, and now we're about to move out of some kind of larval stage into something that's inconceivable from our present point of view.

Certainly, if we don't find some way to help evolution along, the chances of there being people around much longer can't be good. Our track record so far is terrible. Why should we think it's going to change unless something very drastic happens, like being able to make these biological adaptations? Brion Gysin says man is a bad animal—wherever he goes he destroys all the animals, then destroys the environment. The rain forests have been called the lungs of the world. What other animal systematically destroys its own lungs? I'm very much an animal activist, so it's tragic to see the destruction of, for example, the species of lemurs in Madagascar. The gliding lemurs are quite helpless on the ground, so they can't survive the destruction of their habitat. Neither can the singing gibbon, whose singing has been described as the most beautiful and variegated music produced by any land animal. They live only on one island in the Indian Ocean. The purpose of their singing is to establish a little patch of territory in a rain forest where the resources are very limited. So as soon as the rain forest disappears, they disappear.

JM: What were the origins of your interest in animal activism?

WB: It started with my interest in cats. Cats and lemurs. I prefer cats to people, for the most part. Most people aren't cute at all, and if they are cute they very rapidly outgrow it. And they're not an endangered species at the present time, except for the danger they're bringing on themselves.

JM: What do you think about the prospects for developing some means of communicating with animals—for instance, John Lilly's experiments in interspecies communication?

WB: "Communication" is a bad word to use when you're trying to describe that sort of thing, because the purpose of communication is to keep something at a distance. "Contact" is the word I use, which means *identification. The Western Lands* is very much concerned with animal contact. The title refers to the Egyptian paradise, the western lands.

LM: Your recent books rely more heavily on plotted narratives than did the cut-up books back in the '60s. Has this shift grown out of a conscious desire to appeal to a larger audience? Or have you decided that more traditional forms may be more suitable for expressing your sense of reality?

WB: Mostly it's had to do with selecting a form appropriate to what I'm saying, to my content. If you're going to have a pirate story, you have to have straight narration. It has nothing to do with the facts of perception. It's true that popular novels are usually written in the old-fashioned, nineteenth-century form, but that form is really as arbitrary as something like a sonnet. This doesn't have anything to do with "realism."

The point about cut-ups is that *life is a cut-up*. Every time you look out the window or walk down the street, your consciousness is being intruded upon by all these random factors. The idea that a writer composes in a vacuum is itself a fiction. That was the point in introducing this random factor: it's closer to the way human beings perceive things. That's why painters started using the montage method—which is what the cut-up is, applied to writing. Brion Gysin, who first thought up the cut-up idea, was a painter, and montage was already old hat when we started using the cut-ups in our work. Painters walk down the street and put what they see on the canvas—and what they see is a jumble of fragments. If they put *that* on the canvas, it's not going to look like a representational painting, because they've introduced the time and motion elements. If you sit in front of something and paint it, that's one thing; but if you try and paint what you see when you're moving, you're going to be creating a totally different landscape. You can't put that moving, perceptual landscape—particularly urban phenomena—down on a canvas using the old representational methods.

LM: Still, your recent books seem less discontinuous and "in motion" than your earlier books. Why did you feel that your SF stories back in the '60s didn't require as much straight narrative as, say, the pirate or Western stories in *Cities of the Red Night* and *The Place of Dead Roads?*

WB: This is all a matter of degree. For one thing, a lot of people who are pointing to this major break seem to forget that there was always narrative in all my books. Unless there's some narrative, a book won't hold together. And there are passages in, say, *Cities of the Red Night* that were written in much the same way I wrote in *Naked Lunch*. And there are still cut-up passages in the new stuff. I may cut up a whole page and use a sentence or two, or I may throw the whole thing away. Sometimes I just draw a complete blank. If I don't see where the narrative is going, sometimes I'll get an idea from cut-ups. But I've always believed a fiction writer can't get away from straight narrative completely.

LM: It seems as if some writers' efforts to move away from storytelling are defeating the whole impulse behind writing fiction in the first place. Some of these purely formal fictional experiments can be interesting, in the same way that minimalist painting or conceptual art is interesting. But even very radical minimalist fictions can be shown to have a narrative principle underlying them.

WB: It's important for writers to recognize that you can't apply all of the techniques used in painting to writing. For example, in painting you have minimalist expression—in a certain painting there are very slight changes in color, varying shades of white or blue. Well, if you did the equivalent in writing, no one would want to look at it. Sure, you could have one page written like this, and then another page that would be almost the same, each succeeding page just a little bit different. But no one would read it.

LM: One good thing that came out of the literary experimentalism that took place in the '60s was that writers were able to exhaust certain methods that didn't lead anywhere.

WB: Exactly. You simply reach dead ends. In painting, once you have painters starting to get off the canvas, where do they go? There were all those "happenings." A lot of that was just pretentious nonsense. Where would writing go if you threw away the book? Or got rid of the page?

JM: In your 1965 *Paris Review* interview, you talk about the possibility of people in general eventually becoming liberated from words. That basic change would seem to require a long transitional period.

WB: I'm not sure this is going to happen, but if it does, it's not necessarily going to take a long time. If it happens, it will probably happen quickly, just as these things always have. The beginning of words undoubtedly involved biological changes. Animals are not biologically designed to talk; they don't have the apparatus necessary, the larynx and so on. Since a biological change in the apparatus was implicit in the origins of speech, maybe another biological change could produce some other new form of communication. Words did not arise to convey information in the first place, so it's easy enough to imagine that some-day information will be conveyed in an entirely different manner. No, the origin of words was probably emotional and had nothing to do with conveying information. You'd be surprised at how few words are really necessary. You go into a shop and see something you want—you don't need any words in that kind of situation. You need words for something that isn't there.

An Interview with

Octavia E. Butler

Although labels distort what is unique about an author's work, to say that Octavia Butler is a "black feminist science fiction writer from Southern California" serves to open up a discussion of her work, rather than to narrowly pigeonhole it. As Butler herself puts it, "I really have three fairly distinct audiences: feminists, SF fans, and black readers." The way her work weaves these three strands into a provocative whole is what makes her fiction so unusual and compelling.

Butler made these observations to Jim McMenamin and me at her home, a modest duplex in a middle-class, primarily black neighborhood located near the absolute center (if such a point exists) of Los Angeles. It was a glorious July afternoon in 1988, and although we conducted most of the interview on a park bench overlooking the La Brea Tar Pits, our brief interlude at her home provided numerous clues about the seemingly paradoxical elements of her intellectual and literary sensibility. While Butler was signing some of her books for us, we busied ourselves examining her bookcases, which contained (in addition to the expected rows of SF novels) a revealing selection of scientific texts, anthropology books, volumes devoted to black history, albums (jazz, rock, blues), and an impressive number of cassette tapes, which turned out to be mostly National Public Radio selections that she listens to on her Walkman, mainly while riding the bus or walking. (Like Ray Bradbury, Butler does not drive a car.)

Octavia Butler has been publishing SF novels since the mid-1970s. Her early work received excellent critical notices and reviews, but only during the past several years has she begun to attract significant attention from outside SF's insular community. Her fiction has its roots in her experiences as a black woman growing up in a society dominated by white people, particularly white men. With the publication of her Patternist novels, she immediately signaled her interest in anthropological, racial, and political themes.

Given her background, we might naturally expect Butler to focus specifically on racial and sexual issues—and to use science fiction to suggest alternatives to our own society's sexual and racial structures. On one level her works do exactly that. For example, two of her most expansive and provocative novels, *Kindred* (1979) and *Wild Seed* (1980), employ time-travel premises that permit strong black heroines to roam through prior historical periods; Butler uses these confrontations with actual historical circumstances to create fresh, revealing perspectives about past and present racial and sexual biases. In *Kindred,* a strong, adaptable black woman is cast back to the early days of slavery in pre–Civil War America—a wonderfully simple but suggestive vehicle for developing juxtapositions between our own age's assumptions and those of earlier eras. Such interactions are further developed in *Wild Seed,* which moves across two continents and spans over two hundred years. *Wild Seed* traces the evolution of an unlikely love affair between Anyanwu (an African sorceress and shape-shifter) and Doro, a vampirish figure who is intent on establishing a superhuman race by selectively breeding individuals who possess "special" traits. Part of the success of *Wild Seed* is due to Butler's meticulously detailed and vivid renderings of the various environments through which Anyanwu passes. Each of these cultures—a neolithic African village, a slave ship, eighteenth-century New England, and antebellum Louisiana—provides her with an opportunity to examine societal and personal attitudes that not only gave rise to slavery and gender stereotyping but also contribute to contemporary prejudices.

What gradually becomes clear in both *Kindred* and *Wild Seed,* however, is that the dilemmas facing the heroines arise not only from specific, locatable sources of racial and sexual oppression but also from larger political, economic, and psychological forces. The struggle for power, control, and individual dominance/mastery over other creatures and the natural environment is a primal struggle common to all creatures— and it is in this sense that Butler's best work, for all its vivid particularities and subtle treatment of psychological issues, transcends narrow categorization as "black" or "feminist." Anyanwu is probably Butler's most complex and fully realized character to date, possessing the inner strength and nurturing tendencies we associate with many recent feminist authors; she is also a fierce and violent woman who is not reducible to familiar stereotypes. Butler uses race and gender to explore the universal issues of human isolation and our mutual desire for power and transcendence—and the longing for means to bridge this isolation via community, family, and sexual union.

These issues are developed throughout Butler's Patternist novels, including *Patternmaster* (1976), *Mind of My Mind* (1977), and *Survivor* (1978), which move backward and forward through past and future histories on Earth and in outer space. The unifying motif in all these works is the linking of minds through telepathy; but unlike most of the notable previous treatments of mental telepathy (for instance, Theodore Sturgeon's *More Than Human* or Arthur C. Clarke's *Childhood's End*), Butler's communities are racked by internal conflicts and are portrayed in distinctly ambivalent terms.

Most recently, Butler has been expanding similar themes in her Xenogenesis trilogy. *Dawn* (1987), *Adulthood Rites* (1988), and the recently completed *Imago* (1989) examine a postholocaust humanity that has been sterilized and genetically altered by the alien Oankali. Rescued from an ecologically devastated Earth and forced to accept alien intervention in order to procreate, Butler's humans face the ultimate confrontation with the Other. The impetus of these novels is the human's xenophobic fear of the Oankali, who provide the only hope for survival—through mutation and an acceptance of a broader interpretation of the designation "human."

Larry McCaffery: In one way or another, all your books seem to explore different forms of slavery or domination.

Octavia Butler: I know some people think that, but I don't agree, although this may depend on what we mean by "slavery." In the story "Bloodchild," for example, some people assume I'm talking about slavery when what I'm really talking about is *symbiosis.* That's not to say that I haven't dealt with slavery or that I don't think about it—*Kindred* and *Wild Seed* deal very directly with slavery. Let me tell you an anecdote about slavery. When I was about thirteen I found out on a visceral level what slavery was; before that I hadn't understood why the slaves had not simply run away, because that's what I assumed I would have done. But when I was around thirteen we moved into a house with another house in the back, and in that other house lived people who beat their children. Not only could you hear the kids screaming, you could actually hear the blows landing. This was naturally terrifying to me, and I used to ask my mother if there wasn't something she could do or somebody we could call, like the police. My mother's attitude was that those children belonged to their parents and they had the right to do what they wanted to with their own children. I realized that those kids really had nowhere to go—they were about my age and younger, and if they had tried to run away they would have been sent right back to their parents, who would probably treat them a lot worse for having tried to run away. *That,* I realized, was slavery—humans being treated as if they were possessions. I stored that away in the back of my mind, without realizing I was doing it, until at a certain point in my work I needed to call it up. The nice thing about being a writer is that anything that doesn't kill or dismember you is typewriter fodder. Whatever it is, no matter how terrible, can be used later.

Jim McMenamin: Even books like *Wild Seed* and *Kindred,* in which you investigate aspects of black experience, seem to suggest something that transcends specific racial or cultural situations.

OEB: I hope so. When I put together my characters, it doesn't occur to me to make them all black or all white or whatever. I never went to a segregated school or lived in a segregated neighborhood, so I never had the notion that black people, or any other ethnic or cultural type, made up the world. When I write, I'm very comfortable not seeing things in terms of black or white. If I feel self-conscious about something, I don't write about it; I *write it out*—that is, I write about it and think about it until it is so familiar that it becomes second nature—not like some of the early SF writers who include a black character to make a point about racism, or the absence of racism. I want to get to the point where these things can be in the story but are incidental to it.

LM: What has drawn you to writing SF?

OEB: SF is what I like to read, and I think you should write about what you enjoy reading or you'll bore yourself and everyone else. I started writing SF when I was twelve. I was already reading SF, but I hadn't thought of writing it—I was writing fantasy and romance, both of which you know a lot about at ten or eleven, right? What happened to me sounds like a cliché but it's true: I was watching a movie on television, *Devil Girl from Mars,* and I thought, I can write a better story than that. So I turned off the TV and started writing what was actually an early version of one of my Patternist stories. The short stories I submitted for publication when I was thirteen had nothing to do with anything I cared about. I wrote the kind of thing I saw being published—stories about thirty-year-old white men who drank and smoked too much. They were pretty awful.

LM: Joanna Russ told me the same thing—that when she was in high school she thought if she didn't write about men going off to war or hunting big game then she didn't have anything significant to say.

OEB: Right. And a slightly different problem was that everything I read that *was* intended for women seemed boring as hell—basically,

"Finding Mr. Right": marriage, family, and that's the end of that. I didn't know how to write about women doing anything because while they were waiting for Mr. Right they weren't doing anything, they were just waiting to be done unto. Since I didn't know what else to do, in those early Patternist stories I more or less copied the boys' books. I eventually got very comfortable with that approach, but there are stories that were written in the mid-1970s where the strain really shows.

JM: In *Patternmaster* Amber says, "When I meet a woman who attracts me, I prefer women . . . and when I meet a man who attracts me, I prefer men." Talk a bit about the sources of this openness.

OEB: Because of the way I looked, when I was growing up I was called various and sundry unsavory names by people who thought I was gay (though at the time nobody used that word). I eventually wondered if they might not be right, so I called the Gay and Lesbian Services Center and asked if they had meetings where people could talk about such things. I wound up going down there twice, at which point I realized, Nope, this ain't it. I also realized, once I thought it over, that I'm a hermit. I enjoy my own company more than I enjoy most other people's—and going to parties or trying to meet Mr. or Ms. Right or whatever simply doesn't appeal to me. At any rate, I was intrigued by gay sexuality, enough so that I wanted to play around with it in my imagination and in my work. That's one of the things I do in my writing: either I find out certain things about myself or I write to create some context in which I can explore what I want to be. You can see how this works in the way I created Mary, in *Mind of My Mind.* I wanted to become a bit more forward, not so much to take charge (although sometimes it comes to that) but to take responsibility for what happens to me. I made Mary an extremely feisty, not very pleasant woman and then inhabited her life so I could see how it felt. I even had her live in my old Pasadena neighborhood, in the house my best friend lived in.

JM: Do you transpose these specific biographical elements into your work on a regular basis?

OEB: I use actual details only when I feel they'll *work*. For example, all the street names in *Mind of My Mind* parallel Pasadena street names, some in English and some in Spanish, though reversed. I really enjoy doing this sort of thing—along with going back and winning some of the battles I actually lost.

LM: Your father died when you were a baby and you were raised by your mother and grandmother. Did that experience affect your work in any direct way? In *Patternmaster,* for example, the kids are raised elsewhere, protected from their parents.

OEB: Growing up without a father influenced my life and, undoubtedly, my work because I didn't have that one male person around to show me what it means to be male; instead, I would watch my uncles and wonder why they did things the way they did, which may be why I later became interested in anthropology. Certainly, though, my childhood had something to do with the way I sometimes present parents as not being able to raise their own children. In *Mind of My Mind,* the parents can't stand being close to their children and hearing all that undisciplined mental shrieking. And in *Patternmaster* you have a society formed by a psychotic individual who is doing the best he can with what he has. He's not a good person—among other things, he sees the rest of humanity as food—and the daughter he raises is not a good person. But how can she be? She wouldn't survive if she were "good."

JM: Throughout the Patternist series you have different hierarchies yet the same kinds of control mechanisms we see around us.

OEB: No, they're *worse,* because the mutes don't know what's happening to them. If you know that you've been completely taken over, if you're aware of this happening, you might be able to fight it. But if you don't know about it, you don't have a chance.

LM: The idea of control being exercised through mind operations that the victims are unaware of has its parallel in our own society— you go out to buy a Bud Light or a Toyota without being aware that you've been programmed to do it.

OEB: Exactly. And even if you are aware of these forces, they can still possess or control you because you're not necessarily aware of exactly what they're doing when they're doing it. I remember going through a period in my teens when I was very depressed about my writing. I had no siblings—I was basically a solitary person anyway— so I would spend hours watching old movies and whatever series was on TV. After a while, it seemed that everything I'd ever wanted to write about had already been condensed and trivialized on television. I couldn't articulate this at the time, of course; nor could I write much of anything, at least not that I'd show to anyone.

LM: What sorts of SF did you read while you were growing up?

OEB: Until I was fourteen I was restricted to a section of the library called the "Peter Pan Room." That had the effect of stopping me from going to the library much, because after a while I felt insulted by the juvenile books. Before I got into SF I read a lot of horse stories, and before that fairy tales. For some reason I didn't read Asimov until later, but I did read Heinlein and the Winston juveniles (with those fantastic inside pictures of all sorts of wonderful things that never happened in the book). My first experience with adult SF came through the magazines at the grocery store. Whenever I could afford them I'd buy copies of *Amazing* and *Fantastic;* later I discovered *Fantasy and Science Fiction* and eventually *Galaxy*. After I got out of the Peter Pan Room, the first writer I latched onto was Zenna Henderson, who wrote about telepathy and other things I was interested in, from the point of view of young women. I'd go down to the Salvation Army bookstore and buy copies of *Pilgrimage* for a nickel and hand them out to people because I wanted someone to talk to about the book. Later I discovered John Brunner and Theodore Sturgeon. I can remember depending on people like Eric Frank Russell and J. T. MacIntosh to give me a good, comfortable read, to tell me a story. Whether they told me anything I didn't know or hadn't thought about or read someplace else was another matter. Later I read all of Marion Zimmer Bradley's Darkover books. I especially liked Ursula Le Guin's *Dispossessed,* and the original *Dune* by Frank Herbert was another favorite of mine. I read Harlan Ellison's stories and also John Wyndham, Arthur C. Clarke, A. E. Van Vogt, Isaac Asimov—all the SF classics, whatever I got my hands on.

LM: I remember being drawn to a certain kind of SF that seemed very different from what I was used to—works by people like Robert Sheckley and Alfred Bester, for example.

OEB: I think they were writing a sort of humorous, satirical SF that I felt totally alienated from, probably because I had little sense of humor as a kid. The stuff I was writing was incredibly grim—so grim that teachers would accuse me of having copied it from somewhere.

JM: What about the books that Samuel Delany was writing back in the '60s?

OEB: No. I didn't even know he was black until I was at Clarion. I got *Nova* when I was a member of the Science Fiction Book Club in my early teens, but I couldn't get into it. I did read some of his stories but none of his recent work, except his autobiography, *The Motion of Light in Water.*

JM: Were you into other types of reading when you were growing up—comic books or *Mad* magazine, that sort of thing?

OEB: I didn't discover *Mad* until 1962 or 1963, when my mother brought home a couple of issues that someone at work had given to her. She didn't have any idea what they were, even after she leafed through them, but she gave them to me anyway. I got hooked on *Mad* but from an emotional distance—since I didn't really want to write anything funny, I thought I shouldn't enjoy reading anything funny. From the '60s through the early '70s I was also very much into comic books—the Superman DC comic books first, then Marvel, and so on. I went around to all the secondhand stores and bought up the back issues as fast as I could. I was living in a world of my own then—or, I should say, in the worlds of other people—and I had no one to talk to about what I was interested in. I don't think I would have enjoyed being involved in a network of SF fans—I've noticed that people heavily into fandom have a lot of little squabbles, which eats up valuable time and energy and doesn't accomplish anything, so I'm glad I wasn't involved with it back then. What I *would* have enjoyed was having one or two people to talk to about all the strange things I was reading and writing about.

LM: I spoke with Delany about the relationship of black culture to science and SF and why there aren't more blacks writing SF. He said that in some ways it's very obvious.

OEB: He's right. Writers come from readers, and for a long time there simply weren't that many black SF readers. I got used to reading books in which everyone was white, but a lot of blacks didn't—they just stopped reading or read books they were told were realistic, like historical romances, spy stories, detective novels. For some reason they didn't get into SF, although they later got sucked in by the *Star Wars* and *Star Trek* movies. I remember talking to a young black student at a conference in Michigan who told me she had thought about writing SF but didn't because she had never heard of any black SF writers. It never occurred to me to ask, If no one else is doing it, do I dare to do it? But I realize that a lot of people think if there's no model, then maybe there's some reason not to do something.

LM: You said that when you were starting out, your work consisted of versions of the Patternist series.

OEB: For one thing, I never wrote anything "normal"; I never really wanted to. I was fascinated with telepathy and psionic powers and eventually stumbled upon some old J. B. Rhine books, as well as other, more fantastic stories that announced, "You, too, can develop ESP!" I fell in love with that kind of material. About the only genre I never cared for was the ghost story, probably because I stopped believing in the afterlife when I was around twelve—although I didn't get up the courage to tell my mother until I was seventeen or eighteen. What set me off, I think, was going to church one Sunday—I was raised a born-again Baptist—and hearing the minister read a passage from the Bible and then say, "I don't know what this means, but I believe it." Somehow you're supposed to believe and have faith but not worry about having any *evidence* to support that belief and faith. That just doesn't work for me, and I never went back.

LM: Although a lot of your work is about immortality, then, it's not so much about life after death as about finding a way to be immortal while you're still alive.

OEB: You're right. When I was in my teens, a group of us used to talk about our hopes and dreams, and someone would always ask, "If you could do anything you wanted to do, no holds barred, what would

you do?" I'd answer that I wanted to live forever and breed people—
which didn't go over all that well with my friends. In a sense, that desire
is what drives Doro in *Wild Seed* and *Mind of My Mind.* At least I
made him a bad guy!

LM: What was it that drew you so strongly to the idea of breeding
people? Was it the ideal of being able to control the direction of life?

OEB: Basically, yes. I didn't really understand the direction of my
thoughts on this topic until sociobiology became popular and unpopular
at the same time. I kept reading things like, "The purpose of such-and-
such a behavior is so-and-so"—in other words, the assumption that
every behavior has a purpose important to survival. Let's face it, some
behaviors don't; if they're genetic at all, they only have to stay out of
the way of survival to continue. Then, just a year or so ago, I read one
of Stephen J. Gould's books in which he says much the same thing. I
was relieved to see a biologist write that some things—physical characteristics or behaviors—don't kill you or save you; they may be riding
along with some important genetic characteristic, though they don't
have to be. Also, to whatever degree human behavior is genetically
determined, it often isn't determined *specifically;* in other words, no
one is programmed to do such-and-such.

JM: Could you talk about how your Xenogenesis trilogy deals with
the downside, with the possible dangers of sociobiology?

OEB: What scares me now is the direction genetic engineering is
taking. I don't mean creating monsters and other terrible things—
although that might happen—but the idea that "familiarity breeds
contempt." I deal with this in *Imago,* where the genetic engineer talks
about the fact that it can't mate within its own kinship area because it
thinks "familiarity breeds mistakes." I'm concerned that once humans
feel more comfortable with genetic engineering, we're not going to
exercise that caution and we'll be more likely to do terrible things just
because someone isn't paying attention.

LM: Of course, this immediately raises the question of the purpose
of these experiments by whom, and for whose benefit?

OEB: They're going to be put to whatever purpose appears to make
the most money at the time. Right now we seem to be operating on
the principle that we'll realize something is going terribly wrong before
it's too late. But when you're confronted with toxic and nuclear waste
problems, the destruction of the Amazon rain forest, the depletion of
the ozone layer, and so on, it should be obvious that it may already be
too late.

LM: You seem to be interested in exploring the issue of where intelligence fits into the scheme of species evolution. In my view, we may
be getting too intellectually advanced for our own good—that is, our

intellects have evolved more rapidly than our ability to emotionally deal with what we're uncovering in areas like nuclear power and genetic engineering.

OEB: Intelligence may indeed be a short-term adaptation, something that works well now but will eventually prove to be a kind of destructive overspecialization that destroys us. What I'm exploring in my Xenogenesis series is the idea of two competing or conflicting characteristics: intelligence being one of them and hierarchical behavior, simple one-upmanship, the other. Since the tendency toward hierarchical behavior is older and more entrenched—you can trace it all through the animal species of this planet and into the plants, too, in some ways—hierarchical behavior is self-sustaining and more in charge of the intellect than it should be. Whenever we look at the degree to which our behavior is predetermined genetically—and this is where sociobiology comes into play—we get hung up on who's got the biggest or the best or the most, on who's inferior and who's superior. We might be able to stop ourselves from behaving in certain ways if we could learn to curb some of our biological urges.

LM: We see this with birth control, for example.

OEB: Yes, and also in our everyday behavior. If you become angry with me, you probably won't pull out a gun and shoot me or reach across the table and grab me (although some people will). Yet a politician may become angry and say, "I'm not going to let this bill go through, even though it will help millions of people, because you didn't respect my authority, my personal power." Of course, politicians never actually say that, but we know it happens. The same kind of destructive struggle for domination occurs in some doctor/patient relationships, where patients wind up suffering.

LM: That seems to be one of the underlying concepts in *Dawn*— that we are biologically programmed for self-destruction.

OEB: It's less a matter of being programmed for self-destruction than it is that self-destruction occurs because we're not willing to go beyond that principle of who's got the biggest or the best or the most. We can; in fact we do, individually. And if we know we are like that, we ought to be able to go beyond it. In *Adulthood Rites,* the aliens say, "We know you are not going to make it, but we are going to give you a second chance anyway." The constructs (that is, the new generation of mixed children) convince their alien relatives to give humans another chance at simply being human.

LM: In all of your work there is a complex balance between the need for beneficial change versus the feeling that such change will produce a loss of humanity.

OEB: There are a lot of people (unfortunately, some of them are writers and editors) who seem to see things strictly in terms of good and evil: the aliens either come to help us get our poor heads straightened out or they come to destroy us. What I hope to wind up with in my work are a series of shadings that correspond to the way concepts like "good" and "evil" enter into the real world—never absolute, always by degrees. In my novels, generally, everybody wins and loses something—*Wild Seed* is probably the best illustration of that—because as I see it, that's pretty much the way the world is.

LM: What was your original conception for the Patternist series? I know, for example, that they weren't published in the order in which you wrote them. Did you have an outline for the whole series?

OEB: No, they were in my head for so many years that I didn't need an outline. I conceived of the first three books dealing with three different eras: *Mind of My Mind* takes place in the present, *Patternmaster* is set on Earth in the distant future, and *Survivor,* which occurs in the nearer future, deals with those who got away but who didn't fare well because they were so strong in their religion that they couldn't consider self-preservation. "Bloodchild" is also a survivor story, though the characters react differently: they survive as a species, but not unchanged. This idea of change seems to me to be one of the biggest challenges I face as a writer—and the inability fo face this is a big problem in a lot of SF. Some kind of important change is pretty much what SF is about.

JM: When you actually started to work on this series, did the books take shape independent of one another?

OEB: No, they were all going at once and for a long time I couldn't finish any of them. I had been able to finish some short stories, which were about twenty pages long, and I finally decided to try writing twenty-page chapters until I finished each novel. Of course, the chapters all ended up being different lengths, but having that goal helped me trick myself into completing the first novel.

LM: You seemed to have developed a fairly elaborate overall concept before you completed the first book.

OEB: I enjoy working with the effects of difficult human situations. The complexity of the Patternist series resulted from the fact that I'd been in that universe, in my mind, for so long. At the time I was writing *Wild Seed,* for example, all I had to do was see that the numbers and dates were accurate—to make sure that Anyanwu and Doro weren't the wrong ages, that sort of thing. I felt I could do almost anything because I was so comfortable in that realm. But I had problems in the Xenogenesis universe because I hadn't inhabited that world, imaginatively, long enough. I had to look back to see what I had said and to make sure everything held together and wasn't contradictory.

LM: The disease described in *Clay's Ark* seems oddly prophetic, given what has happened with AIDS. Had you heard of AIDS when you wrote that book?

OEB: No, I didn't hear of AIDS until later. The disease I wrote about was based on rabies, which I had read about in an old book of mine. I was fascinated by the fact that one of the side effects of rabies is a briefly heightened sensitivity. I always thought it would be great to contract a disease that was both contagious and a real physical boost. So in *Clay's Ark* I wrote about a disease that would be great for you — if you survived.

JM: *Kindred* seems like a very conscious break from what you were doing in the Patternist series.

OEB: Actually, *Kindred* was supposed to be part of the series but it didn't seem to fit, probably because I wanted to be more realistic than I had been in the earlier books. In fact, *Kindred* grew out of something I heard when I was in college, during the mid-1960s. I was a member of a black student union, along with this guy who had been interested in black history before it became fashionable. He was considered quite knowledgeable, but his attitude about slavery was very much like the attitude I had held when I was thirteen — that is, he felt that the older generation should have rebelled. He once commented, "I wish I could kill off all these old people who have been holding us back for so long, but I can't because I would have to start with my own parents." This man knew a great deal more than I did about black history, but he didn't feel it in his gut. In *Kindred,* I wanted to take somebody with this guy's upbringing — he was pretty much a middle-class black — and put him in the antebellum South to see how well he stood up. But I couldn't sustain the character. Everything about him was wrong: his body language, the way he looked at white people, even the fact that he looked at white people at all. I realized that, unless I wanted to turn *Kindred* into a wish-fulfillment fantasy, I simply couldn't make the main character a male. So I developed an abused female character who was dangerous but who wasn't perceived as being so dangerous that she would have to be killed.

LM: It's interesting that *Kindred* was published as non-SF.

OEB: Yes, and that was one of the things reviewers complained about. The idea of time travel disturbed them. Their attitude seemed to be that only in the "lower genre" of SF could you get away with such nonsense, that if you're going to be "realistic," then you must be *completely* realistic. Yet readers will accept what someone like García Márquez is doing without complaining. I remember hearing Mark Helprin being interviewed on the radio about *Winter's Tale.* When the interviewer referred to it as fantasy, Helprin became upset and said that he didn't think of his work in those terms, in spite of the flying horse and all the other fantastic elements. The implication was that if a work is fantasy or SF, it can't be any good.

LM: Like Márquez, Toni Morrison uses seemingly fantastic elements in some of her work—flying, magic, ghosts—yet her stories are considered realistic.

OEB: Realism in Morrison's work is blurred. There's a scene in *Sula* where two little girls accidentally drown a much younger child and don't tell anybody about it. That's grotesque, maybe even fantastic, but I believed every word. I don't think it's at all unlikely that the girls would try to "Who, *us?*" their way out of it. There are several other things Morrison does in the book that are equally strange, but they rang absolutely true.

LM: At the opposite extreme, we have the "hard SF" party line, which argues that relying on any fantasy elements is a cop-out.

OEB: What's usually important to the hard SF people is the logic of what they're dealing with; as a result, some of them fail to develop their characters—I call this the "wonderful machine school of storytelling" approach. Why can't writers play around with actual science and still develop good characters? I think I accomplished that in "The Evening and the Morning and the Night," which is the most carefully developed story I've written from a hard SF standpoint. It deals with medicine— I used three existing diseases as the basis of the disease in the story. A doctor I know called to tell me how much she liked it, which is probably the nicest compliment I could have received.

JM: What was the origin of *Wild Seed?*

OEB: I had a lingering sense that *Kindred,* which I'd just finished writing, had once been a different sort of novel that somehow involved Doro and Anyanwu in early America. But neither character appears in *Kindred* because *Kindred* didn't really belong in the Patternist universe—it was too realistic. Because of the nature of the research—slave narratives and history—*Kindred* was a depressing book for me to write. By contrast, I thoroughly enjoyed writing *Wild Seed.* In terms of research, it's one of the hardest novels I've written, because I initially thought that dealing with the Ibo would only involve one people and one language—I didn't realize how many dialects there were. I found a huge ethnography about the Onitsha Ibo that was very useful; and before somebody torched the L.A. Public Library, I also found a book called *The Ibo Word List,* with words in five different dialects. It was a wonderful old book, shabby and falling apart, and it helped me get the language I needed.

LM: How did your conception of *Wild Seed's* main female character take shape?

OEB: For a while I didn't know how I was going to relate Anyanwu to the Ibo. The solution came from a footnote about a woman named Atagbusi in a book called *The King in Every Man,* by Richard N. Henderson. Atagbusi was a shape-shifter who had spent her whole life helping her people, and when she died, a market gate was dedicated to her and later became a symbol of protection. I thought to myself, This woman's description is perfect—who said she had to die? and I had Anyanwu give "Atagbusi" as one of her names. I gave Doro his name without knowing anything about his background, but later on I looked up "doro" in a very old, very tattered Nubian-English dictionary and discovered that it means "the direction from which the sun comes"— which worked perfectly with what I was trying to do. And Anyanwu ties into that, since "anyanwu" means "sun."

LM: What inspired you to develop the Xenogenesis series?

OEB: I tell people that Ronald Reagan inspired Xenogenesis—and that it was the only thing he inspired in me that I actually approve of. When his first term was beginning, his people were talking about a "winnable" nuclear war, a "limited" nuclear war, the idea that more and more nuclear "weapons" would make us safer. That's when I began to think about human beings having the two conflicting characteristics of intelligence and a tendency toward hierarchical behavior—and that hierarchical behavior is too much in charge, too self-sustaining. The aliens in the Xenogenesis series say the humans have no way out, that they're programmed to self-destruct. The humans say, "That's none of your business and probably not true." The construct character says that, whether the humans are self-destructive or not, they should be allowed to follow their own particular destiny. The idea is that Mars is such a harsh planet—and so much terra-forming has to be done by the people who are living there (even though they get some support from the outside)—that perhaps it will absorb whatever hostilities and problems of dominance arise. It ain't necessarily so, but at least it was something to hope for.

LM: When you decide to use, say, Mars as the backdrop for one of your books, do you actually research the planet?

OEB: In this case, no, since none of the scenes take place on Mars— all I really did was check on the Martian environment, to see if the aliens, who work with biological tools, could do what I wanted them to do. I decided that I could write about them doing it without actually *showing* them doing it because that process is not what the novel is about.

Another idea I wanted to examine in the Xenogenesis trilogy (and elsewhere) was the notion of cancer as a tool—though I am certainly not the first person to do that. As a disease, cancer is hideous, but it's also intriguing because cancer cells are immortal unless you deliberately kill them. They could be the key to our immortality. They could be used to replace plastic surgery—that is, instead of growing scar tissue or grafting something from your thigh or somewhere else, you could actually grow what you need, if you knew how to reprogram the cells. I use this idea in the third Xenogenesis novel, but I haven't really done what I want to with it. Probably it's going to evolve the way shape-shifting did from *Wild Seed* to *Imago*. I'll do something more with it.

LM: How much of the Xenogenesis series do you have worked out in advance?

OEB: I have the ending worked out, not that it will necessarily stay that way. I find that when I begin to write I need two things: a title and an ending. If I don't have those things I just don't have enough. Sid Stebel, one of the teachers with the Writers' Guild, would make us state the premise of a story in one sentence—"This is the story of a person who does such-and-such." It's important to me that my stories are about people who *do* such-and-such, rather than about people who *are* such-and-such—the latter can make for a very static story that is all describing and explaining and doesn't really go anywhere. When I write, I sometimes put huge signs on the wall: Action, Struggle, Goal. I tend to be too nice to my characters, and if I'm not careful, nothing particular will happen that taxes them in any way. That doesn't make for as good a story.

JM: The Bible seems to provide an underpinning to your work. Is that because you see it as a compendium of fantasy?

OEB: I've always loved the Bible for the quotable things I could borrow from it. All the subtitles in *Wild Seed* are biblical, and in *Dawn* I name one of the characters Lilith, who according to mythology was Adam's first wife and who was unsatisfactory because she wouldn't obey him. *Brewer's Dictionary of Phrase and Fable* defines "Lilith" first as a Babylonian monster. I wonder whether her terrible reputation results from her refusal to take Adam's orders. So yes, I have a lot of fun with names and references; I like to use names that work with who my characters are. For instance, according to its roots, Blake suggests "white" or "black"; and Maslin is a "mingling." Until I've settled on a character's name—and I frequently use name books to help me—I can't really work with that character. Some of this probably comes from being taken to the cemetery a lot as a kid. Half my relatives are buried in Altadena, and my mother used to take me with her when she went there to leave flowers. I remember running around copying names off headstones—somehow, having those names made me feel connected to those people.

JM: Do you think of your work as a self-conscious attempt to break down the white-male-oriented traditions and biases of most SF?

OEB: My work has never been traditional, at least not since I stopped writing those terrible stories about thirty-year-old white men who drank and smoked too much. It's interesting that you use the word "self-conscious," though—I don't think I'm self-conscious in the way that you're suggesting. I write about what I'm interested in, not what I feel self-conscious about. Often, that means writing about a world that seems a bit like the one I inhabit. Let's face it, people who write about whole universes filled with American whites probably can't deal with the real world, let alone alien worlds. I remember walking down a street in Cuzco, Peru—I went there with a UCLA study group—with a blonde woman about my height. Everybody around us was brown and stocky, about a foot shorter, with straight black hair. The two of us agreed that this was probably one of the few places in the universe where we looked equally alien.

LM: SF would seem to be a useful area for feminists and people from other cultures to explore, in order to explode some of the biases.

OEB: True, but there's a trap. Fiction writers can't be too pedagogical or too polemical. If people want to be lectured to, they'll take a class; if they want to hear a sermon, they'll go to church. But if they want to read a story, then it had better be a fairly good story, one that holds their attention *as a story*. It's got to compete with TV, movies, sports, and other forms of entertainment, not to mention vast amounts of fiction.

LM: There has been a lot of SF in the last, say, fifteen years, by feminists working with utopian models.

OEB: Yes, and I have some major problems with that—personally, I find utopias ridiculous. We're not going to have a perfect human society until we get a few perfect humans, and that seems unlikely. Besides, any true utopia would almost certainly be incredibly boring, and it would be so overspecialized that any change we might introduce would probably destroy the whole system. As bad as we humans are sometimes, I have a feeling that we'll never have that problem with the current system.

LM: Have you received any response from radical feminists criticizing the way the masculine and the feminine in your works seem to be trying to find ways to coexist? I'm thinking specifically of Sally Gearhart, who says that we must do something very radical—like completely getting rid of males—if the planet is to survive.

OEB: No, I haven't—but does she really think that? Getting rid of all males (except for breeding purposes) or totally emphasizing the feminine won't solve our problems. If females did manage to take over, through violence or some other means, that would make us a lot like what we already are—it would wind up being self-defeating. I think we humans need to *grow up,* and the best thing we can do for the species is to go out into space. I was very happy to read that it's unlikely there's life on Mars or anywhere else in this solar system. That means, if we survive, we have a whole solar system to grow up in. And we can use the stresses of learning to travel in space and live elsewhere—stresses that will harness our energies until we've had time to mature. Not that we won't continue to do terrible things, but we'll be doing them to ourselves rather than to some unfortunate aliens. Of course, we probably won't get to the nearest stars for quite a long time. I like the idea.

An Interview with

Samuel R. Delany

By the time of the interview, when we first see the living writer, we've already roamed around in some very intimate parts of his or her mind. We've decided some basic things about the person's concerns, anxieties, and vision of an ideal world. In some ways we know this person we've never met better than we know our mother-in-law, our son. In the case of Samuel R. Delany, who becomes Chip as soon as you meet him, the preconceptions Sinda Gregory and I had seemed bound to influence our view of this black, gay, SF writer. In his Upper West Side Manhattan apartment, Delany blasted through those preconceptions during a series of conversations held in the mid-1980s.

Few writers are as rigorous as Chip Delany in analyzing the cultural, sexual, linguistic, and aesthetic biases that control our lives. What follows is a much-abbreviated version of our conversations. Chip talks faster than most people read; and he commands an encyclopedic range of disciplines that allows him to discuss his debts to the poststructuralists and deconstructionists at one moment, the aesthetic implications of how time can be frozen in comic books at the next, and—minutes later—why Rimbaud, Huysmans, and Proust have been such problematic models for certain postmodernists.

Summarizing the personal, intellectual, and artistic influences on Delany's career is difficult because of the many interactions and paradoxes involved. Imagine a personality shaped equally by Harlem (where Delany was born in 1942 and where he grew up) and one of New York City's most prestigious schools for the gifted, the Bronx High School of Science—on top of a lifetime battle with dyslexia. Add the counterculture revolution of the '60s, a writerly imagination that has been affected in equal measure by pulp SF and by the textural explorations of Roland Barthes, by French Symbolism, by the linguistic investigations of Saussure, Wittgenstein, Quine and the mathematics of G. Spencer Brown, by both rock and contemporary classical music, and (of increasing importance) by structuralist and poststructuralist thinkers such as Lacan, Kristeva, Derrida, Felman, and Foucault. This unlikely confluence of influences supports a body of SF that is probably unrivaled in terms of intellectual sophistication and formal ingenuity.

In Delany's work perverse, primordial passions collide headlong with intellectual abstractions, and SF's exotic alien encounters become multilayered vehicles for exploring sexuality (who else would write a sword-and-sorcery tale about AIDS?), the effects of language on perception and identity (like the Neo-Empiricists, Delany believes that there's no such thing as this last), and the way artists can generate beauty and meaning in our random, ambiguous cosmos governed by the second law of thermodynamics—and the similarity of the whole artistic process to crime. What chiefly characterizes Delany's work is both the rigor of his methods and his impressive invention of other-worldly cultures that critique our societal givens, cultures that demand that we recognize all *meanings* as (first) social and (second) part of a larger play of *différances*.

Most critics divide Chip Delany's career into two phases. During the '60s, between age nineteen and age twenty-five, Delany wrote nine science fiction novels, including *Babel-17* (1966) and *The Einstein Intersection* (1967)—both of which won the prestigious Nebula Award—and *Nova* (1968). In the second phase, signaled seven years later by the publication of *Dhalgren,* his magnum opus, Delany's fiction had become more textured, more dense, more difficult, and more clearly influenced by critical theory.

Dhalgren remains the pivotal book in Delany's career. This massive (almost 900 pages), ambitious, unclassifiable novel presents unparalleled challenges for SF readers. *Dhalgren* transfers the exoticism of other worlds to a surreal, nightmarish urban landscape, a twisted, disrupted vision of Harlem and America's other decaying inner cities. Like all of Delany's major novels, *Dhalgren* explores the relation of men and women to the systems and codes around them. His central character is an artist whose doomed efforts to make sense of the chaos become an emblem of all our similar attempts. What is especially interesting about *Dhalgren* is the way its phantasmagoric, prismatic approach to its own structure defeats the reader's efforts to create a single interpretation of what occurs. The book is part myth, part dream, part verbal labyrinth.

Delany's post-*Dhalgren* fiction has continued to evolve and mutate, displaying his deepening appreciation for poststructuralist critical theory. *Triton* (1976) not only rivals Ursula Le Guin's *Left Hand of Darkness* and Joanna Russ's *Female Man* as one of SF's most penetrating studies of sexuality, but its experimental formal features (for instance, the manipulations of point of view, the use of Borgesian epilogues to open up other perspectives on the novel) illustrate the way Delany's recent fiction reflexively explores the codes and narrative conventions of SF—and, by extension, of all texts. *Stars in My Pocket Like Grains of Sand* (1983) is a dense but vividly textured space opera that, among other things, reflects the exuberant and exotic atmosphere of gay life in pre-AIDS America. His personal innvolvement in Manhattan's wide-open gay sexual scene is boldly described in *The Motion of Light in Water* (1988), a meta-autobiographical text that presents an evocative, openly provisional account of his life and career up through the 1960s.

Delany's most important fiction of the '80s, however, is his four-volume Neveryon series: *Tales of Neveryon* (1979), *Neveryona* (1983), *Flight from Neveryon* (1985), and *Return to Neveryon* (1987). These works represent an extended foray into the sword-and-sorcery genre—and into the multivolume series structure; predictably, however, Delany so thoroughly expands, deepens, questions, and undercuts the premises of this genre that the result is absolutely original. Inspired in part by the appearance of a comparative translation from several ancient languages of a brief narrative text known both as the Culhar' Fragment and the Missonlonghi Codex, the Neveryon series depicts life in an ancient, fabled land. Although the narrative drive of these works is fueled by various stock features of sword-and-sorcery—quests, romance, initiation, the struggle of individuals against tyrants—Delany, with his usual meticulous attention to details, creates in Neveryon a land that mirrors (often darkly) our own. Very loosely following the rise of Gorik, a slave miner who subverts the slave trade in Neveryon and eventually becomes Gorik the Liberator, the tales of Neveryon create an interlocking sequence of fictions that examine the way cultural codes and power relations in all their guises—political, personal, economic, sexual, and literary—arise and establish themselves.

Appropriate for a writer whose works display such a keen and sensitive awareness of literary history and critical theory (particularly poststructuralist criticism), Delany in 1988 began to teach full time as a professor of literature at the University of Massachusetts.

Larry McCaffery: Science fiction would seem to provide ideal territory for exploring racial issues, but you are one of the few black SF writers. Is this mainly a sociological situation, as with golfers or tennis players?

Samuel Delany: Well, black golfers and tennis players are actively not wanted by an overwhelmingly white audience and white administration that considers both sports highly elite. Althea Gibson, the first black to play—and win—at Wimbledon, had some pretty hairy stories about her road there. But it's an interesting comparison.

SF starts in most people's minds as something highly technical, full of dials, switches, and things that glitter. Images like that serve as social signs. People learn to read them very quickly. They're like placards on the clubhouse door: No Girls Allowed. They say very clearly: "We don't want any blacks, we don't want the poor, we don't want Hispanics." But finally the door gets broken in when somebody says, "Wait, *I* want to see what's going on in there."

Because SF, unlike the world of professional golf and tennis, is not a real club where people are pushing on a tangible door, nothing stops people from reading SF if they want to. Still, in something as complex as a specific practice of writing, you can't have minority writers until you have minority readers. Once you have the readers, the writers start tumbling out the door. Having said that, I've got to add there *are* black—and native American, and Asian American, and a whole lot more non-Caucasian—SF writers working in the United States, many of them spectacularly good: Octavia Butler, Steve Barnes, Charles Saunders, Creig Street, Russel Bates, Lawrence Yep, Samtow Suchkeritkil . . . but still not as many as there should be, when you consider that SF makes up nearly 16 percent of *all* new fiction published in this country each year.

LM: You said once you'd like readers to see in your works that "behind a deceptively cool, even disinterested, narrative exterior you can hear the resonances of the virulent anti-white critique that informs all aware black writing in America today." Early on, this critique seems to inform your work mainly in the way you say it does even in fascist works, like Heinlein's *Starship Trooper,* by your almost casual inclusion of black characters in positions of power and authority. But later, in *Dhalgren,* for instance, and in the Neveryon books, you seem to take up the issue of racism more directly.

SD: I suppose that quote was my way of saying: "Hey, my experience as a black American runs all through my work. But why do you assume its traces will be such stereotypes?"

Somehow black critics—and three or four, if not five or six, have written the odd article on me—just don't seem to be all that interested in how black a black writer's work is. Or when they are, they express that interest in—how shall I say?—a different tone of voice. The whites, worried about some black's "blackness," always seem to be expressing the troubling anxiety that, indeed, you may not really *be* black and therefore, somehow, they've personally been duped, either by your manipulative intentions or by some social accident. Black critics are perfectly aware that you *are* black; I mean, if you're born black in this country, you're going to know what it means to *be* black in this country. They're just kind of curious, therefore, to know what's going on with you.

I've said, with more than a little belligerence, to a number of whites who've chosen to question my blackness (and you'd have to be black yourself to realize the astonishing number of whites who seem to have nothing else to do but worry about whether or not their black acquaintances are actually black *enough*): "Look, I *am* black. Therefore, what I do is part of the definition, the reality, the evidence of blackness. It's *your* job to interpret it." I mean, if you're interested in the behavior of redheads, and you look at three and think you see one pattern, then you look at a fourth and see something that for some reason strikes you as different, you don't then decide that this last person, despite the color of his hair, isn't really red-haired—not if you and yours have laid down for a hundred years the legal, social, and practical codes by which you decide what hair is red and what hair isn't, and have inflicted untold deprivations, genocide, and humiliations on those who've been so labeled by that code.

LM: What is involved here obviously has to do with the relation of politics to art. How would you describe your perception of this relationship?

SD: The aesthetic bias I share with a lot of others is that you can't propagandize directly in fiction. You have to present politics by indirection, by way of allegory—and complex allegory at that. You have to resort to figurative means. When you just break out and start preaching, however right your sermon might be, it's still propaganda and hence awkward art. You're stuck with the need to allegorize, but you have to do so in a rich way, not in a simplistic way.

Certainly, the *way* I allegorize has shifted. (I wasn't yet twenty-five when I wrote most of those earlier books.) In my Neveryon stories, for example, it should slowly creep up on readers that the barbarians, who have just come to the city and who are creating many social problems, are blond and blue-eyed, while the indigenous citizens are dark. The dark-skinned citizens learn to live with and/or ignore the blond barbarians in some public space that's, say, the prehistoric equivalent of a bus terminal, as if the barbarians weren't there—like middle-class New Yorkers avoiding the many people who hang out and even live in the Port Authority bus station. This kind of reversal serves to distance the contemporary situation. At the same time one recognizes it as *structure,* rather than as *content;* the reader sees a set of relationships, largely economic, a set of positions that anyone might fill, regardless of color—rather than a collection of objects, dark-skinned folks and light-skinned folks, each with an assigned value.

Of course, from a certain standpoint, everything one writes is propaganda. (Wittgenstein used to say that his writings were propaganda for his particular way of thinking.) Certainly, the fact that I'm black and have had certain kinds of experiences, not only as a black person growing up in Harlem and New York, but also as a black person going down to the Port Authority, is why I've chosen to write about the particular relationships I've seen.

Sinda Gregory: So there was never a moment in your career when you sat down and thought, I want to deal with racial issues more directly?

SD: A moment? No. A period, perhaps. Also, some work just demands a more direct approach. If, as in the Neveryon stories, I'm writing about a culture where there's still real slavery, since most of my great-grandparents were slaves and I grew up with my grandmother telling me tales of slavery times that her mother told her, then even if I don't use any of her specific stories, I *have* to handle the racial aspects of the situation more directly. The work requires it.

SG: Your view that allegory and indirection are the most likely means of getting people to respond to political issues seems a far cry from what we heard in the '30s—when most politically committed writers seemed to feel the need to deal with issues directly, in socially realistic terms.

SD: True. But there's another side of the subject that can't be forgotten. Because of all the social pressures placed on black people, the structure of black life is very different, especially at the lower economic levels. I'm talking about the experiential specificity of black life. If we—the black writers—are writing directly about the black situation, we use this experience directly. But if we're writing in a figurative form, as I am most of the time with SF or sword-and-sorcery, we have to tease out the structure from the situation, then replace the experimental terms with new, or sometimes opaque, terms that nevertheless keep the structure visible. The new terms change the value of the structure. Often they'll even change its form. I think the figurative approach is more difficult, but it's the best way to say something *new*.

SG: Your exploration of gay and bisexual relations seems more open from *Dhalgren* onward. Was this a reflection of your own sexual development?

SD: Mainly it's a reflection of what was going on in American culture, certainly not just with me. Sexual areas have been opened up for more discussion on every level. One thing that opened them up was, of course, the women's movement, which created a damning critical dialogue with the so-called sexual revolution. In the late '60s and early '70s, as the women's movement was getting itself together, I was very aware of the similarities between its problems and the problems of the black movement some years before. You saw a lot of the same arguments going down, both pro and con, and you recognized the form. It took a very small leap to see that the movement for gay rights was going to have to go through similar arguments. The gay rights movement probably went through the early stages more rapidly, because it had those two examples to use as models. Not that any of the three situations have been solved. But some progress has been made in all of them.

SG: Probably the most famous SF treatment of sexuality, after the early days of Sturgeon and Farmer, is Le Guin's *Left Hand of Darkness*. It's received some heavy criticism.

SD: There's much in it that's extraordinarily good, and we should keep this in mind when we criticize its shortcomings—especially since it wasn't written as a tract. It's a novel. Certainly you can question its presentation of sexual roles. Ideology (at least in readerly or writerly matters) is a set of questions you're predisposed to ask *of* the text, not something materially situated *within* the text itself; and there's nothing to stop you from asking those questions that reveal the book's lacks: Who, in this ambisexual society, takes care of the children? Why, in a society where everyone can get pregnant and deliver and nurse a child, is everyone called *he?* And, yes, it's terribly easy to read some of the novel's situations as ordinary clichés about homosexuals—from the intrigues and backbiting at the Court of Karhide to the scene with Genly and Estraven on the ice. There were an awful lot of '50s gay novels with terribly similar sections, where the hero discovers he just can't make it with the other guy, at which point one character crashes his car into a tree and conveniently and tragically dies, thus solving the problem.

On the other hand, Le Guin has created a true three-handkerchief climax that's made a million-plus readers weep their hearts out; and it's not easy to write one of those. In that sense, I think she did what she wanted. But more to the point, the book starts its younger readers *thinking*—as well as feeling. Young gay readers who come to *this* book are *not* wondering where in the world they can sneak off to find *any* novel about gay life at all, the way I had to when I was a kid. The novels that ended with the car crashes (or the electrocutions, or whatever) were the closest you could get to any rich literary description of gay life in 1955. It was that or read the appendix to some bizarre self-help book by Erich Fromm, which told you in its final pages that if you *were* gay you could expect to die of alcoholism—if you hadn't already committed suicide, thanks to your miserable, meaningless life.

LM: In all fairness to Le Guin, when we talked with her about this issue, she mentioned that she now realizes the limitations of *The Left Hand of Darkness*. She said that it was written during a period when her own consciousness was just being raised, and that from today's perspective it could have been handled more effectively. But she did the best she could at the time.

SD: And that's one reason why she's a fine writer. She has a sense that there *is* a potential political dimension to a text that may sprout later on. It suggests that the seeds of growth are there in her book— even if they haven't necessarily flowered in that particular story. Having made perfectly valid criticisms of Le Guin's book, I think there are much richer answers suggested in the book than *some* of the people who are looking only for right answers have seen. And she opens up a lot of questions that many writers don't even acknowledge, which puts her books head and shoulders above many, many novels written in the years just before and after them. Besides, you don't castigate Jane Austen for her appalling classism in *Emma;* you extol her for her astonishing and satisfying novelistic dance.

LM: Unlike Kurt Vonnegut, you have openly and proudly proclaimed your writing to be science fiction. Indeed, in your critical writings you have suggested that SF is a genre in its own right, not merely a subgenre of "mainstream" fiction, or of the romance, or whatever. You have resisted the notion that recent SF is "re-entering" the realm of serious fiction. Could you talk about these controversial notions, explain how you arrived at them, and why you feel they're important?

SD: The easiest place to enter your question is at the idea of SF's re-entering the realm of serious fiction. To be re-entering anything, SF has to have been there once before (presumably in the seventeenth, eighteenth, and nineteenth centuries' "feigned histories" and "utopias," from Kepler and Cyrano to More and Bellamy); then it has to have left (no doubt when SF stories began to appear in the adventure and pulp magazines of the early part of this century); and now, according to some people, it's coming back. According to me, it isn't. That whole model of the history of SF is, I think, ahistorical. More, Kepler, Cyrano, and even Bellamy would be absolutely at sea with the codic conventions by which we make sense of the sentences in a contemporary SF text. Indeed, they would be at sea with most modern and postmodern writing. It's just pedagogic snobbery (or insecurity), constructing these preposterous and historically insensitive genealogies, with Mary Shelley for our grandmother or Lucian of Samosata as our great-great grandfather.

There's no reason to run SF too much back before 1926, when Hugo Gernsback coined the ugly and ponderous term "scientifiction."

Look. Currently our most historically sensitive literary critics are busily explaining to us that "literature" as we know it, read it, study it, and interpret it hasn't existed for more than one hundred years. Yet somehow there's supposed to be a stable object, SF, that's endured since the sixteenth century—though it only got named in 1926? That's preposterous.

Now, there've been serious writers of SF ever since SF developed its own publishing outlets among the paraliterary texts that trickled out on their own toward the end of the nineteenth century and that, thanks to technical developments in printing methods, became a flood by the end of World War I and today are an ocean. Some of those SF writers, like Stanley G. Weinbaum, were extraordinarily fine. Some of them, like Captain S. P. Meek, were unbelievably bad. And others, like Edward E. Smith, while bad, still had something going. But what they were all doing, both the bad ones and the good ones, was developing a new way of reading, a new way of making texts makes sense—collectively producing a new set of codes. They did it by writing new kinds of sentences and embedding them in contexts in which those sentences were readable. Whether their intentions were serious or not, a new way of reading *is* serious business.

LM: Until recently, most critics have—fruitlessly, it seems to me—tried to define literary differences in terms of subject matter: one text deals with outer space and the other deals with the mundane world. But you rely on an essentially semiological argument that the sentences in SF "mean" differently from the sentences in ordinary fiction.

SD: The fact that some academic critics still seriously try to present an exhaustive discussion of SF in terms of traditional themes is just a sign of how unsophisticated much academic criticism of SF is. Robert Graves noticed years ago that all poems tend to be about love, death, or the changing of the seasons. A clever observation, and insightful. But in the long run, we still have to say that a poem *can* be about anything. Just as sword-and-sorcery stories tend to be about the changeover from a barter economy to a money economy, SF stories tend to be about the changeover from a money economy to a credit economy—also insightful. Still, SF stories (like sword-and-sorcery stories) can be about anything too.

I've written a number of essays that have employed as examples strings of words that, if they appeared in an SF text, might be interpreted one way but that, if they appeared in a mundane text, might be interpreted another: "Her world exploded. / He turned on his left side." The point is not that the meaning of the sentences is ambiguous but that the route to their possible mundane meanings and the route to the possible SF meanings are both clearly determined. And what's clearly determined is overdetermined. I've also written an essay on the way readers who have only acquired the literary codes of interpretation can go about misreading a typical SF phrase (just a fragment of a sentence): "The monopole magnet mining operations in the outer asteroid belt of Delta Cygni. . . ." The reader who doesn't know what monopole magnets are, who isn't sure if the mining is done *for* the magnets or *with* the magnets, who has no visualization of an asteroid belt, outer, inner, or otherwise, or who wonders how mine tunnels get from asteroid to asteroid—that reader is having the same kind of problem with the SF text that the contemporary reader of Elizabethan poetry is likely to have encountering, say, the opening clause of Shakespeare's "Sonnet 129": "Th' expense of spirit in a waste of shame / Is lust in action. . . ." You have to know that "expense" here doesn't primarily mean cost; its first meaning here is expenditure, or pouring out. You have to know that "spirit" here only secondarily means soul; its primary meaning here is volatile liquid, such as alcohol. And "waste" doesn't have a primarily verbal thrust here; its nominal meaning here is desert. "To act from lust is to pour out alcohol in a desert of shame . . ." was the immediate semantic perception for your ordinary Elizabethan—well before the level of interpretations began that set double (i.e., onanistic and commercial) meanings at play throughout this clause, the conclusion of its sentence, and the rest of the poem.

Before you can deconstruct a text, Robert Scholes writes somewhere, you have to be able to construe it. It's sobering to discover how many otherwise literate people have trouble with SF just at the construction level. And frequently these are the first people to condemn it as meaningless. Since the complex of codes for SF (like that of Elizabethan poetry) *is* overdetermined and segues into and mixes inextricably with the codes for many other kinds of reading, one way to learn the SF complex is to read a lot of it—with a little critical help now and then. That's the way most twelve-year-olds do it. But these codic conventions operate at many levels. They not only affect what one is tempted to call the "what" of the information but also the "way" the information is stored. And I see this storage pattern as fundamentally different for SF and literature—and that difference holds for all the subpractices of literature, too: poetry, realistic fiction, literary fantasy, philosophy.

SG: Do you feel this distinction is true even if the literary text you're reading is a fantasy—say, something by Kafka?

SD: All right. You have a text in front of you. For overdetermined reasons you know it's literature—it's in a large book called *The Norton Anthology,* and there are seventeen books in *your* local library alone about the writer, this Kafka fellow. You read the first sentence: "One morning, waking from uneasy dreams, Gregor Samsa, still in bed, realized he'd been transformed into a huge beetle." Because we know it's a literary text, certain questions associated with literature immediately come into play. The moment we recognize the situation as fantastic, yet still within the literary frame, we prepare certain questions: What could this non-normal situation be saying about the human personality? Is he, perhaps, insane? If not, what in the range of *real* human experience is the *fantastic* situation a *metaphor* for? And we pick out two areas in which we expect those answers to lie: one is that of a certain kind of psychosocial alienation associated with other literary characters (e.g., Conrad's Mr. Kurtz, Dostoyevsky's Underground Man, and Sartre's Antoine Roquentin from *La Nausée,* although there are many others); the other area we've already marked out to explore in the metaphoric light of the text is the area of artistic creativity itself. And you would be hard-pressed to find a discussion of "The Metamorphosis" that, to the extent it sees the story as interpretable at all, does *not* present its interpretation as falling more or less under one or both of those rubrics. Even Kafka, in his diaries, talks about his writing as "a talent for portraying my dreamlike inner life" (he specifically does *not* talk about it as portraying or critiquing his outer world), and we have very little choice but to take this inner life for the inner life of the writer, or of alienated man and his psychological relations, no matter how objective the causes of that alienation may in fact be.

All right. There's a text in front of you. For overdetermined reasons you know it's SF—it's in a mass-market paperback anthology with the initials "SF" in the upper left-hand corner above the front-cover repeat of the ISBN. And though you only vaguely recognize the writer's name, the blurb above the title tells you she won a Hugo Award for best novella sometime in the early '70s. (Stories in SF anthologies often have introductory editorial paragraphs, as though they were all textbooks. But that's because SF has so little formal historiography.) You read the first sentence: "One morning, waking from uneasy dreams, Gregor Samsa, still in bed, realized he's been transformed into a beetle." The moment we recognize the situation as non-normal (because it's SF, in most cases we don't even cognize it as fantastic), certain questions that are associated with SF come into play: What in the *world* portrayed by the story is responsible for the transformation? Will Samsa turn out to be some neotenous life-form that's just gone into another physical stage? Or has someone performed intricate biomechanical surgery during the night? We want to know not only the agent of the transformation—Kenneth Burke's "dramatism" covers that very nicely, as it covers fantasy—but also the *condition of possibility* for the transformation. That condition may differ widely from SF story to SF story, even when the agent (a mad scientist, perhaps) and the transformation itself (the disappearance of an object, say) are the same, and I know of no literary or literarily based narrative theory that covers this specific SF aspect of the SF text. Most of our specific SF expectations will be organized around the question: What in the portrayed *world* of the story, by statement or by implication, must be *different from ours* in order for this sentence to be normally uttered? That is, how does the condition of possibility in the world of the story differ from ours? But whether the text satisfies or subverts these expectations, the reading experience is still controlled by them, just as the experience of reading the literary text is controlled by literary expectations. Because they are not the same expectations, the two experiences are different.

SG: You're saying that a reader's expectations or mind-set makes SF texts different from ordinary fiction?

SD: Mind-set creates the SF text—or the literary text, for that matter? No. You remember that phrase I was worrying over—"The monopole mining operations in the outer asteroid belt of Delta Cygni"— well, even without a predicate it states something; it's a statement about mines, as they exist in the world today. It says that the object, the location, the methodology, and the spatial organization of mines will *change*. And it says it far more strongly than, and well before, it says anything about, say, the inner chthonic profundities of any fictive character *in* those mines or about the psychology of the writer *writing* about them—which is where, immediately, the expectations of the literarily oriented critic are likely to lead her or him in constructing an interpretation.

Any faster-than-light spaceship drive met in the pages of any SF text written to date, be it mine or Isaac Asimov's or Joan Vinge's, basically poses a critique of the Einsteinian model of the universe, with its theoretical assertion of the speed of light as the upper limit on velocity: those FTL drives are all saying, very conscientiously, that the Einsteinian model will be revised by new empirical and theoretical developments, just as the Einsteinian model was a revision of the older Newtonian model.

When Heinlein casually placed the clause "the door dilated" in one of the sentences of his 1942 novel, *Beyond This Horizon,* it was a way to portray clearly, forcefully, and with tremendous verbal economy that the world of his story contained a society in which the technology for constructing iris-aperture doorways was available. But I don't think you can properly call the ability to read and understand any of these SF phrases, sentences, or conventions a matter of mind-set, anymore than you can call the ability to read French, Urdu, or Elizabethan English poetry a matter of mind-set.

Another interesting point where a rhetorical convention has different meanings when it shows up in two different fields: the FTL drive that so delighted the audiences of *Star Wars* and *The Empire Strikes Back* simply doesn't carry the same critical thrust as the FTL drives that appear in written SF. As a number of SF writers noted when *Star Wars* first came out, perhaps the largest fantasy element in the films was the *sound* of the spaceships roaring across what was presumably hard vacuum. In a universe where sound can cross empty space, an FTL drive just can't support that kind of critical weight against the philosophy of real science. Fifteen years ago, the Australian SF critic John Foyster wrote: "The best science fiction does not contradict what's known to be known." When it does, at too great a degree, it becomes something else. Science fantasy, perhaps.

LM: But wouldn't you agree that whenever a reader (or viewer) encounters a work of art—a situation that, as you've said, is circumscribed by all of these overdetermination factors that direct our responses in specific ways—we are in effect entering these experiences as different people (with different mind-sets)?

SD: I'm the same person when I read an SF short story by Sturgeon or an SF novel by Bester and when I read a literary novel by Robert Musil or a literary short story by Guy Davenport—or when I listen to a David Bowie song or see a George Lucas film. Someone's *making* all these interpretations. Do differing mind-sets allow me to make them? Am I happy at one? Sad at the other? Serious and critical at one? Lighthearted and frivolous at the next? Yes, I interpret one differently from the other. And to whatever extent you agree with me, *you* recognize these different interpretations as valid. Do you, then, indulge several mind-sets at once to comprehend my several interpretations if, say, two of them arrive in the same sentence? I think you'd have to work too hard to specify what you meant by mind-set in order to have it cover the needed situations.

In terms of reader expectation, what makes SF different from literary fiction—naturalistic, fantastic, experimental, or surreal—is of the same order as what makes poetry different from literary fiction. Let's start with the overlap, since it's the biggest part, despite the fact that it's the least interesting. A good prose writer is going to pay close attention to the sounds of the words in her prose; and a good poet *of course* pays attention to the sounds of the words in his poem. But that "of course" covers a multitude of expectational differences. Both John Gardner and William Gass are very phonically aware prose writers. Assonance and alliteration, not to mention phonic parallels and parallels disrupted, tumble from their sentences. But precisely what makes them dazzling and stimulating prose writers would make them gross and clumsy poets, assuming they didn't curb it hugely. And that's all controlled by poetic versus prosaic expectations.

SF is a paraliterary practice of writing; its mimetic relation to the real world is of a different order from even literary fantasy. It grows out of a different tradition. It has a different history. I enjoy working with and within that tradition and struggling with and within that history.

SG: Of course, there was a lot of controversy when *Dhalgren* came out because a lot of people were claiming that you *weren't* writing SF, that you had gone outside the tradition.

SD: Perhaps when a book sells seven or eight hundred thousand copies the controversy contributes to the acceptance. You might even say the controversy *is* the acceptance—in which case the acceptance of *Dhalgren* was rather small. Most of the American reading public was quite oblivious to any controversy at all. I never saw any *serious* controversy over whether or not *Dhalgren* was SF. When the idea was put forward at all, it was more in the line of name-calling. You know: "*That's* not science fiction! That's just self-indulgent drivel!" To me it seemed a much more modest argument—between the people who didn't like the book and the people who did. And my impression was that the contention centered mainly on discontinuities in the action and the lack of hard-edged explanation for the basic non-normal situation . . . along with the type of people I chose to write about. This last is a point it's polite, today, to gloss over. But at least one academic (of highly liberal if not leftist tendencies) told me straight out: "I'm just not interested in the people you write about. I can't believe they're important in the greater scheme of things." What makes this significant is that the vast majority of fan letters the book received—many more, by a factor of ten, than any other of my books have ever gotten— were almost all in terms of: "This book is about my friends"; "This book is about people I know"; "This book is about the world I live in"; "This book is about people nobody else writes of." These letters came from SF fans and from non-SF fans. For these readers, the technical difficulties of the book, the eccentricity of structure, and the density of style went all but unmentioned. After all, if the book makes any social statement, it's that when society pulls the traditional supports out from under us, we all effectively become, not the proletariat, but the *lumpen* proletariat. It says that the complexity of "culture" functioning in a gang of delinquents led by some borderline mental case is no less than that functioning at a middle-class dinner party. Well, there are millions of people in this country who have already experienced precisely this social condition, because for one reason or another their supports were actually struck away. For them, *Dhalgren* confirms something they've experienced. It reassures them that what they saw was real and meaningful; and they like that. But there are many others who have not had these experiences. Often they are people who have been threatened by the possibility of their social supports all going, who fought very hard against it, and who have worked mightily to stabilize their lives. Needless to say, these readers do *not* like the book. For them, it trivializes real problems and presents as acceptable things (and I *don't* mean sex) they have specifically found unacceptable—and are to be avoided at all costs. But the arguments between those people who disliked the book intensely and those people who liked it exorbitantly helped it to become somewhat more widely known—and, presumably, to reach an even larger audience.

SG: It's hard for me to think of a mainstream book as long and difficult and experimental as *Dhalgren* that has sold 700,000 copies. (I doubt if even *Gravity's Rainbow* has sold that many.) That seems to be another possible advantage to the SF field: an ambitious, serious writer who is interested in formal experimentation (even if this *is* part of the tradition) may have a greater chance to get his or her book out.

SD: *Dhalgren* has outsold *Gravity's Rainbow* by about 100,000 copies—we share a mass market publisher and statistics leak—but *Gravity's Rainbow* is a fantasy about a war most of its readers don't really remember, whereas *Dhalgren* is in fairly pointed dialogue with all the depressed and burned-out areas of America's great cities. To decide if *Gravity's Rainbow* is relevant, you have to spend time in a library—mostly with a lot of Time/Life books, which are pretty romanticized to begin with. To see what *Dhalgren* is about, you only have to walk along a mile of your own town's inner city. So *Dhalgren's* a bit more threatening—and accordingly receives less formal attention.

Sadly, your description of a field of writing open to experimentation and ambition better fits SF when I began publishing in the early '60s than it does today. The period in the late '50s and early '60s known as the "paperback revolution" created a flood of books—and with it a relatively friendly climate for new writers. William S. Burroughs published his first novel, *Junky,* with Ace Books back in 1953. Those same economic forces probably account for why Vonnegut's books were, indeed, appearing as paperback original SF novels in the '50s and early '60s. Carl ("I'm with you in Rockland") Solomon, of *Howl* fame, worked at Ace. And when, in 1962, Ace became a publication possibility for me, I spent the odd minute smiling over the fact that names like Burroughs and Solomon seemed pretty good writerly company.

LM: Many writers I've talked with over the last decade—Robert Coover, Ron Sukenick, Steve Katz, Joanna Russ, William Gibson—

have pointed to this commercial shift away from experimentalism toward more conservative approaches. Everyone seems to agree that *economic* factors — the takeover of publishing houses by multinationals, different tax laws, the Waldenbooks syndrome — are certainly responsible for this editorial bias against serious, innovative approaches.

SD: True, the economic crunch in the last decade has left the publishing world far less accepting and more suspicious of the new and the vital. Add to our economic hassles the current blockbuster mentality that's infected the book business via the movies and you have a really nasty situation for any serious writer. It strikes me as a very different situation from the particular style of commercialism rampant in book publishing since it came under its present distribution system just after World War II. (Most people are unaware that book distribution companies today are much bigger than book publishing companies.) Today, everybody in publishing is pretty well convinced that the court of sales has been hopelessly corrupted, by hype and other nameless pressures, so that an editor who says, "I think there is an audience (however small or large) that will enjoy this book," is no longer considered to be making a rational statement in business terms. The only statements considered rational in commercial publishing today are those that speak to the questions: How can it be hyped? How can it be made bigger than it is? *What* is being pushed is of secondary or even tertiary importance. Today's publisher would much rather publish a book that sounds catchy when described in three sentences than a book that affects it readers deeply and profoundly. This not only ends up reducing everything to the lowest common denominator; it lowers the denominator itself.

SF benefitted hugely from those early years of the paperback revolution. Joanna Russ, Thomas M. Disch, Ursula K. Le Guin, Roger Zelazny, R. A. Lafferty — the number of markedly exciting SF writers whose careers were strongly shaped by that revolution makes your jaw drop. In 1951 there were only fifteen volumes published that, by any stretch of the imagination, could be called SF novels, while last year SF made up approximately 16 percent of all new fiction published in the United States. When, by the mid-1970s, crunch-crunch was undeniable, there still seemed to be some factors built into the geography of our particular SF precinct (or ghetto, if you like) that kept the damages at bay a little longer than in some other fields — primary among them, the vitality and commitment of SF's highly vocal and long-time organized readership.

LM: I heard that very early in your career you self-consciously resisted jumping on the treadmill of quick-writing-for-quick-money that exhausted writers like Philip K. Dick and others. What gave you the nerve to say to the SF publishing establishment, "Look, I'm going to take my time and write a good book—not in six weeks or six months, but in however long it takes me"?

SD: As an anecdote, it sounds very brave and moral; and I'm willing to take a *modest* bow. But the simple fact is that I'm constitutionally incapable of writing quickly. I'm highly dyslexic. That means, among other things, I must write slowly and revise endlessly, if only to get right what are so cavalierly called, by the lexic, the "basic mechanics." With all the time I spend looking for the dropped, misspelled, and transposed words that litter my early drafts, I might as well, while I'm at it, *X* the odd adjective, clarify a parallelism here, strengthen an antithesis there. It goes, as they say, with the territory. Any text I write, I'm going to have to stay with a while—longer, anyway, than the lucky talents who whip out journeyman-like first drafts. It behooves me to think about what I'm doing a little more, if only to make sure it's complex enough to hold my interest during the extra time I have to live with it.

SG: Do you think your dyslexia may be one of the sources for your emphasis on the fragility and elusiveness of language's relationship to reality?

SD: I'm sure it is. A lot of Kid's perceptions of the world, in *Dhalgren,* are simply any dyslexic's perceptions of what goes on. Maybe once a week I used to go down to see my agent in the Village, and I would ride back and forth on the subway. Every few trips, my home subway station would turn up on the other side of the train—some trips it would be on one side, and others it would be on the other side. I'm forever getting up and going to the wrong door. I've been traveling this route for seven or eight years, yet, when I pull into the station, it's a toss-up—for *me*—which side of the train the station will be on.

That confusion is dramatized by Kid's misremembering distances, misjudging sides of the street, and even watching people changing the street signs as he goes by. That part of *Dhalgren* is very self-conscious borrowing from my dyslexia. Some things are also taken from my being somewhat ambidextrous—which often goes along with my particular sort of dyslexia. It's a learning disability that has many forms.

LM: That process seems related to your hyperawareness of the difficulties of the language process, your emphasis on the right word, your view of SF as a poetic genre. (I'm reminded of Kid saying, "I live in the mouth.")

SD: *Possibly* the dyslexic writer is more aware of what he or she does as a craft. But that may be too broad a generalization. There have been a number of dyslexic writers, of course; Gustave Flaubert and William Butler Yeats are among the best known. Dyslexic writers tend to be slow and painstaking. The fascination of what's difficult, Yeats wrote, had dried him up and left him old. But for a writer who, like Yeats, didn't really learn to read until he was sixteen, more things are going to be difficult than most people might expect. Such a writer has a push to substitute quality for quanity—which isn't *entirely* moral. A writer like Joyce, on the other hand, was as lexic as they come. When he wanted to, he could write like a speed demon: fully a third of *Ulysses* was written in galleys, over 250 of its 765 pages! Even in Paris in the '20s, you had galleys only for a couple of months, at the outside. I could no more write 250 pages of fully realized fiction in two months than I could fly to the Moon. And the more I'd thought about it and the more complicated a structure I'd planned it out to have, the longer it would take me actually to set it down.

SG: Your books have explicitly dealt with some very controversial subject matter. Take, for example, your treatment of three-way or multiple sexual relationships, of gay and bisexual relationships (and all sorts of subgroups) in *Triton,* and your general call for the need to explore male and female sexual roles in all their guises. Has working in the SF field given you more freedom to explore these areas? I'm thinking of the controversy that surrounded, say, Norman Mailer's *American Dream* or Philip Roth's *Portnoy's Complaint*—books that are very mild in their sexual presentation compared with what you are dealing with in *Dhalgren* and *Triton.*

SD: For a number of reasons, from my racial makeup to my sexuality to my chosen field of writing—or even because, in this society, I've chosen to write at all—my life has always tended to have a large element of marginality to it, at least if you accept a certain range of experience that overlaps that of an ideal white, middle-class, heterosexual male as the definition of centrality. To write clearly, accurately, with knowledge of and respect for the marginal is to *be* controversial—especially if you're honest about the overlaps. Because that means it's harder to regard the marginal as "other." And at that point, the whole category system that has assigned values like central and marginal in the first place is threatened.

SG: Would you say that SF is somehow constitutionally more tolerant of what is usually called "the marginal"?

SD: It would be nice to think that because SF itself has traditionally been considered a kind of marginal writing, it recognizes the problems of life on the edges and welcomes them with insight and compassion. But that may be a somewhat naive anthropomorphism.

The same play of social forces that lays down constraints (in sexual matters, say) that are internalized by individuals also lays down constraints for the various practices of writing—what, in practical terms, is generically acceptable and what isn't. But writers are not assigned their genres by God. Nor do they really choose them by conscious and considered acts of will. They move into them, even into literature, by a kind of ecological process.

All through my adolescence I wrote novel after novel, pitched at the center of the literary tradition as I mistily saw it: you know, out of Hemingway by Faulkner and Joyce, with a good nineteenth-century underpinning. That was my adolescent reading history, at any rate. I sent them to publisher after publisher, but although they got me a couple of scholarships, and some of my shorter pieces even won me the odd amateur prize, they were all finally rejected. Then I wrote an SF novel. Actually, it was rather borderline SF. (I had to go through four published SF novels before, in the fifth, I got brave enough to put in a spaceship!) And it was accepted, published, reviewed . . . !

Now there's a developmental aspect here that must be taken into account. I'm sure the SF novel I wrote at nineteen was, indeed, a *little* better than the literary novels I wrote at sixteen, seventeen, and eighteen. But even in my teens, what I was being *told* by literary editors was that the final reason the novels weren't being published was that they were *too* literary—and weren't commercial. There's a bottom-line situation here: literary publishing wasn't very accepting—they didn't accept me through a *whole* lot of tries—while SF publishing was. Even during my first couple of years in the field, the genre tended to say to me, "You can do what you want." Now that's not "Anyone can do anything he or she wants." Rather, that's "The kind of things *you* seem to want to do are more or less within acceptable bounds."

LM: But what seems striking—and significant to me, in terms of literary "history"—is that it *was* SF and *not* the literary "mainstream" that was saying to you that what you wanted to do was within the acceptable bounds of something it would be willing to publish. And obviously what you wanted to do was something very different from what most SF authors were doing at that point.

SD: If you look over my first four SF novels, all of which were written during my first three years in the SF field, you won't find spaceships. What you'll find is characters quoting poetry at each other. There's more than a passing interest in the female characters. Small sections are in play form; other sections are in stream-of-consciousness. (The books that followed were, if anything, more technically conservative.) Bits of the story are told from multiple points of view.

None of this is terribly profound as far as experimentation is concerned. The point is only that the SF publishing situation could accept it. For what it's worth, the books are still in print. This is a very different situation from the one in which a literary editor in 1960 at Harcourt Brace, who liked an early novel of mine enough to recommend me for a scholarship to the Bread Loaf Writers' Conference, said to me about similar devices in the book I'd submitted: "Well, if we *do* publish it, those are the first things that will have to go in the editing." Then she looked at me rather sadly and said: "Chip, you tell a good story. But right now, there's a housewife somewhere in Nebraska, and we can't publish a first novel here unless there's *something* in it that she can relate to. The fact is, there's *nothing* in your book that she wants to know anything about. And that's probably why we *won't* publish it." After two more readings and an editorial conference, they didn't.

The housewife in Nebraska has, of course, a male counterpart. In commercial terms, he's only about a third as important as she is. But his good opinion is considered far more prestigious. He's a high school English teacher in Montana who hikes on weekends and has some military service behind him. He despises the housewife—though reputedly she wants to have an affair with him. Needless to say, there wasn't much in my adolescent "literary" novels for him either. But between them, that Nebraska housewife and that Montana English teacher tyrannized mid-century American fiction.

Most of us have a conflict model for writer/publisher differences in which each is assumed to be after different goals and playing by different rules. But a better model is a game where both sides have internalized all the rules. An aesthetically significant conflict with a publisher is rather like a single player trying to get a team to run a new play when nobody quite understands how it will work or why it will be effective. The resistances—or, to call them by their right name, stupidities—you have to deal with are very much the collective sort; and if you have a truly new idea, you have to deal with that resistance in more or less the same way you would with a team. Any other approach dooms you to frustrating failure.

LM: How does this team model apply to the cyberpunk phenomenon of the mid-1980s?

SD: Cyberpunk involved a new and interesting bunch of SF writers, doing something timely and energetic. But it's important to put all this within a specific context. Cyberpunk has been an exciting phenomenon operating pretty much outside editorial resistance—or readerly resistance. It produced a lot of exciting speculation and argument that woke many of us up to various nuances of writerly tone; it made us look at possible new relations between SF and the world; it foregrounded a real and important attitude toward technology that was constituted as much by numbness as by accessibility. The working-class heroes, the streetwise cynicism, the glut of mini-technologies—some of the points where cyberpunk was congruent to the world that is the case—all this make SF interesting for a notable portion of the readership.

SG: But wasn't there considerable *resistance* to cyberpunk within SF?

SD: There was a lot of criticism. There was a lot of argument, back and forth. Male critics—forever uneasy about paternity—pointed out origins left and right. Feminist critics (most notably Jeanne Gomoll) pointed out the silent and unacknowledged appropriation by the cyberpunks of the last ten years of explosive feminist SF. All of it made a bright and informative dialogue. But within the SF field there was little or no *resistance* to cyberpunk. And why should there have been? (Polemic, criticism, and argument are not resistance; it's how polemic, criticism, and argument are *received* that constitutes resistance.) It was turning everybody on—from feminists to *Analog* fanatics. When I say it was turning them on, I don't for a moment mean that everyone *liked* it! I mean it was making everybody articulate positions, reassess current practices, review the tradition, and say how he or she felt about the world, about writing in general, and about SF in particular. To my mind, that's a good thing.

LM: Have you ever been tempted to try your hand at mundane fiction?

SD: Not since I was a kid. As I once said in an essay, that's like asking a twelve-tone composer to go back and compose diatonic music. It's asking you to give up half your vocabulary. There's little you can do in mundane fiction that you can't also do in SF. But you can do a whole lot of things in SF that are unavailable to the writer of mundane tales. You're not forbidden the subject explorations in SF, but you can relate them to the object explorations. For a certain kind of writer, that's a very exciting freedom. I might try mundane fiction as a sort of five-finger exercise. Chances are it wouldn't be terribly good. It would probably, at best, read like a five-finger exercise and at worst, like Schönberg in one of those Wagnerian pieces—*Pelléas und Mélisande* or an early unnumbered string quartet. You listen to those pieces and they sound like oatmeal—diatonic oatmeal. Oh, I suppose the *Gurrelieder* are kind of wonderful—still, I doubt that any mundane fiction I could write would be very interesting. If I were going to broach another genre, I think I'd prefer nonfiction.

LM: *Tales of Neveryon* and *Neveryona* are obvious departures from your previous books. Instead of being set in some imagined future, both are set in some magical, distant past, just as civilization is being created. Do you consider them SF?

SD: They associate with SF via a subcategory, sword-and-sorcery, SF's despised younger cousin. Certainly, one thing that must have drawn me to SF in the first place was a propensity for working in despised genres. What's intriguing about sword-and-sorcery is that it takes place in an aspecific, idealized past rather than in Rome or Egypt or Babylonia or Troy. This means that whatever happens *doesn't* filter through any recognizable historical events—the Diaspora, say, or the Peloponnesian or Gallic wars. So once again—and this should sound familiar—it lets you look at the impact of certain cross-cultural concepts (like money, writing, weaving, or any early technological advances—the *techne* Pound got so obsessed within the "Rock Drill" *Cantos*) that go so far in overdetermining the structure of the historical biggies: a war, a change of government, a large migration from country to city. But what makes sword-and-sorcery historically aspecific also makes it rather anachronistic. In most sword-and-sorcery you find neolithic artifacts cheek by jowl with Greek and Roman elements, all in the shadow of late medieval or High Gothic architecture.

SG: The Neveryon stories all seem to deal with power—all kinds of power: sexual, economic, even racial power via the issue of slavery.

SD: All four of my grandparents were children of at least one parent born in slavery. Manumitted when she was eight, my great-grandmother Fitzgerald still told my grandmother stories about slave times, as did my grandmother's grandparents, with whom my grandmother stayed in the summer when she was a little girl in Virginia—stories my grandmother, who was alive till only last year (she died when she was 102), told me. In imaginary Neveryon, slavery is an economic reality (fast fading into a historical memory) but also a persistent fantasy. It's a speculative endeavor; and, however interesting or stimulating (or, indeed, crushingly trivial) people find the suggestions that grow out of it, it's still play. But that's different from what I assume would be the corresponding literary endeavor: to sketch a psyche, a character, a mind caught up with such a fantasy (say, slavery), with the world shown only as the necessary frame to hold the canvas to shape. To me, right now, that just wouldn't be very interesting.

LM: What overall plan have you been following in these books?

SD: Only the traditional form SF has developed for its own brand of series stories. In the late '30s and all through the '40s, the overwhelming majority of American SF appeared in the pulp magazines. Many of these stories, by individual writers, would return to the same world or universe and pick up the time stream at different points. Sometimes there would be continuous characters, sometimes not. Clifford Simak's *City* was such a series, and so was Heinlein's Future History series and Asimov's Foundation series.

The particular form I'm talking about is probably clearest in the Foundation tales, though you can trace it out in almost all the others. Put simply, the first story poses a problem and finally offers some solution. But in the next story, what was the solution of the first story is now the problem. In general, the solution for story N becomes the problem for story $N + 1$. This allows the writer to go back and critique his or her own ideas as they develop over time. Often, of course, the progression isn't all that linear. Sometimes a whole new problem will assert itself in the writer's concern—another kind of critique of past concerns. Sometimes you'll rethink things in stories more than one back. But the basic factor is the idea of a continuous, open-ended, self-critical dialogue with yourself.

SG: This supports a particular relationship of author to text that has a lot of formal implications very different from those of most fiction. In effect, it's an open-ended, ongoing structure rather than the closed, "finished"' structure that most fiction presents itself within. A very postmodernist notion, if you will.

SD: Exactly. And it's this very flexibility that is so often misunderstood (and misrepresented) by readers and critics. Here's a short story. Next's a bulky novel. That can be followed by a novella, or another novel, or another short story. When publishers first began to collect SF series together in volume form, they did everything they could to try to make the resultant books look like novels. Because of that back-looking critical process, however, often a writer would have set a story further back in time from an earlier tale, instead of moving continually forward in strict chronological order. When the stories appeared over months in magazines, this was no problem. But when the stories were collected, invariably they'd be put in chronological order, no matter how this obscured the self-critical development. I'm sure you can understand how, if a reader picks up the book version of one of these series, thinking it's an SF novel (and there's often no way to tell, since separate stories are frequently renamed "chapters"), and begins it with the expectations ordinarily brought to a novel, the book's going to read strangely; and the self-critical development, especially if it's not blatantly obvious, might just slip by because the reader isn't looking for it.

In one sense, the SF series is something like a prose narrative version of that quintessentially American form, the open-ended serial composition poem—Pound's *Cantos,* Olson's *Maximus Poems,* Diane Wakoski's *Greed,* or Robert Duncan's *Passages.* You also find the same self-critical thrust at work there. But that's shock analogy. You can only take it so far.

SG: Were you reading anything that specifically influenced the directions the Neveryon books take? In addition to the sword-and-sorcery genre, Larry and I were both reminded of Italo Calvino's *Cosmicomics.*

SD: Just more sword-and-sorcery, particularly, I guess, Joanna Russ's Alyx stories—a marvelous series of sword-and-sorcery tales that suddenly, in the middle, becomes SF. Russ grabs up all her opportunities and juggles them marvelously. I'd fooled around with a couple of incomplete fragments of a sword-and-sorcery tale back when I was living in England, but finally I lost the manuscript. Then, when I returned to the States, I was commissioned to write an introduction to Russ's stories, which were coming out in a library edition. Practically the day after I finished my introduction, I sat down and started writing the Neveryon tales. Russ's stories showed me that you really *could* make the richest and most satisfying art out of sword-and-sorcery. I just had to try it.

SG: Your childhood—growing up in a middle-class black household in Harlem, being somewhat of a child prodigy—has been fairly well documented by now. But there are a few things we'd like you to comment on. The first is being taken from Harlem to Dalton Elementary School in midtown Manhattan. You've described this trip, which you made five times a week during the school year, between the ages of five and thirteen, as follows: "I was subjected to a virtually ballistic trip through a socio-psychological barrier of astonishingly restrained violence."

SD: Of course it affected me. And obviously my white classmates—unlike my few black ones, who were also Harlemites—didn't have the clear visual switch between the kind of neighborhood I grew up in—132nd Street and Seventh Avenue, with a "Housepaint and Hosiery" store on one side and a small family grocery on the other, and the people I saw daily out in the street—and Park Avenue. I was intensely aware of that twice-a-day transition, but as one is aware of the totally normal. It was a violent transition, but it was also my total surroundings. It had to emerge in some form in my writing.

LM: Your father was an undertaker, and when you were a child your family lived above the funeral parlor. Did that leave any lasting, perhaps subliminal, impression? I'm not just thinking of fairly obvious things, like Rydra's visit to the morgue for a needed crew replacement (in *Babel-17*), but of the overpowering presence of death in *Dhalgren*.

SD: The first thing that occurs to me is Yeats's comment that the only two topics worthy of the serious mind are sex and death. I went back and forth, many times and with astonishing speed, from being a very silly to a very serious little boy. It's rather hard to be a living creature without being concerned about what death is. If anything, living over a funeral parlor made me easier with some of the overt manifestations of death. I saw corpses almost every day, and they never plagued me with nightmares; that experience may even have gotten certain images out of the way for me. I certainly remember that living where I did gave me an intriguing power over my contemporaries—you know, "Come on into the funeral parlor—ha ha ha! I dare you!" When I was seven or eight, they'd all tiptoe in after me; when we'd get about halfway through the office, I'd laugh ghoulishly. And the four or five of them would shriek and run out. My father did *not* approve of this.

LM: Your presentation of the city in *Dhalgren* seemed very primordial, something out of a childhood nightmare.

SD: Understand, you're talking to a man with a great distrust of the primordial. I find it a very superficial construct. Still, I suppose in one sense *Dhalgren* has largely to do with the fact that the Harlem of my childhood isn't there today. Just as I distrust the primordial, there's a whole concept of nostalgia that I find equally distasteful. I'm not at all interested in presenting a romanticized picture of long-vanished singing and dancing (or sweating and dope-dealing) darkies. They just weren't there, at least not as they're nostalgically pictured. My way of dealing with the obliteration of my landscape is to observe very carefully what's there now. If you travel in Harlem today, you'll see that buildings are now unoccupied, much of it is burned out. Here and there, small oases of intense community life are surrounded by blocks of devastation, run through by the most tenuous of public transportation. It's much the same on the Lower East Side, where I spent my next near-decade; and it's much the same in practically a third of every big city in the United States. There are all these ruined urban areas. Walk through that landscape and there's a great feeling of death. (Far more than there ever was around my father's funeral parlor. Actually, as such neighborhood businesses go, it was a pretty social spot.)

Dhalgren rings its changes on those current urban images; that, I think, is what its readers first recognized. It's basically an expression of a very depressed part of the city—and of the kind of life that nevertheless goes on there. These images are what inform the dialogue *Dhalgren* tries to set up with the glass and aluminum and poured concrete of the office buildings and the shopping malls and the other brave new acres of our urban and suburban megalopolis.

SG: Was Rydra in *Babel-17* based on your ex-wife, Marilyn Hacker?

SD: Not really. Very rarely do I base characters consciously on real people—though often people, even ones who know me, are sure I do. Marilyn and I had a dear friend, an older gentleman who died just last year, who'd known us since we were teenagers. He was a sometime psychotherapist who went to his grave convinced that he was the model for Dr. Markus T'mwarba, Rydra's psychiatrist. I never had the heart to disillusion him.

Rydra and Marilyn are both poets, and here and there I undoubtedly borrowed some of Marilyn's poetic concerns for the book. But I suspect that Rydra is more me than Marilyn—and, indeed, not all that much either of us. Rydra has one speech—on page 16, if you're interested—that I once made, in an attack of postadolescent grandiosity, *to* Marilyn. But for the rest, it's pretty much invention. Rydra is a twenty-six-year-old Oriental woman from the Outer Satellites who lives two hundred or so years from now. Marilyn was — at least when I wrote the book — twenty-two, Jewish, and from the Bronx. But there are people, some of them rather close friends, who are never going to believe that.

What I try to go through, especially with my major characters, is something like this. On the one hand, I want my characters to do things that I've done myself; that's so I'll know what it *feels* like to be in their situation. On the other hand, I want to have seen at least one other person do the same things; I also want to know what it *looks* like. But to try to associate my major characters with me — or with anyone I know — is a thankless task.

SG: I was struck by how authentic you make your female characters. This is rare for a male author. What's your secret?

SD: It's hard for me to tell how authentic my characters seem to others. When you're standing inside the balloon, it's hard to see what shape it is from the outside. Many years ago, I was thinking about the problem of writing characters of any sort and trying to analyze what seemed to be wrong with the women characters in most modern American fiction. As early as 1959 or 1960, I'd noticed that there was something terribly wrong with the female characters in most novels I was reading. Most of the writers (men and women) tended to conceive of their male characters as combinations of purposeful actions, habitual actions, and gratuitous actions. A female character, in contrast, would be all gratuitous action if she was a "good woman," with no purposes and no habits; if she was a "bad woman," she would be all purpose, with no gratuitous actions and no habits. This seemed silly. Very early on, I tried to think about women characters in terms of all three — actions purposeful, habitual, and gratuitous. And I tried (I almost want to say "manfully") to make sure that my female characters indulged in all three. When I would try to put this into practice, almost always the "natural workings" of the story seemed to conspire to exclude this diversity of action from the women.

SG: Most stories don't provide a place for the kind of variety you're talking about.

SD: Today, we'd say that the basic templates for bourgeois fiction are themselves sexist, patriarchal, and oppressive. Twenty years ago, when, in endless dialogue, Marilyn and I were first figuring this out, I just thought they were psychotic. The standard narrative templates for male characters are richer than those for women, and writers follow them without even thinking. There was a whole twenty years in American fiction when women were *never* portrayed as having any same-sex friends; during the same period, the American "buddy novel," from *The Reivers* to *On the Road,* was endemic. Consider the number of women characters who run through American narratives at all levels, from the best novels to the worst films, about whom you never know how they make their money. Once you start asking, "But who's *paying* for all this?" a whole lot of bad narrative falls apart. Making the artistic representation *of* their place so completely unrealistic is an insidiously effective way to keep women *in* their place.

LM: What literary interests did you have as a child?

SD: Until I wrote my first SF novel, I wasn't particularly interested in SF other than as a reader; I was interested in writing. I'd been trying to write novels since I was fourteen, which isn't *that* odd—some people just know that's what they want to do. During my teens, I was omnivorously reading the kind of things any bright, literarily inclined kid would be reading in the '50s—along with a lot of SF.

SG: No writer really stood out as an inspiration or model?

SD: I guess the writer I was most impressed with as a teenager was Theodore Sturgeon—who happened to be an SF writer but who could do more with a sentence than anyone else I'd ever read. He'd give you the flicker of sunlight through blowing leaves on a bellied-out screen door, in a phrase so vivid that it made you reach to feel the snagged and gritty mesh. He wrote about human emotions as though they were solid objects, with shapes and colors, moving through the body so you could feel their friction. No matter where he set the story, whether in an October suburban schoolroom or in a spaceship cabin between planets or in a village of telepathic aliens under a distantly clouded sun, it was equally sharp and immediate. Later, I began to encounter a few other writers who could do somewhat the same thing—Nabokov, Updike, Barth; and still later, Gass and Gardner; and more recently Guy Davenport—at least with realistic settings. But Sturgeon was the first and, for a young reader, the most astonishing.

When I was seventeen, Marie Ponsot, an older poet (that is, she was twenty-five or twenty-six at the time), gave me a copy of Djuna Barnes's *Nightwood.* That's got to be the single novel I've reread more than any other—about twenty times at this point. Like everyone else back then, I *loved* Baldwin's essays. I had the traditional '50s awe of Joyce and Eliot and Woolf and Pound. And I always liked Gertrude Stein. So there really wasn't anything too unusual about my interests.

SG: Your fiction has often been called poetic, and references to poetry and poets abound there. Certain forms of poetry, especially symbolism (à la Rimbaud in *Babel-17*), have affected your concept of the craft of writing. Why haven't you pursued poetry more often yourself?

SD: I've used poetry as a topic in some of my works because making poems is a good metaphor for the language-making process, the art-making process in general. But it can serve as a metaphor for the latrine-digging process or the dry-cleaning process, too. When I was a kid, I wrote a very few, very bad poems. But that doesn't make me a poet. I've watched a few people who are good poets do their work. That was enough to convince me that it just wasn't something for which I had a talent. I'm an enthusiastic poetry reader, and because my temperament lets me enjoy reading it—enjoy it deeply—I'm *very* grateful. But any poem I wrote would, I suspect, be too much *me* in the worst and most uninteresting way.

LM: A number of other "poetic" prose writers have told me that they have remained in fiction because they are interested in "story." Is that true for you as well?

SD: No. "Story" as it's usually conceived seems to me the most boring thing about fiction. "Story" is a way of talking about the dullest part of the reading experience. You have the experience of "story" at very few points in the text—often only for a moment or two, sometimes just at the very end. Get back from the writerly canvas and you'll see certain things. One thing that emerges, when you're at a certain distance, is, of course, the "story," so at least it's a real category for *readers* to think about. But for the writer who has to work right up next to the canvas all the time, "story" dissolves into so many other things that it's almost pointless to think about it directly. From the viewpoint of the writer, I'd say "story" doesn't exist. It's just not a valid writerly category. Writers face off against the page, put one letter down after another to make a word, one word after another to make a sentence—the sentence has to have a certain shape, a certain melody. Then you have to make another sentence. Then you have to make sure the two of them harmonize—at every level, from sound to semantics. "Story" vanishes in this process. Move back far enough and, yes, a story emerges at a certain point—in the same way that, if you move back even farther, you can see the story's theme; and, if you can get back farther still, you can see its genre. But up close, it's just words and sentences and sounds and syntax, one following another in a variety of patterns, while you try to make those words relate to all the others you've put down in a variety of ways—a very few of which *may* relate to "story."

SG: This sounds a lot like what poets do.

SD: Yes. And if you substitute the idea of "brush stroke" for "word" or "sentence," it sounds much like what painters do. All we're saying, really, is that the construction process in any art tends to follow the same atomic process. This isn't to minimize the important differences of the different elements involved in this process. I begin a sentence lover, which is why I'm drawn to prose rather than poetry. Poetry is made of words, Mallarmé told us a hundred years back. But prose is made of sentences. I'm forever delighted, then delighted all over, at the things sentences can trip and trick you into saying, into seeing. I'm astonished— just plain tickled!—at the sharp turns and tiny tremors they can whip your thoughts across. I'm entranced by their lollop and flow, their prickles and points. For me, the word is a degenerate sentence, a fragmentary utterance, something incomplete. The Russian critic M. Bakhtin hit on the radical notion of considering the word not a locus of specified meaning but rather an arena in which all possible social values that might be expressed with and through it can engage in contest. But what calls up those differing values? What holds them stable long enough to let their dander up, if not the other words about, along with the punctuation that, here and there, surrounds and, there and here, sunders—in short, the different sentences the word occurs in? Without the sentence, the arena of the word has no walls, no demarcation. No contest takes place. All this makes it seem to me that the sentence is certainly the better model of the text.

LM: How did *Dhalgren* begin?

SD: Conceptually, I suppose, it started with Mann's notion that "Nothing is truly interesting save the exhaustive." I wanted to write a big, exhaustive book. As far as incident, it began with the present beginning—the woman turning into a tree. Then it stopped for a while, until I had my next structural notion, the idea of building the novel around two parties, the dinner at Mrs. Richards's and the party at Calkins's mansion. I got the idea partly from Jane Austen's notion that "Everything happens at parties." I'll also confess that I was thinking of the two great Proustian parties at the beginning and the end of *Remembrance of Things Past*. Indeed, you can look at the whole *Recherche* as a movement from the dinner party at Madame Verdurin's to the soirée, years later, at the Princesse de Guermantes's.

LM: You mentioned the relevance of Harlem to *Dhalgren,* which portrays the contemporary urban experience—especially the marginal life of poor people and racial minorities.

SD: Urban life is what I know. The motto I chose for the book was from a conversation with the West Coast poet George Stanley, back in 1969 or 1970, when he and Marilyn and I were having dinner at the Savoy Tivoli, in North Beach: "You have confused the true and the real." But the motto could just as easily have been "I love New York." I had a lot of cities in mind while I was writing *Dhalgren*—in a sense, the city there is Every City, Any City. One person said, with some truth, that *Dhalgren* is a book in which the exteriors are New York and the interiors are San Francisco. Well, a lot of the first draft of *Dhalgren* was written while I was living in San Francisco. That's not to say I was transcribing my life during that period, though some of the things that had been going on in the years before—for example, the kind of life I described in my nonfiction book *Heavenly Breakfast*—certainly resonate throughout the novel. I suppose the central conceit is that what is traditionally socially marginal is re-placed at center stage; there's also an economic distortion at work, and a distortion of the landscape, that allows the marginal to take over. All the "decent people" have left the city, leaving only the marginals, who can then go on leading their lives however they want, without the usual exterior pressures. There's still plenty of interior pressure, though. Another oblique influence was probably Marge Piercy's *Dance the Eagle to Sleep:* the first third seemed so brilliant when I first read it, while the last two-thirds seemed to me . . . well, unrealized.

LM: I felt that *Dhalgren* was, among other things, a very personalized exploration of your own psyche.

SD: I've always hated the idea of art as therapy, yet putting a lot of the confusion and pain and other materials of one's life into a formal pattern *can* make it easier to deal with these things—or at least make them a little less terrifying. Although some of the experiences behind what happens to the adult Kid in the book happened to me when I was a child, I tried to retain what was most important about each incident—the response.

LM: You raise a point that other writers have mentioned: one draws from one's experience when writing, but the effective writer must find a way to transform experience into art. Reality isn't "shapely."

SD: The fiction-making process—and the shape of other stories—can blind you to what's interesting (or, indeed, needed) in life. When I'm teaching a creative writing course, I find this happening time and time again. Precisely when the students think they're really writing about "what happened to them," that's when they are most in the grip of literary clichés and stereotypes. What excited them to write about an incident in the first place was that the reality was already so close to the cliché: that's what made it seem like such good story material. Then all those changes they make so that it will seem more like good fiction manage to take a half-cliché and turn it into a whole one. And once they've got it on paper, they can no longer see their own distortions.

The problems of representation are very real. Nobody denies it. You cannot say everything about any situation, and there is no way to verify that any of what's been said or written is true without a situational context to appeal to. But there is a great rhetorical battery, much of it extant and more of it still inventable, that *can* talk about the world in a recognizable way. To do it takes a great sense of responsibility, some aesthetic sensitivity, and a lot of discipline. But it's also possible that even to have the problem means I'm deluding myself about my own writerly strengths.

SG: When you were writing *Heavenly Breakfast,* did you find the process fundamentally different from your fiction writing?

SD: No. Some people read *Heavenly Breakfast* as autobiography, you know — though it says right in the introduction that "persons are combined to make" single characters and "atomized to make several" and that dates are shifted and incidents are shuffled between cities. Well, what sort of autobiography is that? But, again, I was trying to maintain the structure of the characteristic incidents.

The difference, I suppose, is that in fiction the process happens against a much finer grid. You take a bushy eyebrow from a subway conductor, the red cheeks from your Uncle Lucius, a snowy November evening from a weekend in Milwaukee a half-dozen years ago, a cornice decoration from a church in Thessalonica you saw a dozen years before that, and a wholly invented stained-glass window — though the dirt in the corner is the dirt in the corner of your office window as you're writing. You put them all together into a scene where, one snowy November evening, a bushy-eyed, red-cheeked man stops before a stained-glass window outside a church on the outskirts of Secaucus, New Jersey (where you've never been, though you once read about some colorful characters in a bar there, in somebody's poem), beneath a chipped cornice. Any talk about whether the character is *really* your uncle or a subway conductor is, at this point, silly; so is any discussion about whether the church is really in Greece or New York (or Milwaukee or Secaucus). It's a text. No more — but no less.

In *Heavenly Breakfast,* the grid was much coarser. I was trying to take whole incidents, rather than eyebrows and cornice decorations; I was trying to preserve *some* continuity of discourse. That's what makes it nonfiction. Only the continuity of character, or of gross location, and the chronology were fictive. Those fictions didn't seem great enough for me not to call the work nonfiction — not to call it an essay. Yet those continuities — character, place, and time — are so often seen as one with reality by readers who assume all novels are really romans à clef (most of D. H. Lawrence's critics, for example).

SG: You have said that writing *Triton* was easier than any book you'd written since you were a teenager, yet Bron was the first unsympathetic central character you'd created.

SD: Sometimes it's much easier to write a hate letter than to compose a thoughtful, supportive, positive one. The initial impetus behind *Triton* was to construct a merciless analysis of a monster. It's a kind of monstrosity that many of us share, but it's monstrous nevertheless. Here comes another of those preposterously pretentious declarations: The model for *Triton* was *Madame Bovary,* in the sense, say, that *La Princesse de Cleves* was the model for Radiguet's *Bal du Comte d'Orgel* (rather than in the sense that Bester took the plot of *The Stars My Destination* from *The Count of Monte Cristo*). I wanted to do a psychological analysis of someone with whom you're just not in sympathy, someone whom you watch making all the wrong choices, even though his plight itself is sympathetic. That's the case with Bron. He's constantly taking the easy way out, and finally he destroys himself. He doesn't commit suicide at the end, like Emma, but he's left pretty hopeless. He simply cannot distinguish truth from lies, cliché from reality. It amounts to a kind of madness. Anyway, after five years of writing endless sentences for *Dhalgren* at the head of notebook page after notebook page and revising them, one at a time, down to the bottom margin, then mortaring them back into place—after that, *Triton* seemed to flow very easily. In one sense, *Dhalgren* was a five-year exercise in empathy. *Triton* was a nine-month orgy of antipathy.

LM: You said *Triton* erupted after you had written the "kiss-off" letter Bron reads in chapter 6—and that the rest of the book evolved around that letter. Is that the way your books have tended to proceed for you—in a nonlinear way?

SD: Usually they proceed in a more orderly fashion. I have to have a pretty good idea of what's going on all through them before I start. Still, I usually begin from the beginning and work through to the end— at least for the first draft. Revisions, of course, come more piecemeal— though even the second draft *usually* proceeds from one end to the other. The third and up? Well, that can happen any old way. Still, in that sense *Triton* was unusual. I wrote out a draft of what you called "the kiss-off letter" first—sitting in Heathrow Airport, waiting with Marilyn for a plane to Paris—before going back to start with chapter 1.

LM: Can you point to anything that tends to begin a work for you— a character, an image, a plot idea, a theme, a metaphor?

SD: Usually the books begin with a character in a landscape. Once a draft of that letter was out of the way for *Triton,* the thing that gave me the beginning of the book was the hope that readers would initially think Bron was just an ordinary guy living in a sterile, depressing, gaudy, but ultimately repressive society. Then, as the book goes on, you slowly realize that the society is not so bad—but this *guy* is just *awful!* A switch takes place. I want you to end up feeling that Bron is completely hopeless but that the society is certainly no worse than ours—probably a lot better in some ways. So, again, the book began, as it were, with a character in a place. Then the view of the place—and the character— changed.

LM: Those appendixes and reports at the end of *Triton* and the Neveryon books actually seem integral—discourses that open up what seemed to be the closed system of the novel. What was the inspiration for that approach?

SD: I first found it, of course, in the "Consequential Data," "Notes on the Text," and "workpoints" at the ends of the various volumes of Durrell's *Alexandria Quartet.* That was another spectacularly enjoyable read for me when I was a teenager. Then there were the various journals, fictive and actual, at the end of Gide's *Les Faux Monnayeurs.* Of course, there's a whole tradition in SF novels of having appendixes like those in *Dune* and the glossary in *The Left Hand of Darkness;* so I thought I'd have a go at it. The appendixes to the Neveryon books function a bit differently. They're really a kind of scholarly game. All the people cited in the first one are real—except for K. Leslie Steiner. Interestingly enough, I got a call from someone reviewing the book who had just interviewed Schmandt-Besserat, one of the archaeologists whose theories are discussed in the appendix to *Tales of Neveryon.* The reviewer was quite sure that if someone that obscure (to most people) was real, then *everyone* in the essay must be real, including Steiner.

LM: Are there any contemporary writers, SF or otherwise, whom you particularly admire?

SD: Like a lot of other people, I find it harder and harder to read fiction. I don't know if that's because of the fiction or because I'm getting older. Probably both. Every once in a while, though, I find a writer who wakes up my appetite for fiction. I've already mentioned Guy Davenport, for example. I find the short stories of John Varley very exciting, though I don't enjoy his novels as much. I like William Gass's criticism a lot. I admire Walter Abish's work—*Alphabetical Africa* is one of the most delightful books I've ever read, and the somewhat more traditional *How German Is It* offers all kinds of challenges. I'm sure there are all sorts of interesting fiction writers out there, but my reading in that area has just fallen off. I'm mainly interested in critics, such as Shoshana Felman, Barbara Johnson, Paul de Man, Jane Gallop.

LM: You were a musician yourself for a while, and musicians and musical analogues appear frequently in your works. It seems to me that you consider the elements of your craft—words, symbols, motifs— somewhat abstractly, as materials to be manipulated, in much the way that musicians do.

SD: I've always felt attracted to Walter Pater's notion, "All art aspires to the condition of music"—a phrase which, when I first ran into it, immediately seemed somehow right. In high school, I had a friend who was a composer; for a time, we were also part of a folk-singing quartet together. Somewhere during the autumn of 1961, when he was in his second year of college and I had dropped out, gotten married, and was writing my first SF novel, he completed an interesting musical composition that was to be performed at a concert of new music at Hunter College. It was complex, atonal. At any point in the piece, the dozen-odd instruments would be playing all twelve notes of the scale save one; through the course of the composition, the missing note moved up and down through the cacophonous sonorities, so that the "melodic line," if you can call it that, was a silence that progressed, as a sort of absent melody, through it all. During rehearsals, while I turned pages for the clarinetist, something became clear: When the piece, or more usually a stretch of it, was performed very, very well by all the players, with the dynamics and intonations truly under control and great attention fixed to its overall cohesion, then the traveling silence became clearly audible and its effect striking, disturbing, even moving. If, however, one or two of the players lost their concentration, or there was the least little dynamic wandering, or there was any noise at all in the rehearsal room, or, indeed, if the attention of the listener strayed a moment, then the whole thing dissolved into acoustic mush.

My friend's piece became a kind of model for me of the situation of the serious writer—if not the artist in general. I thought about it a lot then, and I've thought about it a lot since. It doesn't seem to matter whether the writer is a "hard-hitting journalist" or the farthest out constructor of experimental poems. All the writer's noise is finally an attempt to shape a silence in which something can go on. Call it the silence of interpretation, if you will. But even that's too restrictive. The silence of response is probably better—if not just silence itself. The writer tries to shape it carefully, conscientiously; but both forming and hearing it today can be equally hard. The journalist may want a very different kind of thing to go on in that silence from what the experimental poet wants. One may well want the audience to use it as a lucid moment in which to make a decision for action, while the other may want the audience only to hear that it is there and to appreciate its opacities and malleabilities, its resistances to and acceptances of certain semiotic violences. The SF writer may want the audience to observe in it the play and fragile stability of the object world its malleabilities and opacities alone can model. The writer will mold it differently in terms of what she or he wants us to do with it, do in it, using a variety of codes. And the variety of codes that make that writing meaningful will differ here, will overlap there, depending on the writerly mode. Nevertheless, we can still, when it is useful, designate all writerly enterprises with the same terms: shaping the silence.

Patti Perret

An Interview with

Thomas M. Disch

Tom Disch is the closest American SF has ever come to a true Renaissance man. Best known for his intellectually challenging, formally innovative SF novels, including the dazzling, dystopian New Wave classics *Camp Concentration* (1968) and *334* (1972) and the equally impressive *On Wings of Song* (1979), Disch's restless literary imagination has often also led him outside SF. He is the author of various critical essays, several collections of poems (a number of which initially appeared in the *Paris Review*), numerous non-SF or quasi-SF novels (including perhaps his most commercially successful novel, *Clara Reeve*, which appeared under the pseudonym Leonie Hargrave), opera librettos, and a computer-interactive text, *Amnesia* (1986); and he is currently the drama critic for *The Nation*.

The editor of a series of highly influential theme anthologies—including *The Ruins of Earth* (1971), *Bad Moon Rising* (1973), *The New Improved Sun* (1975), *New Constellations* (1976; in collaboration with Charles Naylor), and *Strangeness* (1977; also with Naylor)—Disch is now recognized not only as a master of bitterly humorous, often viciously satirical SF short stories but also as one of the best contemporary short fiction writers of any sort. His short stories—some of which can be found in such recent collections as *The Man Who Had No Idea* (1982) and *Fundamental Disch* (1980), as well as in *Getting into Death* (1973), *Fun with Your New Head* (1968), and *White Fang Goes Dingo and Other Funny SF* (1971; an enlarged version of *One Hundred and Two H Bombs* (1966)—operate on the boundaries of SF, postmodern experimentalism, metaphysical fable, and mainstream fiction. In his use of playful reflexiveness, black humor, and a blend of philosophical, psychological, and scientific concerns, Disch can best be compared to other unclassifiable authors of similar speculative, wide-ranging, intensely realized imaginations: Franz Kafka, Italo Calvino, Donald Barthelme, Guy Davenport, Jorge Luis Borges, Vladimir Nabokov (an early and significant influence), and Stanislaw Lem.

From the time Disch first attracted the attention of serious SF fans, he has remained essentially a maverick, working on the fringes of SF. The reason for his relative aloofness is easy to see, once you examine the textures of his fiction. Whereas most SF being published in the early 1960s, when Disch entered the field, was largely adolescent from an intellectual standpoint—full of turgid prose and flashy but ill-conceived speculations concerning cosmic significance and galactic empires— even Disch's earliest apprentice works—*The Puppies of Terra* (1964) and *The Genocides* (1965)—displayed a sensibility as much influenced by Thomas Mann, Marcel Proust, and the absurd authors then being widely translated (Eugène Ionesco, Jean Genet, and Samuel Beckett, for example) as by SF. The result was a blend of self-consciousness, irony, verbal eloquence, and ferociously misanthropic intelligence that was utterly new to SF.

By the mid-1960s, when he became associated with SF's New Wave in general and Michael Moorcock's seminal *New Worlds* magazine in particular, Disch was writing the equivalent of SF for opera fans. And with the publication of *Camp Concentration* in 1968, he joined J. G. Ballard and William S. Burroughs as key figures in the avant-garde, apocalyptically oriented SF movement that would influence not only the American New Wave of the same period but also the cyberpunk movement of the '80s. Emerging from the rampant paranoia and the mixtures of destructive and liberating energies of the late '60s, *Camp Concentration* is a literary and philosophical tour de force with some vague parallels to Kafka's *Castle* and Ken Kesey's *One Flew Over the Cuckoo's Nest*—a sensitive political prisoner is imprisoned by an oppressive system that regards him as little more than a caged animal to be selfishly manipulated. The most striking feature of the novel is Disch's audacious decision to use a first-person narrative voice for his protagonist, who is injected with a syphilis-derivative spirochete that raises his IQ to unparalleled levels. *Camp Concentration* introduces many of the basic concerns explored in Disch's subsequent work: the horror of metaphysical doubt, the longing for, and possible means of, transcending human mortality and decay, entrapment within our own bodies, the Faustian dilemma of making a compact with immoral forces to enhance personal and intellectual power at the expense of the community.

One of the things that struck me as I prepared for this interview was the way Disch's work had evolved over the years in its tone, thematic concerns, and stylistic features. This is especially true of the newer work he sent me prior to our first taping session. His novella "Hard Work, the Secrets of Success," the metafictional fantasy *A Troll in Surewood Forest,* and the computer-interactive text *Amnesia* all displayed a sense of playfulness and optimism that was very different from the profound sense of insecurity and pessimism so elegantly and convincingly displayed in his earlier major works. In both *Amnesia* and *Troll,* Disch has developed highly original formal methods to foreground the constructed, provisional nature of personal identity, literary texts, and meaning structures; he has emphasized, too, the choice-making process generated by what he refers to as "the rain of possibilities" made available by modern technology.

During the interview—which began in June 1986 and continued in a series of conversations at the East Village's Cedar Tavern and at Disch's apartment in June 1988—the reason for the obvious shift in the tenor and tone of his work became apparent: personally and professionally, Tom Disch is a happy man. Part of his philosophical and emotional optimism arises from his stable and mutually supportive personal relationship with Charles Naylor. Equally significant, he no longer feels quite so much the literary outsider. Disch's best work still makes use of anger and bitter irony, but he has added an element of compassion and empathy for human foibles and longings. He has also begun to explore more openly (and ambitiously) features of personal and sexual identity, as in his most autobiographical novel to date, *On Wings of Song.* Clearly, the man who sat across from me was no longer the enfant terrible of SF's New Wave but a lively individual of vigorous middle age possessing a longshoreman's physique (complete with tattoo!), an unexpectedly delicate voice and ready laugh, and a penetrating, wicked sense of humor that he was quite willing to turn upon himself.

Larry McCaffery: When you began writing SF back in the '60s, your work was closely associated with the New Wave, which tended to be deeply pessimistic about the effects of technology and politics. Your recent work tends to present science and technology less grimly, more playfully, even more joyfully.

Thomas Disch: My work and that of a lot of SF in general is indeed less dark, but you have to view this shift within the context of what the technology means today versus what it meant in the '60s. Twenty years ago we had to contend with a vast war machine that had transformed the continent in a short time; it had created the very nation of cars, highways, and suburban tracts young people were rebelling against. These things aren't necessarily horrific, but we were beginning to see the downside of the system that produced them. It was also becoming apparent that the war machine was gearing up for Vietnam, and that certainly wasn't a nice side of technology. As for the space effort, it was obviously a public relations gimmick for the military-industrial complex, a payoff for all the earlier SF that lusted for nothing but the space program. Given that all these things fit together, it was hard not to take a pretty dark view of what was happening with our technological and political systems.

LM: Has any of this really changed?

TD: None of it has gone away. But the cyberpunk generation's live-and-let-live view of technology reflects entirely different scientific tendencies and technical possibilities—for instance, genetic engineering in combination with computer technologies—that didn't exist in the '60s. The computer has shown itself to be a person-to-person rather than a system-to-system technology, and so it represents *freedom*—at least potentially—for the people using it. Cyberpunk is fueled partly by the possibilities inherent in these freedoms. True, we haven't seen the downside of computer technologies yet—though undoubtedly it *will come,* because you can't have black without white. For the moment cyberpunks represent for our time what Jack Williamson's generation of writers did back in the naive '30s and early '40s.

LM: I sense that the optimism emerging in your recent work has a personal grounding.

TD: The books I wrote back in the '60s reflect the social circumstances of a young man in his twenties with a lot of ambition, no money, no prospects, no connections, no assurances of any future—and no love for any of his immediate companions. In those circumstances, you're more likely to write about prisons and cages than about the joy of possibilities. My early work probably registered with a lot of readers because a good many, if not most, young people found themselves in similar situations and latched on to a certain set of stories and images. Now, I'm happier than I used to be, and I have equanimity—I wrote a poem recently called "Ode to Equanimity" that appeared in *Salmagundi*. Equanimity is viewed with great suspicion these days, especially by intellectuals; but I've always enjoyed my vices, and my present vice is equanimity. There's more love in my life than there used to be, and I'm more interested in opening myself to what's available. You'll find this playful notion in texts like *Amnesia* and *A Troll in Surewood Forest,* where I've used it to foregound writerly and readerly choices and manipulations. I want to encourage readers *not* to lead the single life but to enjoy the process of being rained on by the abundance of what there is.

LM: Some people thrive on overstimulation, but others find themselves drowning in technologically produced words, images, information.

TD: One hears a great deal about the dangers of information overload, but I thrive on the superflux of all possibilities. I want to experience as many different textures, sources of information, stimuli as I can — we have maybe seventy or eighty years to use our minds, to explore the world around us. Technology has created all sorts of horrors, no question about that, but it also allows us to seek out and access myriad sensory and intellectual experiences unavailable to previous generations — and that's our salvation.

LM: But in "Hard Work" and *Troll,* you're making fun of the way people are manipulated by these images. Their identities are literally created by others.

TD: True, but I don't think it's necessarily bad that people are encouraged to try out different identities, even if those identities are media projections. I used to take a more cynical, pessimistic view, maybe because I was so protective of the fragile identity I was jealously guarding. But in something like "Hard Work," where people physically undergo changes to exteriorize these new identities, I suggest that moving in and out of these roles encourages different perspectives and provides access to views and experiences they wouldn't ordinarily have. It's really not that farfetched. Most people who have any ambition or self-esteem have a favorite actor or actress, someone we consciously think of as a role model (or at least a style model), someone who influences our decisions about how to act, how to display ourselves. The fact that these ideals are superficial or artificial doesn't make them less "ideal."

LM: Gay men and women would seem to be especially tuned to the necessity (and utility) of shifting roles.

TD: Gays are typically more self-conscious about this simply because they've had to adjust their identities in so many different sets of circumstances. The extravagant queen, for example, adapts his behavior only by overdramatizing it. But role playing doesn't have to be confined to sexuality; in fact, it's a great disadvantage these days to associate the two, partly because that kind of role playing is associated in many people's minds with AIDS. I'm constantly devising different social personas by altering the way I dress; then I confront the world at random with that persona and see who salutes. It's no accident that a lot of the words we use about identity — persona, mask, role playing — come from the theater. Americans have really come to understand the notion of the world being a stage (or at least a movie screen), with everybody at some point in their lives projecting a certain ideal so that it becomes an overt social phenomenon.

LM: *On Wings of Song* deals with gay life in more ways, and more openly, than your earlier works do. Are you consciously exploring gay life in your work?

TD: When I cast a novel, I always look for equal opportunity situations. What my characters do and are is governed by forces beyond my control—by what is dictated by my dramatic imagination. I've certainly consciously avoided the temptation to write about the erotic adventures of gay life. In *On Wings of Song* I deliberately chose not to create an erotic gay bildungsroman because these things have been done so many times that by now they seem dull. I'm certain I'll continue to have gay characters in my work, but I don't want to put them into situations for which they are grotesquely unsuited. I've always thought it was ridiculous in the opera world, for example, that because there are so many great black opera singers, you find a black person cast in a role which creates a dramatically jarring note (conceive of a *Romeo and Juliet* where Juliet is black but her parents aren't!). Gays are in a parallel situation—there are many roles you simply can't cast them in.

LM: Being in tune with the ways in which the sexuality of a character prevents equal opportunity casting, and then figuring out alternatives, is one thing Joanna Russ has written about in her nonfiction. As she points out, this is an enormously complex issue.

TD: And it's complicated in ways that might not occur to most people. For one thing, from the standpoint of developing suitable story structures for gays, they are disadvantaged by the fact that if they lead exclusively homosexual lives, they tend to be social islands. Since they don't often generate families, authors are cut off from using all the dramatic, Oedipal conflicts that are essential to so many fictional treatments of straight people. Gays who make a good accommodation to their situation can become very well adjusted, socially productive citizens, but such people are not the stuff of which *drama* is made.

LM: When you were beginning your career, was there external pressure—say, from your publishers—*not* to write about homosexuality directly?

TD: If there was, I wasn't aware of it. For me, the pressure was entirely internal, because I didn't know I was gay—I didn't fully come to grips with my sexuality until after I wrote *Camp Concentration*. I'd had gay experiences, but I was still pursuing a social existence predicated upon the idea of marrying a woman. That was simply one of the goals of life, and I very much intended to have everything.

LM: So in *The Puppies of Terra,* for example, you weren't using a male-female relationship as a Proustian metaphor for a gay love affair?

TD: Not that I was aware of. Of course, in those days it wasn't a matter of being "gay," was it? Rather, there were *queers* or *homosexuals;* it was like having a disease. Dealing with those possibilities, or even hinting at them, was both wicked and exciting—little did I know why!

LM: Critics have tended to focus on the anger and pessimism in your writing, but even in your early work you seem to balance this darkness with an exploration of faith, with the role of art in providing consolation for a godless people, with the search for transcendence in a world in which death remains the central reality.

TD: Those are the most important issues in my life, so they've naturally found their way into my writing. I'm not sure why critics focus on what I'm saying about the prison rather than the means of escape—maybe it's a prejudice against optimism—but I do know that I'm leery about emphasizing escape and transcendence to the exclusion of other themes. It seems somehow irresponsible to deal exclusively with that side of our shared condition, like obsessively describing the contemplative life of a monk, even if the cloister is of his own making. A novel that deals only with transcendence or escape wouldn't seem relevant to me; it wouldn't reflect the life I've lived.

LM: *Camp Concentration* displays a profound, obsessive concern with death which seems unusual in a novel by such a young author.

TD: My obsession was partly due to the fact that, just before I wrote *Camp Concentration,* my mother died. Also, I'd recently had a bad bout of hepatitis which absolutely laid me out. In retrospect, I see that I was so dumbfounded by the disease itself that it didn't register that I was dying. Then the long convalescence, the incapacity of my body to carry on normally, made me intensely aware of my mortality.

LM: For all its darkness, *Camp Concentration* does exhibit the bravura side of your imagination—the confident, almost swaggering displays of intellect and stylistic diversity that suggest a young author suddenly coming into his own.

TD: *Camp Concentration* is such a piece of showing off! I had just arrived in Europe and was very much the scholarship boy who had done every bit of his homework and wanted everyone to know it. I knew French, Spanish, and German; I'd been reading all the highbrow classics of European culture; I went through Spain, England, and Germany in quick succession, and then I got my first glimpse of Paris. In a sense, I was having the intellectual experiences, in the flesh, that I would describe metaphorically in the novel.

LM: You've said that *Camp Concentration* couldn't stand on its own outside the SF genre. What flaw did you have in mind—some defect in plot or character? Too much intellectual showing off?

TD: Simply this: if you compare it to a truly major work dealing with the same issues—say, *The Magic Mountain*—the defects in my book are obvious: it's too flashy, it doesn't develop the ideas, it skates over the surface of issues possessing great depth. There's some flashy skating there, I'm proud to say, but *Camp Concentration* is very much a young man's novel—"Look how fast I can play the bugle! Can't I get into the orchestra?"

LM: Some of that flashy playing is evident in *The Puppies of Terra*. It can't be compared with any other SF book, but its blend of playfulness, literary allusion, and self-consciousness reminds me of Nabokov's work.

TD: That was my first jeu d'esprit—I can be a fine goof-off when I try. As to influences, Nabokov is evident in that book, as is Proust. About that time I was paying attention to all the postmodernist writers who were larking about, opening up new forms—the only SF writer who impressed me back then was Philip K. Dick—and I certainly felt an affinity with many of the absurdist dramatists ascendant in the '60s— Beckett, Genet (I once taught *The Balcony* as an SF work), Ionesco. I was also an early reader of Gaddis's *Recognitions* and of Barth, although *The Sot-Weed Factor* was the first of his books that I read.

LM: Thomas Pynchon is a conspicuous absentee among those writers.

TD: I have never liked Pynchon. I simply can't stand his tone of voice. It's like having a food allergy—I can read a paragraph of Pynchon and break out in a rash.

LM: In responding to a reviewer who said your work reminded him of Bertolt Brecht and Eugene O'Neill, you once said that SF could learn a lot from both of these authors. Were you suggesting that SF needs to find a way to present ideas more dramatically, less didactically?

TD: SF writers could certainly profit by examining the way Brecht used plot to lift the subtext into the light of day—and with utter lucidity. He had a particular genius for fully stating the obvious without over- stating it, the way SF often does, a wonderful sense of how to use a central distancing metaphor for poetic, dramatic effect. This is some- thing SF writers must learn. The way SF writers are always trying to wrap things up is like a shopping bag lady's encumbering layers of clothes. Brecht uses body stockings.

LM: You've referred to Thomas Mann as the author who most influenced you.

TD: I haven't read Mann in years, but he was my model when I was starting out. I read all his major works once or twice and was enormously impressed with the way he used fiction to explore the major intellectual issues of his day. His work was a major attempt to push prose fiction until it rivaled serious thought.

LM: If you were beginning as an SF writer today, do you think you would—

TD: —I don't think I would write SF if I were starting out today.

LM: Really? Why not?

TD: It's not nearly as appealing as it used to be. In the 1960s, I absolutely *gloried* in what I was doing, in the sense that I was breaking new ground in an art form with riches yet to be mined. And, even better, all the old fuddy-duddies *hated* it! I had an advantage neophytes enjoy: the censure of all the bad parents in the world. So I felt heroic, like Jack the Giant Killer. All these people I completely *loathed* were writing intemperate, pejorative things about me and my work. I was in heaven! Of course, there were a *few* people who recognized that I was doing something nobody else had thought of doing with SF. It's a pity no one else can ever have that feeling again because no one can ever have the same pioneering delight we did. At any rate, SF today is so retrograde that the same ice needs to be broken again, because the pond is frozen solid. But I don't see any bright young writers coming into SF right now. If I were starting out today, I imagine I'd head straight for the media—the movies or TV.

LM: I've been impressed by a number of uncategorizable works that blend SF with other forms—the kind of quasi-SF you find in Denis Johnson's *Fiskadoro,* John Calvin Batchelor's *Birth of the People's Republic of Antarctica,* Carol Hill's *Eleven Million Mile High Dancer,* and my personal favorite, Ted Mooney's *Easy Travel to Other Planets.* They seem to represent what the critic Brian McHale has termed the "science fictionalization of postmodernism," which is also evident in the work of established writers like Margaret Atwood and Doris Lessing.

TD: I usually don't find these mainstream treatments exciting for my own reading purposes. I haven't read Atwood's *Handmaid's Tale,* but I doubt I'd like it. I don't think I'd enjoy Lessing—in fact, on the basis of everything I've heard about her work, I think I'd absolutely loathe it. I've read a little bit of her writing, and I don't see much difference, asthetically or intellectually, between her and Marion Zimmer Bradley—and I don't suppose I could say much worse about any writer than that! One SF work I greatly admire that was written by someone outside the usual circles is Fred Pfeil's *Goodman 2020.* It didn't come out as SF—it was published by a university press—but it's exactly the sort of imaginative, intelligent SF I like.

LM: Don DeLillo's *White Noise* employs some SF features that I enjoyed a lot.

TD: I liked the comedy of *White Noise* but I took exception to the haphazardness of its conceptualizations. I didn't think it was a coherent piece of satire because it seemed to be coming from four different

directions and going off into as many. And all that stuff at the end—
the business about the pills she was taking and illuminating the fear of
death—seemed dumb, not vividly drawn. The crisis that develops and
the driving around in the midst of mayhem was the best and the most
humorous part of the book—that's DeLillo's forte, but it's the sort of
thing any contemporary satirist could be doing. The specifically SF parts
of DeLillo's writing don't work well for me; they don't show much
imagination or lead anywhere. I don't think he plots stories well—he
creates droll situations, but he doesn't know how to create characters
who have enough guts to get a human drama going. He ran into the
same problem with *The Names*. I respect DeLillo's intelligence, but I
don't like his fiction.

LM: Who are some of the contemporary writers, SF or otherwise,
whom you feel are doing significant work?

TD: I've already mentioned Fred Pfeil. I like Lucius Shepard's *Life
during Wartime*—now there's somebody who can incorporate high,
serious drama with a sustained effort to imagine a transformed future.
I like Kurt Vonnegut, though sometimes he can be . . . *diffident,* or else
he's so casual that you become a little bit embarrassed about the safety
pin that's holding up his trousers. But when Vonnegut is good, he's
absolutely marvelous. He was at the top of his form in *Galapagos.*
That's terrific SF even without a lot of technological marvels—a parable
in the grand manner of Anatole France or Aldous Huxley, and funny
as hell. I also admire Elizabeth Jolley, the Australian writer. I reviewed
two of her books for the *New York Times* and then started a correspondence with her. She's written some remarkable books that are as
postmodern as anything you can find—*Miss Peabody's Inheritance,* for
instance.

LM: What about Stanislaw Lem?

TD: I don't like him, partly due to his smugness. He has an absolutely
unwarranted high regard for his own genius, and it shines through every
sentence.

LM: Italo Calvino?

TD: He's terrific, a lovely writer. I've never read a word of his that
wasn't human and witty.

LM: John Crowley and Steve Erickson appear to be developing an
interesting blend of Márquezian magic realism, SF, and fantasy. Crowley's *Little Big* and *Aegypt* are truly major works.

TD: Crowley is quite remarkable. The *TLS* review of *Aegypt* pointed
out that his works have gotten successively larger and correspondingly
greater. I don't think you can possibly become more ambitious as a
novelist than Crowley.

LM: Not even Gene Wolfe? He seems to be aiming at the *really big* issues—the justification of the ways of God to Man in the Miltonian sense.

TD: I've praised Wolfe again and again. He is grandly ambitious in the manner of C. S. Lewis. Wolfe's work lies outside any of the familiar categories, which is probably why it hasn't received more attention. He's not really dealing with modern science or technology or any of those considerations; rather, he's propelled by his own vision, so it doesn't reflect this week's headlines, at least not in any direct way. Wolfe is like John Cowper Powys or Charles Williams, those monsters of high-mindedness of the '20s and '30s—but he's better. His work and Crowley's point to the fact that the world is not lacking in good writers with large imaginations or in good writers with small imaginations who have terrific dramatic capabilities—take Toni Morrison's *Beloved,* a magnificent ghost story, wonderful not for its imaginative pizzazz but for its deeply felt, large emotions that are well translated into visionary prose.

LM: Brian McHale argues in *Postmodernist Fiction* that SF and postmodernism have been heading down parallel streets. Part of this, he says, has to do with their dual focus on "ontological issues"; and, of course, one of the things associated with postmodernism is the breakdown of genre distinctions and the interaction of pop and "serious" art forms. Does the term "postmodernism" mean anything to you, or is it mainly an invention of critics?

TD: More of the latter, certainly. There are too many different items being lumped together to make the phrase serve any useful purpose. How could there *be* such a thing as postmodernism when all of the things that come under the heading are so unlike? The term is useful only when it's simply pointing to *those things that are happening now that aren't absolutely ordinary.* And that, in itself, isn't really very useful.

LM: Still, don't you feel that periods of massive change—the kind of thing we saw after World War I or what's occurring today—must surely produce some kind of shared artistic response? My sense of postmodernism, for example, has to do with expressing the increasingly mediated nature of our existence, the intervention of all the mass-produced media images we were talking about earlier, the things that seem tied to our age very specifically.

TD: I've heard that argument, but I wonder how unified this artistic response really is? I suppose I resist the whole critical tendency to lump things together, to identify common trends and play morphological games. I've never even believed there was such a thing as modernism—the variety of impulses that are assembled under that umbrella have always struck me as utterly irreconcilable. If Hemingway is a modernist, what does that have to do with *Finnegans Wake* or with *The Sound* *and the Fury* or with T. S. Eliot or Pound? And what does their work have to do with Camus? The fact that they all lived under the distressing circumstances of the twentieth century and wrote about them is an unavoidable accident of history. But it seems to me that each one of them is striving for uniqueness—always the main ambition of any serious artist in any era, and always the most distressing casualty of critical terminology. This is just as evident in the visual arts as with literature. The things called "modernist" that came under the heading of visual arts were virtually everything a painter could be inspired to do. When those possibilities were finally laid out in more or less their entirety, modernism was over. Then came postmodernism—which meant that people didn't know any new tricks and simply had to shuffle the old ones around.

LM: But isn't this change in the fundamental categories we use to relate to the world around us—everything from computers, to the impact of the media industry and the shift away from the industrial age to the information age, to the implications of quantum mechanics or relativity or what the semioticians are pointing to—bound to significantly alter artists' views about their craft, especially the formal means at their disposal to render this new sense of what reality "is"?

TD: If even a single writer who appears on the usual list of post-modernists has a greater understanding of those things than most chimpanzees, I'd be astonished—at least with regard to those abstract concepts you mentioned—relativity, linguistics, and so on. Those things simply don't impinge upon the creative faculties of artists. If writers had the intellectual wherewithal to handle quantum mechanics, they'd be physicists, not fiction writers. Since Whistler and down through Warhol, in the visual arts and outside, the basic way to operate is to be a bullshit artist and hype yourself. That's how we get Lawrence Durrell writing all that nonsense about how his stuff connects to Einstein's theory of relativity. And anybody who pretends to take such posturing seriously is naked in the retinue of a naked emperor.

LM: SF writers are the one group who are, by definition, supposed to be dealing seriously with the implications of modern science. Have they at least been seeking a suitable formal means to express this very strange view of the universe and our role within it?

TD: In a word, No! SF writers as a whole are surprisingly old-fashioned, stuck in the mud of their genre. I don't see much actual intelligence in the IQ sense being deployed by my SF peers in working through the aesthetic implications of what they are allegedly talking about. Greg Bear's *Blood Music* is a significant exception in this regard—it's the kind of SF that ought to result from what you were talking about. But I don't see other SF writers following up on the leads of modern science with anything like Bear's élan.

LM: When I brought up this issue with Gregory Benford, he made much the same argument, pointing to cyberpunk's tendency to recycle the familiar hard-boiled plots and motifs.

TD: If the story being told is actually plainer and stupider than the original, which is the case with most cyberpunk novels, then what sort of revolution do we have? Part of the reason for this massive collective failure of will and imagination is that nearly all SF authors are writing for the bulk intelligence of the newest generation of students, who know less than they used to, whose imaginations are impoverished, and who are less sophisticated in terms of social intelligence. Genre writing is dictated by distribution considerations: if the audience wants Conan adventures in outer space, then SF editors are going to provide that sort of thing. The few writers who buck that trend—Le Guin, Russ, Wolfe—are often enough riding hobbyhorses that likewise don't necessarily reflect the most interesting, far-reaching developments of science. Very little of my own SF, for example, has ever reflected state-of-the-art scientific imaginings. I'm much more of a political satirist, I suppose.

LM: When you sent me the manuscript copy of *A Troll in Surewood Forest,* you mentioned that writing this book was easier for you than any other. Why was that?

TD: Believe me, if I could provide a satisfactory answer to that question I would set to work on a similar book! Writing that offers as much fun as I had with *A Troll in Surewood Forest* creates its own reward, and it would be wonderful to reap that reward every time I work on a project—though I don't mean that I'd want to repeat the same sort of book. Right now I hope to find my voice as a playwright, which could mean a long run of writing pleasure.

LM: Your willingness to explore new territory—to work within different forms and develop distinctly different voices, styles, and personas in your writing—is one of the most striking features of your work.

TD: The ideal for me is to produce an absolutely autonomous object of art every time I create something. This goes against what a lot of critics and readers feel a writer should be doing—they want you to keep writing the same kind of novel or story, to develop a style and voice and to stick with it. Poetry, in particular, is celebrated conventionally by declaring that the artist has found his or her "own voice." A review of one of my books of poetry, written by a fairly respectable critic, said that while I wrote poems, I did not write poetry—the implication being that there should be a certain poetic voice a writer carries from poem to poem. I took that as a wonderful compliment. I want

each of my poems to read as though they were written by a different
poet.

———————

LM: The last time we met, in the summer of 1986, you were just
finishing work on your computer-interactive text, *Amnesia,* and you
were obviously exhilarated by the experience of working in one of the
new forms. What has happened with *Amnesia* to this point? Have you
created a novel in computer's clothing?

TD: I'm still not certain what *Amnesia* is, but it's certainly *not* a
novel. By way of trying to peddle my wares, about a year ago I wrote
a piece that was taken by the *New York Times Book Review* but hasn't
appeared yet. In it I invented a name for books like *Amnesia:* "Youdunits"—there hasn't been a name for something like this except "Computer Interactive Fiction," and that's a mouthful. But the problem
extends beyond what it is to what you *do* with it. Do you read it or
do you play it? While I was working on *Amnesia,* I realized it was an
art form unto itself; I saw visions of sugarplums dancing in my head.
Now, all that is but a handful of ashes (along with some other handfuls),
and I'm no longer hyping Youdunits. Quite simply, *Amnesia* has been
one of the quickest disillusionments of my life.

LM: Why?

TD: *Amnesia* died even as it was appearing. It died for wont of
advertising, though it probably received as much attention as something
like that can get—there was something about it in *Newsweek,* for God's
sake—and the reviews in the computer magazines were what amounted
to four-star raves. The real problem is that there's simply no audience
for this material, no one who would respond enthusiastically to what
I do well. Those who buy it, who are aficionados of the form, are
basically those who want trivial pursuits; and to offer them something,
however entertaining, that involved reading and imaginative skills they
did not care to exercise while playing with their computers was foolish.
I feel like de Soto, who journeyed to Tennessee looking for the Fountain
of Youth—an interesting enough trip, but neither of us found what we
were looking for.

LM: When you say that no audience is specifically interested in what
you do well, are you referring to the subtleties (and complexities) of
your overall conception of the work—which are pretty daunting, as I
recall?

TD: Basically, although I don't feel *Amnesia* is *too* complex or ultra-
sophisticated. I've had no negative feedback from anyone who's been
enticed to enter into the game of tennis that's involved—it's just that
the people who want to play this sort of game are looking, I suppose,
for something like Douglas Adams's *Hitchhiker,* where they can have

their familiar experiences replayed. The computer-interactive games that have done well—like the Hitchhiker or Star Trek series—have been tied in with copyrighted materials that have already had success with the target audience in prior literary forms. I don't think the quality of those scripts compares to what I did in *Amnesia*—Adams's scripts, for example, are actually very good *of a kind,* but it's a matter of one little joke after another. The notion of trying to superimpose over this structure a *dramatic conception* other than a puzzle was apparently too much for the audience. In the end, I just produced another literary curiosity.

LM: What did you find to be the most intriguing aspect of working with this new form?

TD: One of the most fascinating things was recognizing that I was in a sense "mathematizing" literature. Every intellectual probably has a respect in which he enjoys being able to analyze what he's doing and to let that analysis somehow be reflected in the work. Chip Delany's vein in this regard is all the semiology you find in his work. I don't have much truck with that, but I do have a predilection toward being self-reflective, not of myself but of the work at hand—that is, I like my work to have its own story and yet to have its own commentary built in. The postmodern bias. Working with *Amnesia* was an opportunity to explore this brand of self-reflection in spades, and to do it with an entirely new aesthetic apparatus. This is not to say that *Amnesia* has to be read like some Borgesian text but to point out that when you're working on this kind of text, you're operating in an entirely different mode from when you're writing other forms of literature. You're not writing in that trance state of entering a daydream and describing what's to the left or right, marching forward, which is how most novels get written. Rather, you have to be always conscious of the ways the text can be deconstructed. In a very literal sense, any computer-interactive text deconstructs itself as you write because it's always stopping and starting and branching off this way and that. You are constantly and overtly manifesting those decisions usually hidden in fiction because, of course, you don't normally show the choices that were ruled out—though in every novel the choices that are *not made* are really half of the work, an invisible presence. With *Amnesia,* I found myself working with a form that allowed me to display these erasures, these unfollowed paths. It's like a Diebenkorn painting, where you can see the lines that haven't quite been covered over by a new layer of paint. There are elements of this same kind of structural candor in a good Youdunit.

LM: One way *Amnesia* differs from earlier computer-interactive texts is not only in its greater formal complexity but in terms of the elegance, self-referentiality, and sophistication of the language, of the text itself.

TD: I had hoped that readers who ordinarily skim past such graces wouldn't be allowed to do that because they'd have to examine the text for clues as to how to respond; they'd have to read slowly and carefully. I thought that was theoretically appealing: a text whose form allowed me a measure of control over the readerly response in ways unavailable to a novelist or short story writer. I've always been frustrated that genre readers are very often addictive readers who will go through a novel in one night. I can't read at that speed—and I don't like to be read at that speed, either.

LM: Were you aware from the outset that *Amnesia* links up with your work in various ways—your focus on memory, for example, or on the fragile nature of identity?

TD: Some of these things I was aware of, but not everything. For example, I have to give Chip Delany the credit for pointing out how often a person's name figures very significantly in my work. People are always complaining that critical insights rarely help you in your work, but since Chip made that comment I've paid close and conscious attention to this issue of names and naming—for instance, in *A Troll in Surewood Forest,* naming is virtually the focus of the book. The names of the people are arbiters of their destiny; they're the carburetors of the plot.

LM: While you were working on *Amnesia,* you must have had an exhilarating sense that you were solving formal problems in this new genre that were intriguingly different from formal problems in literature.

TD: Absolutely. The nature of the inner activity involved generates *fascinating* formal problems, analogous in some ways to what D. W. Griffith or Sergei Eisenstein were grappling with when the cinema was in its infancy. You have to keep the hypothetical reader in mind to an unusual degree, which makes the inventive process more difficult in many ways. Most writers have the same deluded relationship to their stories that they believe their ideal reader will have. I'm sure Flaubert wept tears for Madame Bovary, reviled her for her follies and failures, and dealt with her *in his mind* as though she were quite real. The glory of fiction is that we have this capacity to create affectively real phantasms. But in writing interactive fiction, you're aware of the fictional and mechanical nature of what you're manipulating into the illusion of life. It's the difference between being an actor and being a puppeteer.

LM: But that difference is only a matter of degree, as authors like Thackeray and Nabokov take pains to remind us.

TD: All these things do indeed exist in fiction. However, good writers have an unconscious understanding of how to pedal the bicycle to keep it upright through the whole maze of expectations they are creating in the hypothetical reader—and that's a side of writing that is rarely dealt with, even in writing workshops. In the case of *Amnesia,* where I had to be so thoroughly self-conscious about most of what I was doing, I was still mainly using an unconscious equilibrium system in the creation process.

LM: Timothy Leary, who recently designed some computer software for Electronic Arts, which produced *Amnesia,* has suggested in a number of different contexts that computers have the potential to expand people's minds much the same as LSD—but only if we can convince artists to move into computer software and develop programs with genuinely creative potential. Do you share his optimism?

TD: Sure. For all my grousing, I can see that there's a generation of new writers who are spending a large part of their most energetic intellectual life playing with computers instead of sitting passively in front of TVs, and the brightest of them are probably creating their own programs. However, the generation that can have deep intellectual involvement with computers without becoming hackers doesn't exist yet because, as Leary suggests, not enough software has been developed for that possibility except in the visual arts. For visual artists who have the equipment and the software, the computer has probably already made a significant difference in the character of their work. And for the next generation of visual artists, there's no question that computers will profoundly alter their thinking about what they do, how they work, what their ambitions will be.

LM: William Gibson and the cyberpunk authors have been influenced by computers (and video games!), not just in terms of their themes, but in trying to find verbal equivalents for that new kind of "space" that is basic to computers or video games.

TD: Cyberpunk differs from other SF, not in the human equations you find there or in the way these equations are grounded, but in its development of the notion of an entirely malleable visual reality that is both representative and abstract. What has usually been ignored in the discussions about cyberpunk is what is most interesting and distinctive about it: its ability to create fantastic landscapes out of words that mirror the visual universe lying within the screen of the computer.

LM: It must be significant that Gibson's generation of SF authors is the first for whom the experience of playing video games or working with computers is as natural as watching television or reading a book.

TD: This is the first generation of people who can believe in cartoons with exactly the same faith that they might believe in a movie.

LM: You wrote once, "Consider how often art thrives by the limitations an artist may impose on his task." That points to an interesting tension I sense in your work—between your respect for the conventions implicit within the SF form itself and your desire to disrupt these structures, to resist their limitations, to play with them, even mock them.

TD: It all goes back to what we were discussing earlier with regard to *Amnesia* and the relationship between the writerly manipulation and the readerly expectation. One of the purposes of literary conventions, which are very important from the artist's point of view (and of lesser significance to the audience), is to provide comfort, safety, security, the certainty that whatever happens in the story will eventually be what the reader *wants to happen*. The writer is essentially in conflict with the reader because the writer wants to do something surprising while the reader wants something familiar, and each must necessarily accommodate the other. Even the most solipsistic modernists—Beckett, for instance—are nevertheless writing in a language they share with the reader; writers rarely have the solipsist moxie to invent their own language, their own alphabet. Accommodations must always be made. Of course, the best writers and artists violate *some* conventions, though not all of them, and certainly not all at once; they shift ground, moving the area of surprise away from where it last appeared.

LM: Edmund White has said that in each of his works his aim is to lose the audience he gained in the previous work. You can see this approach in some of our greatest artists—Picasso or Joyce—but there's a tremendous temptation to keep working within familiar forms and voices.

TD: I respect artists in strict proportion to the extent that each of their works is unlike the other works I know. That's certainly my goal in my own work. I'm interested in writing every kind of novel and story and poetry and opera libretto. When I'm finished with, say, a novel, I don't feel like beginning another; I want to try something different.

LM: In one of your autobiographical sketches, you talk about learning to recognize "the occasion of poetry: the phrase of formulation that grows into poems." How does this occasion differ from one that produces a piece of fiction?

TD: With a poem, you're not looking for a dramatic situation but for a *mode of apprehension*. Recently, I read a friend's poem about a railroad trip from New York City to the suburbs. It's a meditative poem, more or less keyed to the hypothetical advance of the train into suburbia, told from the viewpoint of someone living in suburbia. I was transfixed by all the ways *my* imaginary trip out of New York on *my* railroad would be so utterly different. For instance, my friend didn't notice some of the most salient features about leaving New York: going through Harlem, the cemeteries, the station itself, with its dismal, decaying grandeur and all the derelicts. I decided to start my own poem, but the first several stanzas were worthless, probably because I was picking up too much from my friend's poem, trying to apply my own ideas to it. Eventually, though, I found an approach that seemed to work: I placed the poem in the context of a derelict who murders a businessman in the toilets of the terminal, then takes his clothing and his train trip. This established the alien point of view that I kept wanting to find in my friend's poem.

LM: But isn't that the same as creating a dramatic situation in a piece of fiction? How are these "occasions" different?

TD: With this poem, I'm not dealing with these elements to create a story. A lot of poetry is simply making the commonplace be seen through Martian eyes. But with fiction, you focus on the story line, not the surrounding mode of apprehension. Nearly always, there's a deep creative dislocation within a poem that can only rarely be sustained for long, and at such a high pitch, by writer or reader.

LM: You mention in your preface to "How to Fly" that after reading an Apollinaire quote about cubism in a John Berger book—"Already I hear the shrill sound of the friend's voice to me, who walks with you in Europe while never leaving America"—you knew how you would develop the central metaphor of flying in *On Wings of Song*. What was it that was so resonant about that passage?

TD: My reaction has to be put into the context of Berger's essay, in which he's celebrating the way cubism had been such a liberating influence. It's a joyful celebration of certain specific modern experiences and potentials—all those things we take for granted today, like the airplane, electricity, the radio, that seemed at that early moment to be utterly vibrant, new, wonderful, bright. Apollinaire's line has to be seen in that context. It's not a fancy metaphor but an attempt to state an actual, but mind-boggling, possibility: If all these things are possible, what is the furthest limit of such power? The passage also implies the antithesis of the two realms of European and American social and cultural experiences that Berger deals with in his essay. The "shrill sound" has to do with the tinny sound of the telephone, but because of the timbre it also suggests the idea of sexual doubleness. And because a lot of the essay is about celebrating flight, the story that immediately came to me is implicit in that image as well. The gestalt that came together from all these things involved the possibility of flying and not being "here" when you are "here." In the most basic sense this is a common daydream—out-of-body flight; but what I began to think of was a way of giving this daydream a scientific rationale. Once that was provided, the questions that immediately came to mind are: What condition is your body in when you're not in it? Would it be something like the cinema? What if you did not come back? Your body would still physically be there, but who would take care of it? I realized my story had to be that of someone looking after this physical residue. So within five minutes of reading that passage, I had conceived of the basic plot of the book, from beginning to end, and of the relationship of the hero and heroine.

LM: One of the most striking aspects of your treatment of the flying metaphor in *On Wings of Song* is the way you unravel so many different aspects from this central kernel: flying as a metaphor for sex, for transcendence, for death, for music.

TD: How much can the artist bring to bear on a metaphor? *That's* the art of writing. To use a metaphor successfully in a novel, you must first recognize that your central metaphor is capable of supporting an enormous amount of weight. In this case, I knew immediately that I could pile a lot onto the metaphorical scaffolding. The body/soul dichotomy has always been a powerful one for me, something that seems to trigger my deepest hopes, fears, and creative impulses. I was also instantly delighted with the prospect of extensively developing the flying metaphor because it would allow me to use my own flying dreams, which are quite sensational. And it was a subject that had never been dealt with except trivially—the sort of pedestrian thing you see in something like William Wharton's *Birdy*, which was terrible, or *Superman*.

LM: Were you consciously using *On Wings of Song* to explore your past?

TD: Very much so. I saw that I could use the flying metaphor to present the story of my life, insofar as I could make this presentation congruent with the more abstract issues I wanted to deal with. It turned out that I could make things overlap to a great extent because even when those specific events in the novel didn't literally happen to me, the correlative events had occurred, metaphorically. Such autobiographies—the kind of thing you find in Goethe's *Wilhelm Meister*—are often much more revealing than literal treatments.

LM: After you've received the initial inspiration for a work, is there a consistency to the way you proceed in developing the work?

TD: The only two cases where I actually started writing from the moment I got the idea were *On Wings of Song* and *A Troll in Surewood Forest*. Usually, there's some period of incubation while I mentally work out where I want to go with something. Thank God I rarely have to do much rewriting. I would hate to be the kind of writer who has to do seven drafts of a book, all the while sweating and foaming and worrying. In that respect I guess I'm a natural writer.

LM: Would you say that music or any of the other arts has had a direct impact on your literary imagination?

TD: The storytelling we have all absorbed from the cinema and television necessarily affects all writers today. For example, media techniques influence the way we pace the narrative in a novel or a story, the way we choose to present scenes. In my case, this common fund of techniques includes opera, which is my optimal mode of drama or storytelling. I tune in emotionally and imaginatively to a well-produced opera, more than to any other art form, whether on a record or on the stage (and in a sense, it's easier with a record). The payoff from opera is greatest because my engagement in the experience is the deepest.

LM: What is there about opera that produces this profound engagement?

TD: It's Wagner's *Gesamtkunst*—total art. With opera, the libretto should be good poetry in itself, while the music heightens the poetry exponentially, simultaneously underlining and explicating it—and this doesn't even take into account the narrative aspects. Those who can adapt to the total artifice of the opera form open themselves to the largest aesthetic experience available. In opera we find the most considered and deepest statements about mythic materials and about our relationship to the cosmos, to the larger political institutions, to the structure of the family, and to hope, love, and hatred.

LM: Would you say that SF and opera share a basic affinity for relying on a heightened sense of artifice?

TD: SF is certainly equivalent to opera in that, compared to other fictional forms, it too calls for the maximum suspension of disbelief, the maximum amount of stylization. I would argue as well that SF, like opera, provides the maximum impact when all those things are working right. I'm attracted to forms that strive to achieve a certain kind of intensity, that produce the maximum effects, emotionally and intellectually. If you want to achieve this, you must be willing to accept, within the naturalistic context authors always use, the maximum degree of artifice and exaggeration.

LM: Many novice SF readers and first-time opera-goers share the same problem: they literally don't know how to interpret the codes and forms they encounter. Do you agree with Chip Delany's argument that there is a fundamental difference between SF and "mundane fiction"— that SF conventions have the effect of changing the meaning of all the codes, right down to the level of individual words?

TD: Chip focuses on the different ways language functions in different literary texts. But for me, the most fundamental thing happening to a reader in the case of fiction involves *visualizing,* imaginatively, what the author has created. Stories are like dreams, and since the capacity for experiencing vividness in dreams varies, readers' responses to stories are going to vary in terms of imaginative detail or intensity—depending on how well the writer conjurs up the story. The faculty to produce this vivid dream experience for the reader—the specific demands of the internal movie the writer is creating, frame by frame, in a text—is probably what varies most from writer to writer. The best writers are undoubtedly the ones whose visual canvases are the most extensive and the best edited—and it strikes me as strange that this feature of writing has, so far as I know, never been examined by literary critics. J. G. Ballard, for example, has a great painterly imagination and a remarkable ability to evoke images from his primordial landscapes that seem to emerge from our shared unconscious. Yet the critics tend to reduce his work to a set of themes that in themselves are not especially original. In my own work, I include many references to other artworks as a way of suggesting the tone of the visual image I want to elicit from the reader. I'm sure most of my SF audience misses the point—they see it not as one of the few ways available to me to precisely and economically present a context of meaning but as a way to impress them with my knowledge. The reason for alluding to great art is not because you assume other people will know the meaning you're alluding to. Great art is often elusive and enigmatic, but it's incontrovertible exactly in proportion to the extent that it's great. What better form of common reference is available to the writer?

LM: In some of your recent work, you rely as much on pop cultural references as on other artistic references. Was this a conscious shift, maybe an acknowledgment of the blurring between pop and serious art?

TD: It was conscious in the sense that in both "Hard Work" and *A Troll in Surewood Forest* I was writing about the way popular culture can affect our sense of self and the world around us, so placing the emphasis on pop culture when I created allusions seemed only appropriate. The "instant access" provided by technology has certainly changed our relationship to all the arts, maybe for the better. For example, opera is now on television, with subtitles! People can now derive the dramatic meaning of opera without having to learn a foreign language.

LM: Since *Camp Concentration,* you've repeatedly examined the difference between an imaginative system that has a moral vision as part of its structure and a system that has no moral structure, is actively destructive. I gather that part of your attraction to the Faust legend, especially Goethe's version, is the way it deals with this issue.

TD: Goethe centrally formulated the question of the two forms of the imagination. His Faust is constantly tempted by Mephistopheles to accept the use of the imagination that not only excludes morality but is willing to accept others' pain as the price of his own pleasure, and others' diminishment as the price of his own bounty. This is the central dilemma in all issues of political and economic justice: to what extent we can accept the idea that the cost of our advantages should be the impoverishment of others, or the impoverishment of the future, because we are using up our resources with insane prodigality. The Faustian question is the use to which we apply the enormous advantage that modern science gives us as a culture. It's an ethical question of such huge dimension that most of us can never articulate it in a way that makes it relevant to our individual lives, even while we confront a world that is in its very existence threatened by the technology we possess and which we continue to augment.

LM: By its very nature SF writers would seem to be the group best equipped to address these issues imaginatively.

TD: Yes, but ironically SF's influence so far has been largely disastrous. What's happened with SDI is a very telling case in point. A number of SF writers, notably Jerry Pournelle, have become spokesmen for SDI, and more generally salesmen for a high-tech future. I recently wrote an article for *The Nation* about Pournelle and the rocket-boosters because I strongly believe that the particular high-tech future they promote is a disastrous misdirection of the resources of our national economy, and it seemed important to point out the ways in which SF has lent this very inauthentic voice to the promotion of SDI. I would just as soon try to build a paved highway to the moon as develop the system that's being envisioned for SDI—and a consensus of informed scientific opinion agrees. But the difficulty is that Reagan listens to men whose imaginations have developed in the playrooms of SF (and not especially sophisticated playrooms at that). In the article I point out the politics that went along with the high-tech imaginations of these SF authors, and how intimately related these imaginations are to adolescent power fantasies. SDI is simply the latest, most egregious, and most dangerous triumph of the will of a thirteen-year-old nerd—and therefore perfectly suited for the president. We simply have to hope that the next president won't be such a dope.

LM: You've mentioned, in reference to your original intentions in creating *334,* that you conceived of what you were doing as a "scientific experiment" in the manner of Zola. In what sense was that novel a scientific experiment?

TD: I was thinking in terms of a laboratory experiment in which the author would meticulously create an environment (the invariable element) and then place within it the variable elements, the different characters who become the rats moving around in the maze you've built for them. This was actually beyond Zola—he was usually too much the melodramatist to create any sort of truly controlled environment. But I've always believed that it's possible, and *334* is the nearest

I've come to realizing that: to build a scale model, populate it with the likeliest of denizens, and then record the results as neutrally as I could.

LM: I take it, then, that you feel SF can express genuinely prophetic visions of possible futures.

TD: I wouldn't say that *334* is prophetic in the sense that what I described will literally happen—it was more of a thought experiment, a simulated environment that I hoped would be so scrupulously imagined that it would be as believable as a meticulously realistic view of the present. I'm being proven right about one thing, though: the illusion of progress so common a few years ago—those visions of future cities in which helicopters sweep you from one cloud-piercing tower to the next—was never really in the cards. The drollest irony about the future is that, for all the changes time can bring about, things don't change much in the end. The cities of the world are huge systems of inertia, and the conservatives are correct when they argue that inertia is what we must prize most in the world we live in. Inertia keeps the world recognizable, habitable, comfortable, lovely. At any rate, in *334* I was trying to defy the "Gee whiz!" syndrome of making a futuristic invention attractive—fortunately, I waited until I had the skills and maturity I needed to write it. It's my first mature work, maybe my only one.

LM: Pardon my terminology, but *334* struck me as being very postmodernist in its refusal to tie things up neatly and in its encouragement of the reader to become a collaborator by making associations and connections. In other words, your form reinforces a nonreductive view about our problems.

TD: There are usually such formal concerns in any novel, insofar as you can think of the structuring of a drama as being a formal concern. But a novel isn't concerned with form in the way a painting is, where this mass must balance that mass, and so on. In *334* I was certainly aware of trying to devise a form appropriate to my thematic concerns— I was quite conscious, for example, of refusing to supply the usual escapist ending for readers, many of whom must have found this distressing. Unfortunately, the macroscopic problems of life—the depletion of our environment's resources, the inevitability of death and decay, the inertia preventing genuine progress—simply aren't going to be "solved" by government or religion or politics.

LM: One other genuinely prophetic implication of *334* is its insistence that single enemies no longer oppress people and destroy their lives. That is, you don't present us with Big Brother or a single evil nation to be conveniently blamed for everything that's gone wrong.

TD: There isn't a simple evil in my novel because it doesn't exist. Who can point the finger? And at what? Everyone has a favorite fool or criminal, but there's really nobody around whom we can blame for everything. Not even Reagan. People will continue to need that fictional convenience of Big Brother, of a central wrongdoer—like the welfare system—that is the cause of all the problems. But the sources of our oppression aren't so eloquently simplistic. And things are only going to get more complicated.

LM: In *Camp Concentration,* you bring up the association of madness and genius, suggesting that when we adjust to societal norms we surrender something of our potential.

TD: Earlier, we were talking about the notion of identity being discretionary, something individuals can redefine. That doesn't accord with the common wisdom of an analyst or therapist who, by definition, tries to help people build a strong, unified sense of identity. We have all these public institutions, including legions of psychotherapists and psychologists, whose real job is to find methods of fine-tuning the hidden components of a bureaucratic structure. People have to be made to function smoothly and equitably and reasonably with other people in these structures; they've got to be trained to work, raise families, and engage in all those other essential social purposes that give rise to internal conflicts. Psychology often keeps these things running smoothly, but it serves a purpose art doesn't share and isn't likely to profit from, except insofar as artists also must survive socially and develop social skills sufficient to this end. Artists are people whose lives are the experiments by which others try to extend the boundaries of their potential. Art is often a deliberate leap into madness.

An Interview with

William Gibson

In 1984 William Gibson's first novel, *Neuromancer,* burst onto the science fiction scene like a supernova. The shock waves from that explosion had an immediate impact on the relatively insular SF field. *Neuromancer* became the first novel to win the triple crown—Hugo, Nebula, and Philip K. Dick awards—and, in the process, virtually single-handedly launched the cyberpunk movement. *Neuromancer,* with its stunning technopoetic prose surface and its superspecific evocation of life in a sleazed-out global village of the near future, has rapidly gained unprecedented critical and popular attention outside SF.

Prior to the publication of *Neuromancer,* Gibson had published only a half-dozen stories (since collected in *Burning Chrome* [1986]). Although several of these display flashes of his abilities—and two of them, "Johnny Mnemonic" and "Burning Chrome," introduce motifs and elements elaborated upon in the later novels—clearly *Neuromancer* was a major imaginative leap forward for someone who had not even attempted to write a novel previously. The source of all the white light and white heat being generated by this new kid on the block are immediately apparent from the opening words of the novel: "The sky above the port was the color of television, tuned to a dead channel." Dense, kaleidoscopic, fast-paced, full of punked-out, high-tech weirdos, *Neuromancer* depicts with hallucinatory vividness the desperate, exhilarating feel of life in our new urban landscapes.

A number of critics have pointed out Gibson's affinities with certain earlier innovative SF authors: comparisons with Alfred Bester's early novels, with Philip K. Dick's midperiod fiction, and with Samuel Delany's *Nova;* Gibson's reliance on the cut-up methods and quickfire stream of dissociated images characteristic of William S. Burroughs and J. G. Ballard are also noted. But equally significant are the influences from sources either wholly outside SF—the hard-boiled writing of Dashiell Hammett, 1940s *film noir,* the novels of Robert Stone—or only nominally connected with the field—the garishly intense, nightmarish urban scenes and pacings in the work of rock musicians like Lou Reed; or the sophisticated blend of science, history, pop culture, hip lingoes, and dark humor in Thomas Pynchon's work.

What made *Neuromancer*'s debut so auspicious, however, was not its debts to earlier authors but its originality of vision, especially the fresh, rush-of-oxygen high of Gibson's prose, with its startling similes and metaphors drawn from computers and other technologies, and its ability to create a powerfully resonant metaphor—the cyberspace of the computer matrix—where data dance with human consciousness, where human memory is literalized and mechanized, where multinational information systems mutate and breed into startling new structures whose beauty and complexity are unimaginable, mystical, and above all *nonhuman.* Probably as much as any first novel since Pynchon's *V.,* *Neuromancer* seemed to create a significant synthesis of poetics, pop culture, and technology.

Although often overlooked by critics and reviewers in this regard, *Neuromancer* is also deeply rooted in human realities. Gibson's presentation of the surface textures of our electronic age re-creates the shock and sensory overload that define our experience of contemporary life, of having grown up with VCRs, CDs, terrorists broadcasting messages on fifty-channel video monitors, designer drugs, David Bowie and the Sex Pistols, video games, computers. Both disturbing and playful, he also explores much deeper questions about the enormous impact of technology on the definition of what it means to be human. After reading *Neuromancer* for the first time, I knew I had seen the future of SF (and maybe of literature in general), and its name was William Gibson.

Gibson's second novel, *Count Zero* (1986), is set seven years in the future of *Neuromancer*'s world, and to some degree it retains the earlier novel's focus on the underbelly world of computer cowboys, black market drugs, and software. But the pace is somewhat slower, allowing Gibson more time to develop his characters—a mixture of eccentric lowlifes and nonconformists who find themselves confronting representatives of vast egomaniacal individuals whose wealth and power result directly from their ability to control information. More tightly controlled and easier to follow than *Neuromancer, Count Zero* is nevertheless as extraordinarily rich in suggestive neologisms and other verbal pyrotechnics; it's also a fascinating evocation of a world in which humanity seems to be constantly outshone by the flash and appeal of the images and machines that increasingly seem to push people aside in their abstract dance toward progress and efficiency.

When we spoke in August 1986 at his home in Vancouver, British Columbia, William Gibson was working on the screenplay for *Aliens III* and on his third novel, *Mona Lisa Overdrive* (1988), which completes his cyberspace trilogy. *Mona Lisa Overdrive* expands some of the implications of the two earlier novels—for instance, the interface between the human social world and cyberspace is now sufficiently permeable that humans can actually die in cyberspace; Angie Mitchell (who appeared in *Count Zero*) is able to tap into the matrix without a computer; and, once again, we witness people (including Molly from *Neuromancer*) struggling against having their bodies and imaginations manipulated by international corporations who control information and images to suit their own purposes. While these overlaps seem to make *Mona Lisa Overdrive* less startlingly original than the earlier works, Gibson's experiments with prismatic storytelling methods, his ongoing stylistic virtuosity, and his presentation of characters possessing deeper emotional resonances all point to a growing maturation and versatility.

Larry McCaffery: There are so many references to rock music and television in your work that it sometimes seems your writing is as much influenced by MTV as by literature. What impact have other media had on your sensibility?

William Gibson: Probably more than fiction. The trouble with "influence" questions is that they're usually framed to encourage you to talk about your writing as if you grew up in a world circumscribed by books. I've been influenced by Lou Reed, for instance, as much as I've been by any "fiction" writer. I was going to use a quote from an old Velvet Underground song—"Watch out for worlds behind you" (from "Sunday Morning")—as an epigraph for *Neuromancer*.

LM: The breakdown of distinctions—between pop culture and "serious" culture, different genres, different art forms—seems to have had a liberating effect on writers of your generation.

WG: The idea that all this stuff is potentially grist for your mill has been very liberating. This process of cultural mongrelization seems to be what postmodernism is all about. The result is a generation of people (some of whom are artists) whose tastes are wildly eclectic—people who are hip to punk music and Mozart, who rent these terrible horror and SF videos from the 7-Eleven one night and then invite you to a mud wrestling match or a poetry reading the next. If you're a writer, the trick is to keep your eyes and ears open well enough to let all this in but also, somehow, to recognize intuitively what you should let emerge in your work, how effective something might be in a specific context. I know I don't have a sense of writing as being divided up into different *compartments,* and I don't separate literature from the other arts. Fiction, television, music, film — all provide material in the form of images and phrases and codes that creep into my writing in ways both deliberate and unconscious.

LM: Our culture is being profoundly transformed by technology in ways most people are only dimly starting to realize. Maybe that's why the American public is so fascinated with SF imagery and vocabulary — even people who don't even know what SF stands for are responding to this stuff subliminally, in ads and so on.

WG: Yeah, like *Escape from New York* never made it big, but it's been redone a billion times as a rock video. I saw that movie, by the way, when I was starting "Burning Chrome" and it had a real influence on *Neuromancer.* I was intrigued by the exchange in one of the opening scenes where the Warden says to Snake: "You flew the wing-five over Leningrad, didn't you?" It turns out to be just a throwaway line, but for a moment it worked like the best SF, where a casual reference can imply a lot.

LM: In theory MTV could be an interesting new art form, a combination of advertising and avant-garde film, though it seems to be getting worse.

WG: We don't get MTV up here, but from what I've seen of it in the States, there was initially a feeling of adventure that you don't find in the established forms. But you're right — it's getting worse. So is most SF.

LM: How consicous are you about systematically developing an image or a metaphor when you're writing? For example, the meat puppet image in *Neuromancer* seems like the perfect metaphor for how the soft machine of our living bodies is manipulated by outside forces. I assume you arrived at that metaphor from listening to the cow-punk band Meat Puppets.

WG: No, I got it from seeing the name in print. I like accidents, when an offhand line breezes by and you think to yourself, Yes, that will do. So you put it in your text and start working with it, seeing how it relates to other things you've got going, and eventually it begins to evolve, to branch off in ways you hadn't anticipated. Part of the process is conscious, in the sense that I'm aware of working this way, but how these things come to be embedded in the text is intuitive. I don't see how writers can do it any other way. I suppose some pick these things up without realizing it, but I'm conscious of waiting for them and seeing where they lead, how they might mutate.

LM: Sounds like a virus.

WG: It is—and only a certain kind of host is going to be able to allow the thing to keep expanding in an optimal way. As you can imagine, the structure of a book like *Neuromancer* becomes very complicated at a certain point. It wasn't complicated in the "admirably complex" way that you find in Pynchon's novels but simply in the sense that all these odds and ends started to affect and infect one another.

LM: Does knowing that most readers won't recognize many of these references bother you? Obviously, they don't have to know that "Big Science" is a song by Laurie Anderson in order to catch the drift of what you're suggesting; but if they do know the song, it might broaden the nature of their response.

WG: I enjoy the idea that some levels of the text are closed to most readers. Of course, writers working in popular forms should be aware that readers aren't always going to respond to subtleties—though that isn't as weird as finding out that people are missing the whole point of what you think you're doing, whether it's thinking you're being ironic when you're not, or being serious when you're trying to make fun of something. When I was in England in February, I noticed that the response to my work was markedly different: people were referring to me as a humorist. In England they think what I'm doing is *funny*—not that I'm *only* being funny, but they can see that there's a certain humor in my work.

LM: Clearly, in "Johnny Mnemonic" and "Burning Chrome" you were laying the foundation for what you would do later on in *Neuromancer*.

WG: Yes, although I didn't think in those terms when I wrote those stories. Actually, "Johnny Mnemonic" was the third piece of fiction I wrote, and the only basis I had for gauging its success was that it sold. "Burning Chrome" was written later on, and even though it got more attention than anything I'd done before, I still felt I was four or five years away from writing a novel. Then Terry Carr recruited me to write a book, which turned out to be *Neuromancer*. He was looking for people he thought had some promise—he'd offer them contracts and say, "Do you want to write a book?" I said "Yes" almost without thinking, but then I was stuck with a project I wasn't sure I was ready for. In fact I was *terrified* once I actually sat down and started to think about what it meant. I didn't think I could fill up that many pages; I didn't even know how many pages the manuscript of a novel was "supposed" to have. It had been taking me something like three months to write a short story, so starting a novel was really a major leap. I remember going around asking other writers things like, "Assuming I double space everything, how *long* is a novel?" When somebody told me 300 pages, I thought, My God!

LM: What got you going with the book?

WG: Panic. Blind animal panic. It was a *desperate* quality that I think comes through in the book pretty clearly: *Neuromancer* is fueled by my terrible fear of losing the reader's attention. Once it hit me that I had to come up with something, to have a hook on every page, I looked at the stories I'd written up to that point and tried to figure out what had worked for me before. I had Molly in "Johnny Mnemonic"; I had an environment in "Burning Chrome." So I decided I'd try to put these things together. But all during the writing of the book I had the conviction that I was going to be permanently shamed when it appeared. And even when I finished it I had no perspective on what I'd done. I still don't, for that matter. I always feel like one of the guys *inside* those incredible dragons you see snaking through the crowds in Chinatown. Sure, the dragon is very brightly colored, but from the inside you know the whole thing is pretty flimsy—just a bunch of old newspapers and papier-mâché and balsa struts.

LM: The world you evoke in *Neuromancer* struck me as being a lot like the underworld we find in the work of Raymond Chandler and Dashiell Hammett—sleazy, intensely vivid, full of colorful details and exotic lingoes that somehow seem realistic *and* totally artificial.

WG: It's probably been fifteen years since I read Hammett, but I remember being very excited about how he had *pushed* all this ordinary stuff until it was *different*—like American naturalism but cranked up, very intense, almost surreal. You can see this in the beginning of *The Maltese Falcon,* where he describes all the things in Spade's office. Hammett may have been the guy who turned me on to the idea of *superspecificity,* which is largely lacking in most SF description. SF authors tend to use generics—"Then he got into his space suit"—a refusal to specify that is almost an unspoken tradition in SF. They know they can get away with having a character arrive on some unimaginably strange and distant planet and say, "I looked out the window and saw the air plant." It doesn't seem to matter that the reader has no idea what the plant looks like, or even what it is. I think Hammett may have given me the idea that you don't have to write like that, even in a popular form. But with Chandler—I never have read much of his work, and I never enjoyed what I did read because I always got this creepy puritanical feeling from his books. Although his surface gloss is very brilliant, his underlying meaning is off-putting to me.

LM: The other reason I thought of Hammett has to do with your rich, poetic vocabulary—the futuristic slang, the street talk, the technical and professional jargon.

WG: I suppose I strive for an argot that seems real, but I don't invent most of what seems exotic or strange in the dialogue—that's just more collage. There are so many cultures and subcultures today that if you're willing to listen, you can pick up different phrases, inflections, and metaphors everywhere. A lot of the language in *Neuromancer* and *Count Zero* that people think is so futuristic is probably just 1969 Toronto dope dealers' slang, or biker talk.

LM: Some of the phrases you use in *Neuromancer*—"flatlining" or "virus program"—manage to evoke some response beyond the literal.

WG: They're poetry! "Flatlining," for example, is ambulance driver slang for "death." I heard it in a bar maybe twenty years ago and it stuck with me. A drunken, crying ambulance driver saying, "She flat-lined." I use a lot of phrases that seem exotic to everyone but the people who use them. Oddly enough, I almost never get new buzzwords from other SF writers. I heard about "virus program" from an ex-WAC computer operator who had worked in the Pentagon. She was talking one night about guys who came in every day and wiped the boards of all the video games people had built into them, and how some people were building these little glitch-things that tried to evade the official wipers—things that would hide and then pop out and say, "Screw you!" before vanishing into the framework of logic. (Listening to me trying to explain this, it immediately becomes apparent that I have no grasp of how computers *really* work—it's been a contact high for me.) Anyway, it wasn't until after the book came out that I met people who knew what a virus program actually was.

LM: So your use of computers and science results more from their metaphoric value or from the way they sound than from any familiarity with how they actually operate.

WG: I'm looking for images that supply a certain atmosphere. Right now science and technology seem to be very useful sources. But I'm more interested in the *language* of, say, computers than I am in the technicalities. On the most basic level, computers in my books are simply a metaphor for human memory: I'm interested in the hows and whys of memory, the ways it defines who and what we are, in how easily memory is subject to revision. When I was writing *Neuromancer,* it was wonderful to be able to tie a lot of these interests into the computer metaphor. It wasn't until I could finally afford a computer of my own that I found out there's a drive mechanism inside—this little thing that spins around. I'd been expecting an exotic crystalline thing, a cyberspace deck or something, and what I got was a little piece of a Victorian engine that made noises like a scratchy old record player. That noise took away some of the mystique for me; it made computers less *sexy*. My ignorance had allowed me to romanticize them.

LM: What many readers first notice in *Neuromancer* are all the cyberpunk elements—exotic lingoes, drugs, cyber-realities, clothes, and so on. In many ways, though, the plot is very traditional: the down-and-out gangster who's been jerked around and wants to get even by pulling the big heist. Did you make a conscious decision to attach this punked-out cyber-reality to the framwork of an established plot?

WG: When I said earlier that a lot of what went into *Neuromancer* was the result of desperation, I wasn't exaggerating. I knew I was so inexperienced that I would need a traditional plot armature that had proven its potential for narrative traction. I had these different things I wanted to use, but since I didn't have a preset notion of where I was going, the plot had to be something I already felt comfortable with. Also, since I wrote *Neuromancer* very much under the influence of Robert Stone—who's a master of a certain kind of paranoid fiction— it's not surprising that what I wound up with was something like a Howard Hawkes film.

LM: First novels are often the most autobiographical. Were you drawing on a lot of things from your own past in *Neuromancer?*

WG: *Neuromancer* isn't autobiographical in any literal sense, but I did draw on my sense of what people are like to develop these characters. Part of that came from accessing my own screwed-up adolescence; and another part of it came from watching how kids reacted to all the truly horrible stuff happening all around them—that unfocused angst and weird lack of affect.

LM: Did the book undergo significant changes once you knew the basic structure was in place?

WG: The first two-thirds was rewritten a dozen times—a lot of stylistic changes, once I had the feel of the world, but also a lot of monkeying around to make the plot seem vaguely plausible. I had to cover up some of the shabbier coincidences, for example. Also, I never had a very clear idea of what was going to happen in the end, except that the gangsters had to score *big*.

LM: Do you look for specific effects when you revise your prose?

WG: My revisions mainly involve looking for passages that "clunk." When I first started to write, I found that in reading for pleasure I'd become suddenly aware that a *beat* had been missed, that the rhythm was gone. It's hard to explain, but when I go over my own writing I look for places where I've missed the beat. Usually I can correct it by condensing my prose so that individual parts carry more weight, are charged with more meaning; almost always the text gets shorter. I'm aware that this condensation process winds up putting off some readers.

"Genre" SF readers say that *Neuromancer* and *Count Zero* are impossibly dense, literally impossible to read; but other SF readers who ordinarily have no patience for "serious" fiction seem to be turned on by what I'm doing. Now that I've gained some experience writing, revisions take up less of my time; in fact, it's become easier to hit a level I'm satisfied with and stay there. One of the big problems with *Neuromancer* was that I had so much stuff—all this material that had been accumulating—that it was hard to get it into a manageable book.

LM: Has Thomas Pynchon had an influence on your work?

WG: Pynchon has been a favorite writer and a major influence all along. In many ways I see him as almost the start of a certain mutant breed of SF—the cyberpunk thing, the SF that mixes surrealism and pop culture imagery with esoteric historical and scientific information. Pynchon is a kind of mythic hero of mine, and I suspect that if you talk with a lot of recent SF writers you'll find they've all read *Gravity's Rainbow* several times and have been very much influenced by it. I was into Pynchon early on—I remember seeing a *New York Times* review of *V.* when it first came out—I was just a kid—and thinking, Boy, that sounds like some really weird shit!

LM: What was the inspiration for your cyberspace idea?

WG: I was walking down Granville Street, Vancouver's version of "The Strip," and I looked into one of the video arcades. I could see in the physical intensity of their postures how *rapt* the kids inside were. It was like one of those closed systems out of a Pynchon novel: a feedback loop with photons coming off the screens into the kids' eyes, neurons moving through their bodies, and electrons moving through the video game. These kids clearly *believed* in the space games projected. Everyone I know who works with computers seems to develop a belief that there's some kind of *actual space* behind the screen, someplace you can't see but you know is there.

LM: From a purely technical standpoint, the cyberspace premise must have been great to hit on simply because it creates a rationale for so many different narrative "spaces."

WG: When I arrived at the cyberspace concept, while I was writing "Burning Chrome," I could see right away that it was resonant in a lot of ways. By the time I was writing *Neuromancer,* I recognized that cyberspace allowed for a lot of *moves,* because characters can be sucked into apparent realities—which means you can place them in any sort of setting or against any backdrop. In some ways I tried to downplay that aspect, because if I overdid it I'd have an open-ended plot premise. That kind of freedom can be dangerous because you don't have to justify what's happening in terms of the logic of character or plot. In *Count Zero* I wanted to slow things down a bit and learn how to do characterization. I was aware that *Neuromancer* was going to seem like a roller coaster ride to most readers—you've got lots of excitement but maybe not much understanding of where you've been or why you were heading there in the first place. I enjoyed being able to present someone like Virek in *Count Zero,* who apparently lives in any number of "realities"—he's got the city of Barcelona if he wants it, and an array of other possibilities, even though he's actually a pile of cells in a vat somewhere.

LM: Philip K. Dick was always writing about people like Virek who have so many "reality options," so many different reproductions and illusions, that it's difficult to know what reality is more real—the one in their heads or the one that seems to exist outside. That's a powerful notion.

WG: Yeah, it is powerful—which is why it's such a temptation to keep pushing once you've got a concept like cyberspace that creates an instant rationale. I probably was a little heavy-handed in *Count Zero* with Bobby's mother, who's hooked on the soaps, who *lives* in them, but it was just too much to resist. Everybody asks me about Dick being an influence, but I hadn't read much of his work before I started writing—though I've imagined a world in which Pynchon sold his early stories to *Fantasy and Science Fiction* and became an alternate Dick.

LM: One of the issues your work raises is the way information— this "dance of data," as you refer to it—not only controls our daily lives but may be the best way for us to understand the fundamental processes that control the universe's ongoing transformations. It seems significant that mostly SF writers are tuned to this.

WG: Information is the dominant scientific metaphor of our age, so we need to face it, to try to understand what it means. It's not that technology has changed everything by transforming it into codes. Newtonians didn't see things in terms of information exchange, but today we do. That carries over into my suspicion that Sigmund Freud has a lot to do with steam engines.

LM: The various ways you use the dance metaphor in *Neuromancer* suggests a familiarity with the interactions between Eastern mysticism and modern physics.

WG: I was aware that the image of the dance was part of Eastern mysticism, but a more direct source was John Shirley, who was living in the East Village and wrote me a letter that described the thing about proteins linking. That's just another example of how pathetically makeshift everything looks from inside the papier-mâché dragon. It was the same thing with the voodoo gods in *Count Zero:* a copy of *National Geographic* was lying around that had an article about Haitian voodoo in it.

LM: Back in the '60s and early '70s, most of the important New Wave SF took a pessimistic stance toward technology and progress. Although your work has sometimes been described as glorifying technology, I'd say it offers a more ambivalent view.

WG: My feelings about technology are *totally* ambivalent—which seems to me to be the only way to relate to what's happening today. When I write about technology, I write about how it has *already* affected our lives; I don't extrapolate in the way I was taught an SF writer should. You'll notice in *Neuromancer* that there's obviously been a war, but I don't explain what caused it or even who was fighting it. I've never had the patience or the desire to work out the details of who's doing what to whom, or exactly when something is taking place, or what's become of the United States. That kind of literalism has always seemed silly to me; it detracts from the reading pleasure I get from SF. My aim isn't to provide specific predictions or judgments so much as to find a suitable fictional context in which to examine the very mixed blessings of technology.

LM: How consciously do you see yourself operating outside the mainstream of American SF?

WG: A lot of what I've written so far is a conscious reaction to what I felt SF—especially American SF—had become by the time I started writing in the late '70s. In fact, I felt I was writing so far outside the mainstream that my highest goal was to become a minor cult figure, a sort of lesser Ballard. I assumed I was doing something no one would like except for a few crazy "art" people—and maybe some people in England and France, who I always assumed would respond to what I was doing because I knew their tastes were *very* different and because the French like Dick a lot. When I was starting out, I simply tried to go in the opposite direction from most of the stuff I was reading, which I felt an aesthetic revulsion toward.

LM: What sorts of '70s SF did you have in mind? All those sword-and-sorcery books or the hard SF that people like Jerry Pournelle, Gregory Benford, and Larry Niven were writing?

WG: Some of my resistance had to do with a certain didactic, right-wing stance that I associated with a lot of hard SF, but mainly it was a more generalized angle of attack. I'm a very desultory reader of SF— I have been since my big period of reading SF when I was around fifteen—so my stance was instinctual. In the '70s, during the years just before I seriously thought about writing SF, it seemed like the SF books I enjoyed were few and far between. Just about everything I picked up seemed too slick and, even worse, *uninteresting*. Part of this has to do with the adolescent audience that a lot of SF has always been written for. My publishers keep telling me that the adolescent market is where it's at, and that makes me pretty uncomfortable because I remember what my tastes ran to at that age. One new factor around 1975 was that writers started getting these *huge* advances for SF books, and I said to myself, Hey, you can get *big money for SF.* But by the time I started writing SF, those big advances had dried up, because a lot of them had gone to books that had lost money. I had a sense of what the expectations of the SF industry were in terms of product, but I *hated* that product and felt such a genuine sense of disgust that I consciously decided to reverse expectations, not give publishers or readers what they wanted.

LM: How would you describe the direction of your work?

WG: When I first started writing, what held me up for a long time was finding a way to introduce the things that turned *me* on. I knew that when I was reading a text—particularly a fantastic text—it was the *gratuitous* moves, the odd, quirky, irrelevant details, that provided a sense of strangeness. So it seemed important to find an approach that would allow for gratuitous moves. I didn't think that what I was writing would ever "fit in" or be accepted, so what I wanted was to be able to plug in the things that interested me. When Molly goes through the Tessier-Ashpool's library in *Neuromancer,* she sees that they own Duchamp's *Large Glass.* Now that reference doesn't make sense on some deeper symbolic level; it's really irrelevant, a gratuitous move. But putting it there seemed right—here are these very rich people on this space station with this great piece of art just gathering dust. In other words, I liked the piece and wanted to get it into the book somehow.

LM: Precisely these personal "signatures" create a texture and eventually add up to what we call a writer's "vision." You can see this in Alfred Bester, whose books remind me of yours.

WG: Bester was into flash very early. When *Neuromancer* came out, a lot of reviewers said that I must have written it while holding a copy of *The Demolished Man.* Actually, it had been some time since I'd read Bester, but he was one of the SF authors who had stuck with me, who seemed worthy of imitating, mostly because I always had the feeling he had a ball writing. And I think I know exactly what it was that produced that sense: he was a New York guy who didn't depend on writing SF to make a living, so he really just let loose; he didn't have to give a damn about anything other than having fun, pleasing himself. If you want to get a sense of how groovy it could have been to be alive and young and living in New York in the '50s, read Bester's SF. It may be significant that when you read his mainstream novel (which is pretty hard to find over here, but it's been released in England as *The Rat Race*), you can see him using the same tools he used in those two early SF books—but somehow it doesn't work. Bester's palette just isn't suited for convincing you that you're reading about reality.

LM: This business about realism often seems misleading. You said that Bester's SF books gave you a sense of what it felt like to be in New York at a certain time—*that's* realism, though different from what you find in Honoré de Balzac or Henry James; it's the realism that cyberpunk supplies, that sense of what it really feels like to be alive in our place, at our time.

WG: My SF *is* realistic in that I write about what I see around me. That's why SF's role isn't central to my work. My fiction amplifies and distorts *my* impressions of the world, however strange that world may be. One of the liberating effects of SF when I was a teenager was precisely its ability to tune me in to all sorts of strange data and make me realize that I wasn't as totally isolated in perceiving the world as being monstrous and crazy. In the early '60s, SF was the only source of subversive information available to me.

LM: Some of that spirit of subversiveness, that sense of the strangeness of the ordinary, is finding its way into mainstream quasi-SF novels: Ted Mooney's *Easy Travel to Other Planets,* Don DeLillo's *White Noise,* Denis Johnson's *Fiskadoro,* Steve Erickson's books, and recent work by Robert Coover, Margaret Atwood, Max Apple, and Stanley Elkin.

WG: Funny you should bring up Mooney's novel, because I was very jealous of the attention it got. *Easy Travel* is a brilliant book, but I remember thinking, "Here's this guy using all these SF tropes and he's getting reviewed in *Time.*" I was struck with how categories affect the way people respond to your work. Because I'm labeled an "SF writer" and Mooney is a "mainstream writer," people may never take me as seriously as they do him—even though we're both operating on some kind of SF fringe area.

LM: Your work and Mooney's share a hyperawareness that people are being affected in all sorts of ways—psychologically, perceptually—by the constant bombardment of sounds and other data. And you're both willing to experiment stylistically to find a means suitable for presenting the effects of information overload.

WG: I'm very prone to what Mooney calls "information sickness," and I'm having increasing trouble dealing with it. Without doing this too consciously, I had set up my life to minimize input. But now that I've started to make it—even relatively modestly in an obscure field like SF— I've been bombarded with all kinds of stuff. People are coming to my home, stuff arrives in the mail, the phone is ringing, I've got decisions to make about movies and book jackets.

LM: One of the common, maybe simplistic comments you hear about information overload is that the result is a kind of psychological confusion or dislocation. We have all this stuff coming in but we can't seem to put anything together so that it *means* anything. We're only slightly better off than Mooney's characters, with their paralysis and convulsions.

WG: But sometimes you find you can have *fun* with these dislocations. When I said I was prone to information sickness, I meant I sometimes get off on being around a lot of unconnected stuff—but only certain *kinds* of stuff, which is why I'm having trouble handling the input right now. I have a friend, Tom Maddox, who did a paper on my work. He's known what I've been up to for a long time—he says I display "a problematic sensitivity to semiotic fragments." That probably has a lot to do with the way I write—stitching together all the junk that's floating around in my head. One of my private pleasures is to go to the corner Salvation Army thrift shop and look at all the junk. I can't explain what I get out of doing this. I mean, I used to have to spend time there as a survival thing, and even now I'll go in and find something I want.

LM: You said you weren't really reading much SF when you started out as a writer. What got you started writing SF?

WG: A series of coincidences. I was at the University of British Columbia, getting an English B.A.—I graduated in '76 or '77—because it was easier at the time than finding a job. I realized I could get the grades I needed as an English major to keep getting the grants I needed to avoid getting a job. There were a couple of months during that period when I thought very seriously about SF without thinking I was ever going to *write* it—instead, I thought I might want to write *about* it. I took courses with a guy who talked about the aesthetic politics of fascism— we were reading an Orwell essay, "Raffles and Miss Blandish," and he wondered whether or not there were fascist novels—and I remember thinking, Reading all these SF novels has given me a line on this topic—*I* know where this fascist literature is! I thought about working on an M.A. on this topic, though I doubt that my approach would have been all that earthshaking. But it got me thinking seriously about what SF did, what it was, which traditions had shaped it and which ones it had rejected. Form/content issues.

LM: Were there other literature classes that might have influenced your thinking about SF?

WG: Most of the lit classes I took went in one ear and out the other. However, I remember a class on American naturalism, where I picked up the idea that there are several different kinds of naturalist novels: the mimetic naturalist novel—the familiar version—and the crazed naturalist novel—the kind Hammett writes, or Algren's *Man with the Golden Arm,* where he tries to do this realistic description of Chicago in the '40s but his take on it is weirder than anything I did with Chiba City in *Neuromancer.* It's full of people with neon teeth, characters with pieces of their faces falling off, stuff out of some bad nightmare. Then there's the overt horror/pain end of naturalism, which you find in Hubert Selby's books. Maybe related in some way to these twisted offshoots of naturalism are the books by William Burroughs that affected SF in all kinds of ways. I'm of the first generation of American SF authors who had the chance to read Burroughs when we were fourteen or fifteen years old. I know having had that opportunity made a big difference in my outlook on what SF—or any literature, for that matter— could be. What Burroughs was doing with plot and language and the SF motifs I saw in other writers was literally mind expanding. I saw this crazy outlaw character who seemed to have picked up SF and gone after society with it, the way some old guy might grab a rusty beer opener and start waving it around. Once you've had that experience, you're not quite the same.

LM: Has the serious attention you've gotten from the SF world made you feel any less alienated?

WG: Yeah—everyone's been so nice—but I still feel very much out of place in the company of most SF writers. It's as though I don't know what to do when I'm around them, so I'm usually very polite and I keep my tie on. SF authors are often strange, ill-socialized people who have good minds but are still kids.

LM: Who among the current writers do you admire or feel some connections with?

WG: Bruce Sterling is certainly a favorite—he produces more ideas per page than anyone else around. Marc Laidlaw had a book called *Dad's Nuke* that I really enjoyed. And John Shirley, of course. I also admire Greg Bear's work, even though his approach is much more hard SF oriented than mine. Recently I came across some quasi-SF books by Madison Smartt Bell—*The Washington Square Ensemble* and *Waiting for the End of the World*—which are wonderful, brilliant.

LM: What about Samuel Delany? His work seems to have influenced your generation of SF authors in important ways.

WG: There's no question about his importance, and he's obviously influenced me. Those books he was writing when he was twenty-one or whatever were my favorite books when I was fifteen and plowing through all that SF. I'm pretty sure I didn't know at the time that Delany wasn't much older than I was, but I think the fact that I was a kid reading books by a slightly older kid had something to do with my sense that his books were a lot *fresher* than anything else I could find.

LM: You're usually considered the leading figure of the cyberpunk movement. Is there such a thing, or was the movement dreamed up by a critic?

WG: It's mainly a marketing category—and one that I've come to feel trivializes what I do. Tying my stuff to *any* label is unfair because it gives people preconceptions about what I'm doing. But it gets complicated because I have friends and cohorts who are benefiting from the hype and who like it. Of course, I can appreciate that the label gives writers a certain attitude they can rally around, feel comfortable with—they can get up at SF conventions, put on their mirrored sunglasses, and say, "That's right, baby, that's us!"

LM: That was exactly the scene at the recent SFRA conference in San Diego. John Shirley, decked out in a leather jacket and shades, wound up in a screaming match with the hard SF "Killer B's"—Brin, Bear, and Benford—who have their own identity, their own dress code.

WG: Michael Swanwick wrote an article about the split between the cyberpunks and the humanists. He referred to John Shirley as John-the-Baptist-of-Cyberpunk, roaming the wilderness trying to spread the new gospel. Even though I don't agree with everything Swanwick wrote, I do think John has always had this evangelical side to him—though he's less like that now than when I first met him in 1977, when he was into spiked dog collars. No one was ready for his insane novels, which are unfortunately very hard to find. There just wasn't anything else like that being written then—no hook or label like cyberpunk, no opening—so they were totally ignored. If those books were published now, people would be saying, "Wow, look at this stuff! It's *beyond* cyberpunk." Really, though, I'm tired of the whole cyberpunk phenomenon. I mean, there's already bad *imitation cyberpunk,* so you know it can only go downhill from here. All that really happened was that a bunch of work by some new authors landed on some publishers' desks at the same time. People didn't know what to make of us, so they gave us this tag.

LM: The cyberpunk/humanist opposition seems way off base to me. There are a lot of scenes in both *Neuromancer* and *Count Zero* that are very moving from a human standpoint. Beneath the glittery surface hardware is an emphasis on the "meat" of people, the fragile body that can get crushed so easily.

WG: That's my "Lawrentian" take on things. It's very strange to write something and realize that people will read into it whatever they want. When I hear critics say that my books are "hard and glossy," I almost want to give up writing. The English reviewers, though, seem to understand that what I'm talking about is what being hard and glossy does to you.

LM: One of the scenes that sticks out for me is the one near the end of *Neuromancer* where Case is on that beach with the woman. It's a powerful and sad moment even though—or maybe *because*—we know he's in cyberspace imagining all this.

WG: It's great to hear *someone* react that way to that scene, because that passage was the emotional crux of the book, its center of gravity.

I'd like to think that the novel is balanced in such a way that the scene shows how distorted everything has become from several different perspectives.

LM: Another scene that has a peculiar emotional charge is the one where Case is trying to destroy the wasps' nest. What makes the nest seem so primal, so scary?

WG: The fear of bugs, for one thing! That scene evolved out of an experience I had destroying a very large wasps' nest. I didn't know what was inside, didn't know they were "imprinted" that way, so when the nest broke open I was astounded and scared by all the wasps. It probably also helped that I got stung several times.

LM: Do you consciously build a metaphor like the wasps' nest so that it resonates in different ways, or is the process buried in your unconscious?

WG: Once I've hit on an image, a lot of what I do involves the controlled use of collage; I look around for ways to relate the image to the rest of the book. That's something I got from Burroughs's work, and to a lesser extent from Ballard. I've never actually done any of that cut-up stuff, except for folding a few pages out of something when I'd be stuck or incredibly bored and then checking later to see what came out. But I could see what Burroughs was doing with these random methods, and why, even though the results weren't always that interesting. So I started snipping things out and slapping them down, but then I'd air-brush them a little to take the edges off.

LM: Isn't that approach out of place in a field like SF, where most readers are looking for scientific or rational connections to keep the futuristic fantasy moving forward credibly?

WG: As I said earlier, I'm not interested in producing the kind of literalism most readers associate with SF. This may be a suicidal admission, but most of the time I don't know what I'm talking about when it comes to the scientific or logical rationales that supposedly underpin my books. Apparently, though, part of my skill lies in my ability to convince people otherwise. Some of the SF writers who are actually working scientists do know what they're talking about; but for the rest of us, to present a whole world that doesn't exist and make it seem real, we have to more or less pretend we're polymaths. *That's just the act of all good writing.*

LM: Are you interested in developing a futuristic, Faulknerian Yoknapatawpha County in which everything you write will be interconnected in a single fictional world?

WG: No—it would look too much like I was doing one of those Stephen R. Donaldson things. People are already asking me how many of these books I'm going to write, which gives me a creepy sensation because of the innate sleaziness of so much SF publishing. When you're not forced to invent a new world from scratch each time, you find yourself getting lazy, falling back on the same stuff you used in an earlier novel. I was aware of this when I was finishing *Neuromancer,* and that's why, near the end, there's an announcement that Case never saw Molly again. That wasn't directed so much at the reader as at me. If you had told me seven years ago that I would write an SF trilogy, I would have hung myself in shame. Posthaste.

LM: The obsession today with being able to reproduce a seemingly endless series of images, data, and information of all sorts is obviously related to capitalism and its drive for efficiency; but it also seems to grow out of our fear of *death,* a desire for immortality. The goals of religion and technology, in other words, may be closer than we think.

WG: I can see that. But this isn't something that originated with contemporary technology. If you look at any of the ancient temples, which were the result of people learning to work stone with the technology available to them, what you'll find are machines designed to give those people immortality. The pyramids and snake mounds are time machines. This kind of application of technology seems to run throughout human culture.

LM: You didn't start college until the mid-1970s. What were you doing during the late '60s and early '70s?

WG: Virtually nothing. My father was a contractor back in the '40s; he made a bunch of money installing flush toilets for the Oak Ridge projects and went on to the postwar, pre–Sun Belt building boom in the South. He died when I was about eight, and my mother decided to move the family back to this little town in Virginia where they had both come from. I stayed there until I was sixteen or seventeen, a bookish, geekish, can't-hit-the-baseball kind of kid. Then I went to boarding school in Tucson, where I was exposed to urban kids and where I encountered the first wave of hippies pouring over the land from San Francisco. They were older than I was, and they were really into some cool stuff. Eventually, I got kicked out of boarding school for smoking pot. I went back to Virginia, but my mother had died and my relatives weren't particularly sympathetic to my style. So I spent some time bumming around. I more or less convinced my draft board that they didn't want me; in any case, they didn't hassle me, and in 1968 I left for Toronto without even knowing that Canada would be such a different country. I wound up living in a community of young Americans who were staying away from the draft.

LM: Was it pretty much an underground scene? Did it contribute to your novels?

WG: I'm sure it did, in terms of supplying me with some of the offbeat language I use. But to describe it as an "underground scene" would seem funny to anyone who knew me and what was going on. It was really pretty tame compared to what was happening in a lot of places; it was a soft-core version of the hippie/underground street scene, nothing heavy. I did have the small-town kid's fascination with watching criminal things. No question, though, that it made a lasting impression on me. Those were portentous days. Nobody knew what was going to happen.

LM: You weren't giving much thought at that point to being a writer?

WG: Only occasionally. Like a lot of other people, I felt I was living in an age in which everything was going to change very radically, so why make career plans? When things *didn't* get different, except maybe worse, I retreated. I went to Europe and wandered around there for a year—I had enough income from my parents' estate to starve comfortably. I came back to Canada because my wife, Deb, wanted to finish a B.A., and we moved to Vancouver so she could attend UBC. When Deb began work on an M.A. in linguistics, I realized that higher education was a good scam. If I hadn't wandered into SF, I'd be totally unemployable.

LM: Are you interested in trying your hand at non-SF soon, maybe breaking out of the SF ghetto into the mainstream's mean street?

WG: I am, because I'm afraid of being typecast if I make SF my permanent home. But what seems important right now is finding my way out of what I'm doing without losing a sense of what it is I'm doing. I don't want to go back and start over. I have glimpses of how this might be done, but it's a lateral move that has become increasingly difficult to make. It's taken as gospel among SF writers that to get out of SF once you've made a name in it is virtually impossible: "The clout isn't transferable."

LM: That's ironic, given all the mainstream writers doing quasi-SF. Not to mention the Latin American fabulists.

WG: I envy the Latin American writers because they can do what they want. In America, it seems like these influences mostly travel in one direction—mainstream writers borrow from SF, but SF writers seem locked into provincialism. When I was in England, I thought it was interesting that their community of SF writers was enthusiastic about Latin American fabulism. But few people in the equivalent American SF community seem remotely familiar with it.

LM: What can you tell me about your next novel? Have you started work on it yet?

WG: I'm supposed to be working on it, but as you can see by this household's sublime sense of peace and order, it's tough going right now. It's called *Mona Lisa Overdrive* and it's not a linear sequel to

Count Zero—in fact, it bears the same relationship to *Count Zero* that *Count Zero* did to *Neuromancer,* in that each book takes place seven years after the previous one. You glimpse some of the same people, but fourteen years is a long time in a world like this, where things change so fast you can hardly recognize anything from minute to minute. When I was doing *Count Zero,* I had initially intended to pursue what was going to happen to Mitchell's daughter; that seemed like an interesting thread to follow. But I was so anxious to finish the book, so tired of working on it, that I talked myself out of making any judgments about it. It nagged at me, though; I kept wondering what happened to her. She's a permanent interface with the voodoo gods and she's also obviously going to be the next Superstar. Somehow, though, that wasn't enough to get me going. Then I spent a weekend at the Beverly Hills Hotel with some producers, an eye-opening trip. Coming back on the plane, it struck me that for the first time I had actually gotten to see some of the stuff I had been writing about. I had another book I was supposed to start, but when I got back to Vancouver I phoned the agents and told them I wanted to do *Mona Lisa Overdrive* instead.

LM: The Japanese settings you've used, notably in *Neuromancer,* seem right in all sorts of ways. Was any of that based on personal experience?

WG: "Terry and the Pirates" probably had more to do with it than personal experience. I've never been to Japan, but my wife has been an ESL teacher for a long time, and since the Japanese can most afford to send their teenagers over here to study English, there was an extended period when this stream of Japanese students turned up in Vancouver— I'd meet them a week off the plane, see them when they were leaving, that sort of thing. Also, Vancouver is a very popular destination for Japanese tourists—for example, there are special bars here that cater exclusively to the Japanese, and almost no one else goes into them because the whole scene is too strange. I'm sure I got a lot of this in when I wrote *Neuromancer.* Of course, the Japanese have really bought the whole cyberpunk thing. It's as if they believe everything Bruce Sterling has written about it! It's frightening. But one of the things they seem to like about my work is that I don't try to invent Japanese names—I got the street names from a Japan Air Lines calendar. And I got lucky with the geography. I didn't even know where Chiba was when I wrote *Neuromancer*—all that stuff about it being on a peninsula and across a bay came out of my head—so I was really sweating when the book came out. But then I got a map and there was Chiba—on a peninsula! on a bay! Life imitates art. The only culture I've seen firsthand that might have influenced *Neuromancer* was Istanbul, which had a big impact on me even though I was only there for a week or so. Another place that affected my writing was the East Village, which John Shirley introduced me to in 1980. Nothing had prepared me for what I encountered when I stepped out into the street. The buildings were papered with Xerox art as high up as people could reach. From the point of view of somebody who'd been living in a place like Vancouver, the whole scene was total chaos and anarchy. It was weird and frightening and interesting all at the same time.

LM: Do you sometimes wish you lived in New York or Los Angeles so you could draw on the strangeness more directly?

WG: If I lived in a place like that, I'd write about unicorns. I'll leave well enough alone for now.

An Interview with

Ursula K. Le Guin

Ursula K. Le Guin has described science fiction (in her essay "Do-It-Yourself Cosmology") as "a modern, intellectualized, extravagant form of fantasy." Whether that description can be applied to most contemporary SF is debatable, but it is a useful starting point for a consideration of her prolific and varied body of work, which includes poetry, short stories, essays, and young adult fiction as well as a number of major fantasy and SF novels. Like the writings of Italo Calvino, Jorge Luis Borges, Philip K. Dick, and Stanislaw Lem, Le Guin's work defies genre categories. Her fiction typically is a sophisticated blend of myth, fable, political inquiry, and metaphysical parable. A wonderful spinner of adventure tales, she also makes us take note of the codes and cultural assumptions with which we construct our present. Le Guin creates worlds apart and then explores their premises—those central anthropological, semiological, political, ecological, and aesthetic assumptions that define a culture—in meticulous detail. After we put down her fiction, we examine with alien eyes our own cities and social structures, our commonplace truths and "natural" assumptions.

Le Guin began writing novels and stories during the 1950s, but not until the '60s did she find a publishing home in SF. Her early novels, *Rocannon's World* (1966), *Planet of Exile* (1966), and *City of Illusions* (1967), while clearly apprentice works, exhibit her interest in anthropology and Taoism and her skill in embedding symbolic features within exotic contexts. Le Guin's fourth novel, *The Left Hand of Darkness*

(1969), established her as a major new voice in SF—and as one of the leading authors in the budding feminist movement. Her Earthsea trilogy—*A Wizard of Earthsea* (1968), *The Tombs of Atuan* (1971), and *The Farthest Shore* (1972)—brought about comparisons with Tolkien's Lord of the Rings fantasy cycle and further expanded her audience. *(Tehanu: The Last Book of Earthsea* [1990] has recently transformed the series into a tetralogy.) Le Guin's next major work, *The Dispossessed* (1974), reflected her deepening political interests, particularly her sympathy for anarchism (later fully realized in *Always Coming Home* [1985]).

Throughout the '70s and '80s, Le Guin continued to publish widely in SF and fantasy: for example, *The Lathe of Heaven* (1971), *The Word for World Is Forest* (notable for its treatment of Vietnam; 1971), *The Wind's Twelve Quarters* (stories, 1975), *The Beginning Place* (1980), *The Compass Rose* (1983), and *Buffalo Gals* (1986). In addition, there were so-called mainstream works of fiction (*The Orsinian Tales* [1976] and *Malafrena* [1979]), poetry (*Wild Angels* [1975]), and essays (*The Language of the Night* [1979]). By far the most important of her recent works, however, is *Always Coming Home.* Part initiation story, part political allegory, part philosophical meditation, *Always Coming Home* prismatically introduces a rich variety of cultural artifacts of the Kesh, including recipes, music (some editions included an audiocassette), drama, folktales, descriptions of native flora and fauna, and drawings. These artifacts surround and illuminate the central story of a young Kesh woman named Stone Telling whose journey to the land of the Condors sparks her own personal growth and permits Le Guin to establish a series of contrasts between the Kesh (a peaceful hunting-and-gathering tribe) and the condors (whose warlike, acquisitive nature and reliance on abstract modes of thought bring them clearly in line with our own culture). Le Guin's sensuous prose, and the book's roots in science, archaeology, and anthropology, make *Always Coming Home* the highlight of her career to date.

When Sinda Gregory and I interviewed Le Guin in the summer of 1983, the cool, detached observer was nowhere in evidence at her home, a beautiful old two-story house with a picture-postcard view of the Columbia River, the many bridges and highways that crisscross it, and the smoky Portland skyline. We found instead a warm, vigorous, open woman who was full of ideas and who tempered her intellect with a generous and humorous spirit.

Larry McCaffery: As anthropologists, your parents spent a great deal of their professional careers trying, in a sense, to re-create other people's cultures. Is that one of the attractions of SF for you—that it allows you to reconstruct, imaginatively, other cultures?

Ursula Le Guin: Yes. Science fiction allows me to help people get out of their cultural skins and into the skins of other beings. In that sense SF is just a further extension of what the novel has traditionally been. In most fiction the author tries to get into the skin of another person; in SF you are often expected to get into the skin of another person from another culture.

Sinda Gregory: You've said that when you turned to SF writing in the early '60s it was partially out of a desire to find a publishing niche—a place that would allow you to publish the unclassifiable things you were writing at that time. But why this particular niche? Why not, say, detective fiction, or historical romances?

UL: The answer to that is simple: SF was what bought me. The other genres weren't interested. Whatever it is that I write—this general, odd area that seems hard for others to define, although I know in my own mind what it is—didn't sell until it was given to an SF editor. Today, my work sells in other areas, because once you get published it's easier to get published again and again and to enlarge that pigeonhole you've been put in. But in all honesty, my entry into the field of science fiction was largely a matter of chance or circumstance. It finally occurred to me that this kind of editor might buy whatever it was that I was writing.

SG: There's a story about your interest in SF becoming rekindled about this same time by your being given the works of Cordwainer Smith. Did that really happen?

UL: Yes, and I realized that if there was a place for him, there must be a place for me.

SG: What did you find in Smith that got you reinterested in SF? I understand you had been an avid SF fan as a kid but had given up the field in favor of more traditional forms.

UL: Smith had a highly original imagination expressed in original language. His works were certainly much better than the pulp stuff I had been reading when I quit looking at SF back in the '40s. He was not a "literary" writer, but he knew what he was doing as a short story writer—in fact, he was an excellent story writer. And yet here he was, working in the SF mode. To me, encountering his works was like a door opening. There is one story of his called "Alpha Ralpha Boulevard" that was as important to me as reading Pasternak for the first time and realizing that one could write a novel the way he wrote *Dr. Zhivago*. There are these moments in most writers' careers when you discover that someone else has actually written down some of these things that have been going on in your own head; you realize that this isn't just a private experience.

SG: Could you talk a bit about the effects of your remarkable parents on your writing or your imagination?

UL: I find it almost impossible to analyze the effects my parents and their friends had on me. I wasn't exactly a dumb kid, but I was such an unaware kid. I don't think I was as conscious of things going on around me as other kids might have been. I was a nice serious little Germanic girl, a good girl. I have always liked to work. I was very introverted. And I was the youngest and the only girl. My parents never pushed any of us in any particular direction intellectually. They wanted us to be intelligent, and to be intellectuals if we wanted to be. It was important to them that we be educated people. This was during the war; my three brothers went away to the service, which meant that their education was all fouled up. I was the only one who had a normal progress through school. But my parents made absolutely no distinction between the boys and the girl. It never occurred to me that because I was a girl I was expected to do less or do other than my brothers. That was enormously important to my whole attitude.

The intellectual milieu I grew up with was, of course, high powered in a kind of easygoing way. A kid doesn't recognize how unique the situation is, because a kid doesn't have anything to compare it to. I thought that every kid lived that way and had these impassioned, intellectual conversations around the table. To me that was just how it was. I didn't question it; it didn't seem strange. It was a very articulate family—my brothers and I were always encouraged to talk a lot—and there were books all over the place. It was no holds barred, as far as what we could read or talk about. There were also a lot of refugees around the house, and academic friends of my father. One Indian who always came and stayed with us every summer, Juan Dolores, was like a member of the family. As I look back on it, I suppose that was the kind of thing that must have influenced me later on. It's not every child who is lucky enough to have a Papago uncle!

LM: I've heard the suggestion that the Napa Valley country place where your family spent its summers must have been one of the sources for your later wilderness settings. Did you and your brothers ever invent fantasy worlds while you were there, like the Brontë children?

UL: Nothing so elaborate as that. We were a close-knit family and we did what most kids do when they play together. When, for example, my nearest brother was doing *Julius Caesar* in junior high, we'd do our own version at home. We did build some forts, and I had to be the Germans attacking. So we basically played the kind of imaginative games all kids play. When my brothers were off in the war, there were several summers when I was there more or less alone. This was a different experience, since I had the woods to myself. Entirely to myself.

LM: When you said that you had the run of the house as far as books were concerned, it occurred to me that you must have run across a lot of mythology because your works so often seem fascinated with the myth-making process. And *Rocannon's World,* your first novel, was directly based on Norse mythology. That doesn't seem like a coincidence.

UL: No, it certainly wasn't. My mother was the mythology book collector in the family, partly because she liked mythology and partly because she liked it for us. So by the time I came along (I was the fourth kid), there was a lot of mythology around, mostly in kids' versions, but what's the difference? Beautiful big books with lots of illustrations. I plunged around in those books and in everything else; the Norse myths were my favorite. Sometime in here I also came across Dunsany's *Dreamer's Tales,* which proved to be another revelation. Dunsany was important to me because he was the first writer I had come across who wrote what I would call "pure fantasy." Today his works probably seem old-fashioned—I know my kids didn't take to him at all. He wrote in a biblical-grand-Irish-romantic language, a very mannered style. But as a kid in the '30s, I wasn't so far from that early twentieth-century mannerism. What I saw in Dunsany were these absolutely pure invented fantasies: a mythology that one person had made up. The idea that people could invent their own myths, use their imaginations to the limit, was a wonderful discovery.

LM: So it wasn't just the mythic quality of the work but the fact that it was completely made up, not handed down but invented on the spot, that intrigued you.

UL: That was the magical quality. After all, that's the basis of our modern notions of the difference between myth and fantasy: in myth story is handed down, while in fantasy one person is inventing this on his own. This can be quite a revelation for kids. They use their imaginations a lot this way—as with the stories they tell themselves or tell each other before they go to sleep—but they may not realize that adults engage in this fantasy-making activity and are willing to share it. Of course, nowadays fantasy and children's books have become an enormously bigger industry than they were in the '30s and '40s, so probably children often make this discovery a lot earlier than I did; it probably doesn't hit kids with quite the air of glorious revelation that it did me, an introverted kid who needed an *outlet* for a strong imagination.

SG: When I first read *Rocannon's World,* I didn't realize that it was so elaborately based on Norse mythology. When you were conceiving the book, were you using these mythic parallels more or less unconsciously, or were you more systematic about it?

UL: Oh, quite systematic. I was still fairly young when I wrote that novel and rather uncertain of what I was doing—I thought it was SF

I was writing, but now I'd say it's more fantasy. I initially plotted it myself, but somewhere in the building I began to see the parallels with Odin's adventures. So I thought, All right, I'll just use these parallels more systematically. Then I went back and read Padraic Colum's Norse legends, *The Children of Odin,* and I stole various things, like the episode where Odin is standing in the fire—only I put him in that stupid impermasuit. . . . I was a beginner, and *Rocannon's World* is really a beginner's piece, with the charms and many of the limitations of a beginner's piece.

SG: I can't recall any of your other works using specific myths like this.

UL: I never consciously borrowed in that way again, although obviously unconscious residues appear. I must admit that I'm made uncomfortable when a fiction writer systematically uses myth. Oh, Joyce's borrowing—one major writer to another—is all right; but when writers base a fantasy or SF piece directly on some myth, there is often an intellectualization that trivializes both the myth and the novel. I have tried to avoid that and get down far enough inside my own head, where I can at least believe I'm creating while I'm writing. Later on, a critic may get a look at what I've come up with and point out some parallels and explanations, and I say, Oh, *that's* what I was doing.

SG: Rumor has it that you wrote your first story at the age of nine and had it rejected by John Campbell's *Astounding.* That's a pretty early start.

UL: Writing was never a hobby for me. Writing has always been what I've done. Actually, I was so pleased to be getting the same kind of rejection slip that grown-ups did that I wasn't cast down at all.

SG: Did you take creative writing classes in college?

UL: I took one at Radcliffe out of curiosity and a sense of duty. I'd said to myself, Look here, you consider yourself to be a writer, now take a class in writing. But the class was a disaster. I got an *A* and all that, but I didn't belong there. I was also very arrogant. Nobody could teach me nuttin'.

LM: I was intrigued with your reply to the 1976 special issue of *Science Fiction Studies* that scholars might do well to go back and check some of your critical work in college which dealt with Renaissance literature.

UL: I was being facetious. I doubt there's anything of interest in the critical work I did in college. I was training myself to make a living and I knew I couldn't do it writing, at least not for a long time.

LM: What I found interesting about that comment, facetious or not, was that a number of recent writers, including John Barth and Robert Coover, have said that they went back to Renaissance literature and studied it when they were starting out as writers. Both say that they found this area interesting for formal reasons—these prenovelistic, pre-realistic forms opened up all sorts of possibilities for them. The other thing that occurred to me is that Renaissance literature is filled with fantastic voyages, landscapes that fuse inner and outer states, and several other motifs that have found their way into your works. Did your immersion in that area have much of an effect on your work?

UL: Undoubtedly it did because it was such a long and loving immersion. I found that I had an affinity with writers like Ariosto and Tasso, at least to the extent of loving their poetry. But my motivation was basically the opposite of Barth's. I knew I had to earn a living, but I didn't want to try to earn it by writing because I wanted to write what I wanted to write—not what some editor wanted. What I was most suited to earn a living by was scholarly work in literature, and so far as I was concerned it had *not* to be English literature, because I didn't want my studies to get near what I was doing with my writing. So I focused on literature in a foreign language from the relatively distant past. One of my hangups before I left graduate school was that I was going to have to take my orals in twentieth-century French literature and I didn't want to do that reading; I wanted to read only the contemporaries *I* wanted to read, not be *forced* to read anybody. In retrospect I can see that I was protecting my own integrity, my selfhood as a writer, against contemporary writers who might threaten me because they were doing what I knew I couldn't do, or confuse me by excellence into an effort to imitate. I was also trying to protect myself against an intellectualization of what I did. Being an intellectual, I'm extremely aware of the dangers of that. So what I did in school was turn back, in a sense, to an area of literature that seemed safely remote.

SG: So you weren't looking for prenovelistic sources for your own works.

UL: Exactly. But, of course, what happens is that you do find sources, only you distance them enough so they don't overwhelm you. It is a matter of respect for yourself and for the older artists. At twenty-one or twenty-two, both my arrogance and my modesty as an artist led me to work with stuff written in a different language by people who had been dead for four hundred years.

LM: I haven't found much information about Jehan Le Maire de Belges, the subject of your unfinished Ph.D. thesis. Who was he?

UL: He was a fifteenth-century Frenchman, just before the Renaissance, a little after Villon, who was totally medieval, and just before the Pleiade, the great court poets who flowered during the Renaissance. You can tell by his work that he knew something was coming, but he didn't know what. I found him a touching figure in literary history—

there's this young imagination trapped in the outmoded armor of medieval imagery and allegorical forms. Pivotal people are always rather touching. I think any artist will identify with someone struggling to get out of a cocoon. Of course, he never made it—he's a thoroughly and deservedly unknown figure.

LM: Those allegories of Ariosto and Tasso were in some ways very futuristic with those fantastic voyages—they were almost like SF without the science.

UL: Of course, they didn't really have science to use. But they had a similarly disciplined imagination.

SG: Even in your early works that preceded your entry into SF— like the '50s pieces that would later be incorporated in *The Orsinian Tales*—you were doing something quite different from the fairly narrow brand of social realism that most writers were pursuing back then.

UL: That's maybe why I didn't get published during that period. When it comes to writing, I don't think in abstract terms, such as, Am I going to write a traditional or a nontraditional work? I was in college when I started the pieces that eventually became *The Orsinian Tales*. I was trying to write fiction rather than poetry, which is what I was mainly doing up to that point, and I was stuck in that old formula that everyone always tells you to write about what you know, what you've experienced. This is a terrible thing to tell an eighteen-year-old. What does an eighteen-year-old know? I remember thinking, finally, To hell with it, I'll just make up a country. And since most of what I knew came out of books at that point—I'd read a lot more than I'd done— I made up a place that was like the places in books I liked to read. But as soon as I began work in Orsinia, I realized I didn't have to imitate Tolstoy. I had created a place I could write about in my own terms; I could make up just enough of the rules to free my imagination and my observations. This was a big breakthrough for me—to say, All right, I don't give a shit whether I get published or not, I'm not going to write for anybody but myself; I'm going to make these stories good by standards I set for myself. It was a step out of the trap of feeling that I had to get published right away. It was a step inward that finally led me out.

LM: *The Orsinian Tales* seems very "literary" in an almost nineteenth-century European sense.

UL: They had a literary origin, as I said. I was soaked in the Russian novels from the age of fourteen on. I read and reread Tolstoy and Dostoyevsky, and it's obvious to anyone who's familiar with their work that I've been tremendously influenced by them. Another thing important to Orsinia's development was that I became aware politically. The first thing I really noticed and took personally, from a political standpoint, was the invasion of Czechoslovakia in 1947 by the Russians. That's when I came of age and realized I had a stake in this world. And, of course, if there's any country Orsinia is like, it's Czechoslovakia. It's puzzled me that everyone says Orsinia is like Hungary but nobody mentions Czechoslovakia. Writing about Orsinia allowed me to talk about a situation that had touched my heart, yet I could distance it, which was very important at that time. This was during the McCarthy period, and you can't imagine what it was like. Well, maybe you can, these days, because we seem to be trying hard to bring it back. But in a political climate like that, one's imagination begins to look for ways to say things indirectly, to avoid the polemic, the soapbox. You have to decide whether you're going to be a preacher or a novelist.

SG: Was *Malafrena* written during this same period?

UL: I got the original idea for that book in the early '50s, but for a long time it never worked itself out. I would occasionally find myself doing a bash at it, but it wasn't right and I'd put it away again. I had eventually put it away in despair when some editor asked for something, and so I thought I might as well have another look at it. I had to rewrite it almost totally. This time it seemed to work.

LM: It's amusing that so many reviewers kept saying things like, "With *Malafrena* Le Guin has at last decided to work her way into the literary mainstream."

UL: I was surprised and amused as well. There are whole paragraphs and passages that are very old and hadn't been changed at all. But there were things I needed to rethink entirely. Getting the women characters right. Itale was always OK, the men's story was easy, but I had a terrible time with the women. I didn't understand them. I especially didn't understand what was happening to Piera, the heroine. I know now why: I needed to become a conscious feminist to understand why my women were acting this way and what was happening in their relationships. Without the teaching of the movement of the '70s, I would never have got the book unstuck. So although the general conception of the book was twenty years old and bits and pieces of it remain intact, I can't say *Malafrena* was like one of those books found in the bottom of a trunk; it kept coming out of the trunk and being worked on, and then hurled back in despair. Until I finally grew up enough to write it.

SG: In one of the SF journals, you list literary influences, but the only SF writers included are Philip K. Dick and Italo Calvino.

UL: That's why I'll refuse to give you a list—there are so many people I'd be sure to leave out. Wasn't Borges on that list? How could I have left him out? What I've started doing when people ask who influenced me or whom I like is to say whom I *don't* like. That list is much shorter.

SG: Well, whom *don't* you like?

UL: I don't like Nabokov. I'm told I have to read *Ada* because it's an SF novel, but I can't read it. Boring.

SG: The reason I brought up that list of influences was to see if you'd say that your main literary influences were from outside SF.

UL: I wouldn't say that. It would be silly. Obviously, I have been influenced by SF writers in my SF books. If you're going to write SF, within even a moderately narrow definition of the term, you must have read it. If you haven't, you're wasting your time and everybody else's. There are several mainstream writers who have happily launched themselves into the sea of SF because they see what a glorious field it is; and since they haven't read any SF, they do things that were done forty years ago and have been done a hundred times since—a situation embarrassing for everybody. I've read a lot of SF and enjoyed a lot of it, been influenced by it. I'm an omnivorous reader, except for mysteries, which I can't seem to get anything out of; I can enjoy a Harlequin Romance. And, of course, only snobbery or ignorance apologizes for liking SF anymore, with writers like Philip K. Dick and Gene Wolfe around.

LM: *The Lathe of Heaven* obviously owes something to Dick.

UL: Of course. You could almost call it "Homage à Dick." I was openly, I trust, acknowledging the influence. My approach was like saying, This is one great way to write a novel, invented by Philip K. Dick. That's one thing about SF: writers in the genres are less uptight about imitation and emulation than "mainstream" people. Writing should be really more like music, with its healthy spirit of borrowing— as in the period of Bach, as in all healthy artistic periods. Everybody borrowing from each others' tunes and ideas like crazy and nobody worrying. There's plenty of music to go around.

LM: After you listed your literary influences, you mentioned that music may have had as much to do with affecting your works as fiction. Music occurs in your works in many ways, both directly and, I think, structurally. Could you talk a bit about the way music may have affected your literary sensibility?

UL: I made that comment partially because when people ask you for "influences," they almost inevitably mean literary ones. How silly. It's very probable that listening to Beethoven might influence a writer far more deeply than anything read, but only musicians are asked about Beethoven. The same thing is true, of course, with painting. We really ought to run the arts together more.

LM: We talked about several writers who have made much the same point—that various media, like painting, music, television, the cinema, affect the way they think about fiction.

UL: Right. These other media shape your aesthetic sensibility, your intellectual perception of things. Most of my cognition is via art. I think as an artist. I don't think as a thinker. Very often I don't think in words at all. Cognition often comes to me visually or is heard. The trouble is that we don't have a vocabulary for talking about these things. But except for the very purest types of art, these various inputs are bound to have an effect on the creative process.

SG: Let's talk about the specific creative process that allows you to invent whole universes over time and space. For example, when you began the Hainish cycle, did you have a grand vision in mind? Or did you just invent as you went along and not worry about consistencies, linking things up, until later on?

UL: The so-called Hainish cycle wasn't conceived as a cycle at all: it's the result of a pure economy of imagination. I'd gone to the trouble of creating all these planets in that insane universe ("insane" because nothing alive can go faster than light) and had discovered that it's a lot of work to invent a universe. I certainly didn't want to do that work all over again; it would probably have come out pretty much the same since it's all out of the same head. So each succeeding book was placed in a different time but in the same universe.

LM: So you never sat down and charted things out precisely, the way we assume Isaac Asimov or Robert Heinlein did with their macrohistories?

UL: No. My history is really pretty scroungy. I'm certainly not like Asimov, who I've heard has an office full of charts. Of course, when I'm writing a novel I'm very careful about the world. *The Left Hand of Darkness* and *The Dispossessed* both took a year or so of research and planning. I work out the details of the individual world very carefully beforehand. But I'm not very careful about the connections between the different novels. Those connections have never struck me as important; it's merely entertaining for people to have a reference here or there to other books. On the other hand, I created a very detailed map of Orsinia for myself, with all the distances; I had to know, for instance, how long it would take a coach-and-four to get from one place to another. That sort of internal consistency is, I think, important to most novelists. When you build a world, you are responsible for it. You don't want a coach traveling too far in one day. I want these details to be right. They have to be.

SG: Was the map the first thing created for the Earthsea trilogy?

UL: Yes. At first the map could be adjusted to fit the story. This is the beauty of fantasy—your invention alters at need, at least at first. If I didn't want it to take two weeks, say, to get from one island to another, I could simply move the islands closer. But once you've decided that the islands *are* that far apart, that's it. The map is drawn and you have to adjust to it as if it were a reality. And it is.

LM: Obviously, you must have had to think about the geography of the universe in your Hainish works very differently from the more limited world of *The Orsinian Tales* or the Earthsea trilogy.

UL: Actually, there's no geography at all between the worlds in those books; there's only time. The only thing that's interesting is when each book happened, whether events are taking place before or after other books. Time moves closer and closer to now, after starting way in the future. A critic was the first person to point this out to me. I hadn't seen it, nor do I have the faintest idea why I've been developing the books in that way.

LM: One critic suggests that you deliberately don't set things too close to the here-and-now to distance yourself and your readers from painful subjects. But your two novels, *The Lathe of Heaven* and *The New Atlantis,* and quite a few of your stories, are set right here in Portland—and take place not too far in the future. Is there any conscious reason why you might choose to use a real rather than an invented setting?

UL: First off, that critic was on the wrong track. One thing I've noticed about my settings is that when I have something I really don't want to say but which insists on being said I tend to set it in Portland. *The Lathe of Heaven* and *The New Atlantis* are among the saddest things I've written, the nearest to not being hopeful, and they're both set right here. I don't know the reason for this.

SG: In your National Book Award acceptance speech you said, "I think that perhaps the categories are changing like the times. Sophisticated readers are accepting the fact that an improbable and unimaginable world is going to produce an improbable and hypothetical art. At this point, realism is perhaps the least adequate means of understanding or portraying the incredible realities of our existence." Are you dissatisfied with realism because you feel the world is itself, in a sense, less "realistic," more fantastic? Or does this view have more to do with the formal restrictions that realism imposes on writers?

UL: That statement is several years old. I made my comments aggressive to combat the patronization suffered by the fantastic arts and the critics' tendency to undervalue or brush them aside. My comments were therefore deliberately provocative—SF has been spat upon a great deal—and I was getting back at an attitude I deplore. Anybody who loves Tolstoy as much as I do obviously has a strong respect for realistic fiction.

Let me pursue your question, since it's an important one. I do indeed think that at this point the world is in a degree of flux, is more fantastic than the world of the great nineteenth-century realistic novel. Consequently, the description of what's right here in front of us can end up reading more fantastic than any fantasy. That's surely what García Márquez is doing: simply describing what's happened. So in the National Book Award acceptance I was also trying to say, Don't worry about categories, they're becoming irrelevant, or maybe have always been irrelevant.

SG: One other quote I'd like you to respond to: "Science fiction has inherent limitations which may keep it always on the fringe of the greatest potentialities of the novel." What did you have in mind there about "inherent limitations"?

UL: That quote goes even further back. I was thinking of SF in a fairly narrow definition, the way it was conceived about 1967 or 1968. I wasn't talking about fantasy in general. What I was driving at was simply that SF has certain inherent limitations because no genre is going to break all the barriers the way absolute unlimited art forms can. But I no longer believe first-rate SF can be categorized as genre fiction at all. Take Gene Wolfe's Book of the New Sun tetralogy. He calls it "science fantasy." Is it SF? Is it fantasy? Who cares? It's great.

LM: But when you're at work on a novel, isn't it useful for you to make distinctions between SF and fantasy? *Some* sort of definition would seem to be necessary for the artist to know what the boundaries are, what can be done and what can't.

UL: Yes. I've found that I have to make certain distinctions of this sort for myself. When I failed to do this, as with *Rocannon's World,* I wound up with an uncomfortable hybrid between fantasy and SF. Later on I discovered that I personally do much better when I clearly separate straight SF, like *The Left Hand of Darkness,* from straight fantasy, like the Earthsea trilogy. But that's not true for all writers, many of whom work very comfortably within hybrid forms. And as far as critics are concerned, even Darko Suvin's very intelligent attempts to create a classification system for SF and fantasy don't seem very useful.

SG: While we're on the subject of the ambiguity of labels, the importance of true names runs throughout the Earthsea trilogy. This insistence seems a further extension of the idea in your other works that words are slippery and misleading, that they can lock people into modes of thought that often are removed from the essence of experience. This view of language, which may have some connection with your familiarity with anthropology, must occasionally strike you as paradoxical since, as a writer, you must try to have language serve your purposes as precisely as possible.

UL: I'm constantly struck with the paradox you're talking about. George Steiner says that language is for lying. What language is for is not merely to say that what I'm sitting on here is a chair—if that's all we did with language, what the hell good would it do us? Language is for saying what isn't. This is paraphrasing Steiner rather boldly, but I think it's a marvelous approach to the use of words. As for what it is that fiction writers do: I tell lies for a living.

LM: You've said that *The Left Hand of Darkness* began for you with an image of Genly and Estraven pulling a sled.

UL: No, it wasn't as particularized as that. It was just an image of two people (I don't know what sex they were) pulling a sled over a wasteland of ice. I saw them at a great distance. That image came to me while I was fiddling around at my desk the way all writers do.

SG: At what point in your planning of *The Left Hand of Darkness* did you realize that the inhabitants of Winter were androgynous? They weren't that way in "Winter's King," the story on which you based the novel.

UL: I didn't realize their androgyny until early on in the planning of the novel, long after I'd written that short story. At that point I was trying to figure out what exactly this novel was going to be about, what was going on, who these people were, and so on. I had a vision or mental plan and I was beginning to think about the history of the countries, that sort of thing. As I was going through this planning process, I realized there was something strange about the people on this planet—were they all men? At that point, I said to myself, These aren't all men; they're neither men nor women. And both. What a lovely idea.

LM: Have most of your books and stories begun with the kind of visual image that began *The Left Hand of Darkness?*

UL: They've all begun differently. That image from *The Left Hand of Darkness* is a good one to talk about, though, because it's so clear. Angus Wilson says in *Wild Garden* that most of his books begin with a visual image; one of them began when he saw these two people arguing and he had to find out what they were arguing about, who they were. That fits in beautifully with the kind of visual image that started *The Left Hand of Darkness.* But the others have come to me totally otherwise: I get a character, I get a place, sometimes I get a relationship and have to figure out who it is that's being related.

SG: The sexual implications of *The Left Hand of Darkness* seem to have a lot in common with what feminists have been writing about. Were you much aware of these writings while you were developing your conception of what you wanted to do with that book?

UL: This was back in the '60s, before I'd read any of the feminists, except for Virginia Woolf. *The Second Sex* was out, but I hadn't read it yet, and the rest of the American feminists were just writing their books. *The Left Hand of Darkness* served as my entry into these issues—

issues that all we protofeminists seemed to be thinking about at the same time. Of course, if I wrote that novel today I'd do some things differently, perhaps handle certain issues more effectively and dramatically. But that's no big deal. I did it as best I could at the time.

SG: A number of feminists, including Joanna Russ, criticized *The Left Hand of Darkness* for being too "masculine" in its presentation. How do you respond to that sort of criticism?

UL: As I said, I was writing that novel back in 1967 and 1968, and we've all moved on a long, long way since then. When I'm at work on a novel I'm not trying to satisfy anybody who has a specific program they want propaganda for. I dissatisfy a lot of my gay friends and I dissatisfy a lot of my feminist friends because I don't go as far as they would like.

LM: You've mentioned in several places that you don't so much plan your books consciously as "find them" in your subconscious. Could you talk about what you mean by this?

UL: I'm given something like a seed, a beginning. After that the planning, the intellectualizing, and the plotting take place. Let me try to make this process a bit clearer by going back to that vision that started *The Left Hand of Darkness* because it's fairly easy to talk about. I had this vision of the two people with a sled on the ice—that was the generating seed. Well, I already had found out a lot about the Antarctic by years of reading journals from the Scott and Shackleton expeditions; so first I had to figure out if that vision was occurring in the Antarctic. I realized it wasn't the Antarctic, so I had to find out where they were. And I had to find out who they were. As I began to find that out, I began to think, What exactly am I talking about here? Is this a novel? A short story? A novel starts relating to everything and getting bigger and bigger; if it's a story then it's self-limited and intense, it comes as a whole, so that I have to write it all down as fast as possible.

LM: One of the impressive things about your writing is the way you work out the full implications of the premises of your fictions. I mean, if you have a world in which there are tiny people living in forests— as in *The Word for World Is Forest*—then you carefully work out what the implications would be about these people's language, culture, mythologies, and so on. How do you proceed in developing these details?

UL: It's fiddle, fiddle, fiddle, trying to get all the pieces to fit together. It's an enjoyable process, but one you can't work with very fast. What does it really imply that beings exist in a forest? Are they going to clear it? Cut it? Eat it? When I'm developing a novel, which may take two years of planning, everything's a constant jiggling and resorting and figuring out. This means a lot of note taking for me, because I forget details easily. I also lose notes.

SG: What kinds of fiddling were required in *The Dispossessed?*

UL: That book took me the longest. It began as a crappy short story, one of the worst I've ever written. But I sensed that buried in that ten pages of garbage was a good idea. I can't even remember now what the story was, but the beginning of the character of Shevek was in it; he was a man on a sort of prison planet. This was before I had done any reading of the anarchists; but somehow that failed story led me to them. I read Kropotkin and Emma Goldman and the rest, and finally found a politic I liked. But then I had to integrate these political ideas, which I'd formulated over a good year's reading, into a novel, a utopia. The whole process took quite a while, as you might imagine, and there were hundreds of little details that never found their way into the novel.

LM: *The Dispossessed* seems different from your other books in that it presents a vision of society that you seem to want your readers to consider as an actual possibility. Can anarchism work on this planet?

UL: First off, I don't agree with the distinction you're making—I'm completely in earnest in *The Left Hand* and others in the same way that I am in *The Dispossessed.* But in terms of anarchism, the problem is how to get there. As Darko Suvin has pointed out, all utopias tend to be circular and isolated. They tried an anarchist utopia in Spain in the '30s, and look what happened there. The only trouble with an anarchist country is going to come from its neighbors. Anarchism is like Christianity—it's never really been practiced—so you can't say it's a practical proposal. Still, it's a necessary idea. We have followed the state far enough—too far, in fact. The state is leading us to World War III. The whole idea of the state has got to be rethought from the beginning and then dismantled. One way to do this is to propose the most extreme solution imaginable: you don't proceed little by little; you go to the extreme and say, "Let's have no government, no state at all." Then you try to figure out what you have without it, which is essentially what I was trying to do in *The Dispossessed.* This kind of thinking is not idealistic, it's a practical necessity these days. We must begin to think in different terms, because if we just continue to follow the state, we've had it. So, yes, *The Dispossessed* is very much in earnest about trying to rethink our assumptions about the relationships between human beings.

LM: You chose to set your utopian society, Anarres, in a bleak, harsh landscape. Were you trying to suggest that any utopian society is going to have to abandon the dream of luxury and abundance that we take for granted here in America?

UL: The way I created Anarres was probably an unconscious economy of means: these people are going to be leading a very barren life, so I gave them a barren landscape. Anarres is a metaphor for the austere life, but I wasn't trying to make a general proposal that a utopia has to be that way.

SG: Your use of names has intrigued me ever since I saw your comment that to know the *name* of a person or a place is to know that person or that place. Could you talk about the process that's involved in selecting these names? Obviously, with a name like Genly Ai there must be a lot of conscious decision making going on.

UL: Genly's name is "Henry," evolved in time. What happened to the "h" is what the Russians do, and then the "r" became "l." He first came to me as Genly Ao, but I thought that sounded too much like "ow"—as when pinched—so I decided this isn't right. This selection process sounds mysterious, but it isn't really. One listens. You listen until you hear it, until it sounds right. You go: Eye, I, Aye, Ai . . . and "ai" is *love* in Japanese. What more could you ask for in a name? When something like that comes together, you grab it. But it's not really as if I chose it in a truly volitional, deliberate, intentional sense. It's more as if I opened something and then waited until something came out. A box. Pandora and her box?

LM: You've gone on record a number of times suggesting that the specific meaning or significance of the specific episodes in your works is unconsciously produced. Yet when one looks closely at your books, they usually seem extremely carefully put together—for instance, the mythology or background sections in *The Left Hand* seem to have been created with specific intentions in mind. When you're at work on something, are you really not conscious of the specific implications you're developing?

UL: The tricky bit in answering that question is what you mean by *unconscious*. What I mean when I say that I'm not conscious of certain elements or implications of my work is that I don't have an intellectual, analytic understanding of what I'm doing while I'm doing it. This doesn't mean that I don't know what I'm doing: it does mean that there are different modes of knowing, and the analytic mode is inappropriate to the process of making. As the old song says, "I know where I'm going. . . ." I've got a good intellect, and it was fairly highly trained, long ago. But the intellect has to be kept in its place. As the emotions and the ethical sense and intuition have to be kept in theirs. For me, personally, the intellect plays its major part in *revision,* and also at the very beginning, in disallowing an idea that is inherently stupid or self-contradictory. But once it's served there, the analytic mind must serve other functions during the first draft of a piece of fiction; it cannot be the controlling function. If I were thinking while I wrote of whatever it is the Antarctic means to me, let's say, all those snowy wastes that this California kid is always dragging her readers through, if I were thinking of it as a symbol of something else, let's say Snow is Loneliness or whatever—zonk, I might as well drop it and go garden. And once I know what Antarctica means to to me, I won't need it any longer and will have to find a new metaphor. I'm not saying that self-knowledge destroys creation. I'm saying that, for me, self-*consciousness* vitiates creation. A writer like John Barth deliberately plays with self-consciousness; I doubt that Barth thinks much of my writing, and I don't take pleasure in his, but I know he knows what he's doing and I respect him for it. But I don't work that way. My mode is not to intellectualize about what I'm doing until I've done it. And when it's done I don't want to, because it's done and I want to get on with the new work, with what has to be done next.

SG: I'm among those who feel that the Earthsea trilogy is your best work to date, despite being aimed at a young-adult readership. Did you approach these differently, in any fundamental sense, from your adult novels?

UL: Earthsea is the neatest of all my works. In purely aesthetic terms, it seems to me the best put together. When I started out I said to myself that I didn't see why this kind of book had to be different from any other, except for the commonplace that the protagonist had to be young, or there had to be a young viewpoint character. This viewpoint is simply standard for books slanted for the juvenile, but it wasn't hard at all for someone like me, who can drop back into adolescence without noticing it. After an initial self-consciousness, as soon as I began to see the characters and the plot, I wrote the same way I always had done. I don't know of anything you "do" for kids that is different from what you do for adults; there's maybe a couple of things you don't do. There are certain types of violence, for example, that you leave out, and there's a certain type of hopelessness that I just can't dump on kids. On grownups sometimes; but as a person with kids, who likes kids, who remembers what being a kid is like, I find there are things I can't inflict on them. There's a moral boundary, in this sense, that I'm aware of in writing a book for young adults. But that's really the only difference, as far as my feeling goes.

SG: One of the things that surpised me about Earthsea was the way you explore the function of death in human life—I guess I'd assumed I wouldn't find that subject in a young-adult novel. And your exploration of death is done in what seems such a sensible, reassuring manner. Is that the artist talking? Are you personally that accepting of death?

UL: Not at every moment. Not many critics have been willing to notice that the view presented of life and death in Earthsea is not only non-Christian but anti-Christian. This can't be as reassuring as any view of death that includes a real personal immortality. But, sure, that view was written out of personal conviction. Sometimes the idea of becoming grass is pleasant, sometimes it's not. We all have our night terrors. Those night terrors are one of the things you can't dump on a kid. You can share them—if you're able to—but not dump them. Kids want to talk about death. They are often more willing to talk and think about it than adults.

LM: And, of course, a lot of fairy tales deal with death and violence, although usually in disguised forms.

UL: Disguising things, presenting things metaphorically, is the way you generally do it. You don't force; you don't scream. You don't treat kids that way. The metaphor is the means and the end in one. By metaphor we may evade dishonesty.

SG: At what point in your life did you become interested in Taoism, whose influence seems everywhere apparent in your work?

UL: The old Paul Carus translation of the *Tao Te Ching* was always on the downstairs bookshelf when I was a kid, and I saw it in my father's hands a lot. He was an anthropologist and an atheist; I think this book satisfied what other people would call his religious beliefs. He clearly got a great lifelong pleasure out of this book, and when you notice a parent doing something like this it's bound to have some effect on you. So when I was twelve years old I had a look at the thing and I reacted the same way my father had—I loved it. By the time I was in my teens I had thought about it quite a lot. I was never in the position of most kids in having to break with any church. My father was quite strongly antireligious—his generation of anthropologists more or less had to be. He was respectful toward all religious people, but he counted religions as essentially superstitious. There was a certain feeling among intellectuals of my dad's generation that the human race was done with religion, that religions belonged to the past. That, of course, has not proved to be true.

LM: Despite your disavowal of propaganda, your works can often be seen as responses to specific political and social concerns—the elaborate critiques of current political and sexual attitudes in *The Dispossessed* and *The Left Hand,* the satire of the arrogance of many scientists and politicians in *The Lathe of Heaven,* the Vietnam analogies established in *The Word for World Is Forest.*

UL: Sure, I care about what's going on, and my books reflect these concerns. I just hope my ax grinding doesn't intrude too much. Haber in *The Lathe of Heaven* is an almost allegorical figure of what I most detest in my own culture: people who want to control everything and to exploit for profit in the largest, most general sense of exploit and profit. He's the ultimate, controlling man. And Vietnam was very central to *The Word for World Is Forest,* obviously. I was living in London when I wrote that novel. I couldn't march, so I wrote. I prefer, though, to keep my activism out of my art; if I can march downtown with a banner, it seems a lot more direct than blithering about it in a novel. When I was in London, I couldn't do anything and I had an anger building up inside me, which came out when I was writing that novel. It may have hurt that book from an artistic standpoint.

SG: So you feel there's a contradiction between aesthetic aims and moral ones?

UL: No. Art is action. The way I live my life to its highest degree is by writing, the practice of art. Any practice, any art, has moral resonances: it's going to be good, bad, or indifferent. That's the only way I can conceive of writing—by assuming it's going to affect other people in a moral sense. As any act will do.

LM: How does your worry about ax grinding fit in here?

UL: That's different. By that I mean that I don't want to get on hobbyhorses in my fiction, saying that this is "good" in my works and that is "bad." That kind of moralizing is a bad habit and, yes, I wish I were free of it forever. Such approaches are always simplistic and are usually uncharitable. Taken as a whole, overt moralizing is not an admirable quality in a work of art, and is usually self-defeating.

SG: SF seems to appeal to a lot of Americans who are concerned about the things you write about, who feel that something drastic needs to be done before we blow ourselves up or completely destroy our environment.

UL: We have to thank Ronald Reagan and friends for this mood, maybe. They've scared us. Poor Jimmy Carter, who was perfectly aware of what World War III would be like, couldn't get through to the public. We let him do the worrying for us and then blamed him for our problems.

SG: What happened to Carter seems to reinforce the point you make in *The Dispossessed* that even idealistically oriented programs will inevitably become contaminated by the same power structures they're fighting against.

UL: That's what history, unfortunately, seems to teach us. An anarchistic society inhabited by real people; the imaginary garden inhabited by real toads. As soon as you get real people involved in something, no matter how idealistically motivated they are, everything is eventually going to get mucked up. With people, nothing pure ever works quite right. We're awful monkeys.

LM: Is that why all utopias are, as the subtitle to *The Dispossessed* suggests, inevitably "ambiguous"?

UL: I think so. Besides, I'm rather afraid of purity in any guise. Purity doesn't seem quite human. I'd rather have things a little dirty and messy. Mixed up. Mucky.

During the fall of 1988, Ursula Le Guin agreed to respond by mail to the following questions, which were developed jointly by Larry McCaffery and Sinda Gregory.

Q: While most of your work defies easy categorization, you seem to feel most comfortable writing within SF or fantasy forms. What draws you to these forms?

UL: You're applying terms from the marketplace, and from the hierarchy of academe, with which I am not at all "comfortable." I write in a whole range of forms, from pure fantasy and conventional SF through utopian works, "magical realism," slight displacements of reality or history, to completely realistic or mimetic everyday stuff. I'm not interested in barriers or pigeonholes.

Q: Do you think kids today have a different relationship to fantasy and SF? We're wondering if the constant barrage of ads, TV shows, movies, and comic books may have made SF and fantasy somehow seem less exotic than they were for us.

UL: I agree that kids today get a lot of cheap, mass-produced fantasy thrown at them. The main trouble with this barrage is that it is not only full of violence without pain but is also quite mindless. Intelligence is not involved. However, kids are as tough as ever, and they grow out of this junk. I think young people can be trusted to find as much mystery and wonder as old ones.

Q: In our earlier interview, you commented that at eighteen you were stuck having to "write what you know." This formula is unfortunate for any writer, but especially for young women. SF offers women authors an obvious way out of that trap, since it offers the chance to write about situations that needn't derive from immediate experience.

UL: Yes, I agree that in my generation so-called realistic fiction could be quite difficult for a young woman to write. The modes and expectations regarding "proper subject matter" were not only masculine but were, because of the influences of Hemingway, Mailer, and others, aggressively and grotesquely limited to a macho point of view. All that has changed tremendously and is still changing. It is now possible for a woman to write as a woman, without putting on somebody else's suit of armor. The guardians of the canon don't seem to understand what's going on, but perhaps they will eventually.

Q: Earlier you mentioned that you'd do some things differently if you were writing *The Left Hand of Darkness* today.

UL: As a matter of fact, I had the opportunity to "rewrite" *The Left Hand of Darkness* as a screenplay. The changes mostly involved getting rid of the masculine pronoun and trying to show the androgynous characters as really neither/both in gender, instead of being *perceived* predominantly as men.

Q: You also told us that when you went back to *Malafrena,* you found yourself having a difficult time with the female characters in particular ("I didn't understand them"). What was the source of these difficulties? Are there other characters, even within your completed novels, from which you'd now say you feel dissociated?

UL: What I meant was that the women in *Malafrena* were really the center of the book, and I had not understood that in the first versions. But I don't feel dissociated from characters in any of my books. They are, after all, parts of me.

Q: Joanna Russ has argued about the need of women authors to reinvent (or simply invent) myths and mythic roles for female characters. How would you describe your own strategy for combatting the sense that many literary patterns and forms are male-dominated?

UL: I have no strategies. The work itself is the strategy. Sometimes it's clumsy; sometimes it's effective. The more truly I can write from my own experience, the less I have to worry about being dominated by anybody.

Q: How did *Always Coming Home* evolve for you? For instance, did the Stone Telling sections develop concurrently with the other parts?

UL: Everything in *Always Coming Home* had to take shape concurrently and as a whole. It was a long process and involved getting farther into the world of the book than perhaps any other I've written. I had to learn, quite literally, to think like a person of the Valley. It was in this sense an exercise in being a different person, so it was slow, sometimes a bit dangerous, always intellectually and emotionally extremely demanding. It was, in the book's own terms, a *reversal.* My hope is that the book may have a little of that same effect on the reader.

Q: Did any books directly influence your conception of *Always Coming Home?* We were particularly interested in the relevance of Lewis Hyde's study *The Gift: Imagination and the Erotic Life of Property,* or of any recent feminist texts.

UL: Yes, *The Gift* was one of the many books I read while I was learning my way into the Valley. The most useful sources of all, however, were Native American literary texts. I tried not to exploit Native American material in any way, but it served me as an unfailing inspiration for an ethic and aesthetic native to the western American earth.

Q: Several aspects of *Always Coming Home*—your use of the rainbow as a symbol, the way in which you seem to explore the masculine impulse to attain a certain control of our environment—made us wonder if you intended the book to be, in part, a response to Thomas Pynchon's *Gravity's Rainbow.*

UL: I've never read Pynchon.

Q: We were intrigued with your remarks about the limitation of "influences" questions, which tend to focus exclusively on literary influences. You said then that "these various inputs [from other art forms] are bound to have an effect on the creative process," and that "we really ought to run the arts together more." What kinds of integration did you have in mind?

UL: Well, I can answer this most briefly simply by saying that I seem to be a person who is uncomfortable with artificial barriers and distinctions. Although I'm obviously a verbal artist, and only a verbal artist, all the arts transcend their boundaries, and artists are always collaborating with other artists who use other media. Finding this in any way unusual is in itself unusual. Working with Margaret Chodos on the pictures for *Always Coming Home,* with Todd Barton on the music tape, and more recently with the choreographer Judy Patton and her troupe of dancers and three musicians on a performance of dances from the Blood Lodge—all this has been a completely natural process, a tremendously enriching and, to my delight, a very "Kesh" process of working collaboratively, nonhierarchically—everybody "dancing together."

Q: We see your recent work aiming toward that voiceless (or wordless) experience existing outside human perception.

UL: I'm not aiming toward the voiceless or wordless at all—quite the opposite. A lot of my recent poetry is word play and voice play for live performance or for tape. As I said in a poem a while ago, words are my matter.

Q: Do you employ a different mind-set when you're working with different literary forms?

UL: More and more I find our differentiation of literary forms artificial. Of course, there are differences of technique—the work is different, writing a poem or a novel or an essay—but we really must rethink all this pigeonholing and distinction making. What matters is not the label on the work; what matters is the rhythm of the work, the intensity of the feeling, the integrity of the thought.

Q: Could you talk about the way your poetry has evolved?

UL: Early influences would have been mostly nineteenth- and twentieth-century poets in French and English, through Dylan Thomas but totally exclusive of the Robert Lowell school and excluding many high gods of the pantheon, such as Pound and Whitman. Chinese poetry has been a minor influence on me. I suppose the older poets who've in the long run meant most to me are Victor Hugo, Roethke, Rilke, and Yeats. When I learned that women were writing a new kind of poetry, in this decade and the last, it became an unceasing source of pleasure and inspiration. So is Native American poetry, both from the old oral traditions and that being written by Linda Hogan, Joy Harjo, Wendy Rose, Paula Gunn Allen, and others.

Q: Your work shares with that of many other contemporary SF authors an interest in Oriental philosophy and culture.

UL: We're probably all sharing a similar general intellectual drift. I happened to grow up with Lao Tzu. I read *Tao Te Ching* by the time I was thirteen or so, and it just got under my skin. I think the metaphors in *Always Coming Home,* however, owe far more to Native American art than to Far Eastern—except for that area of permanent Taoism that's in all my books.

Q: *Always Coming Home* seems like a major, cumulative work. Was there a letdown once you'd finished it?

UL: Actually, a work of so much energy leaves you kind of energized, ready to spin off in other directions.

Q: Your work has occasionally been criticized as being, in a sense, "antiscience." But the implications of your fiction appear to emerge from the relativistic and pluralistic approaches associated with contemporary science.

UL: I hope I've never been, and am never, perceived as being in any way "antiscience" in my work. Confusion often arises concerning what science and technology are. For example, I thought *Always Coming Home* was a rather interesting work in the technological mode; I had tried to think out carefully and consistently a highly refined, thoroughly useful, aesthetically gratifying technology for my invented society of the Valley. Being an anthropologist's daughter, I think of technology as encompassing everything a society makes and uses in the material sphere. However, a lot of people now use "technology" simply to mean extremely high-tech inventions that are predicated on and depend on an enormous global network of intense exploitation of all natural resources, including an exploited working class, mostly in the Third World. Technology in this sense doesn't strike me as having much of a future, I must admit.

Q: You're aware that some SF critics and authors have found your work flawed by "optimism" about politics and human nature. What's your response to this reaction?

UL: A shrug.

Q: Many of the features ascribed to postmodern art—self-reflexiveness, the breakdown of genre distinctions, the merging of high and low art forms, metafictional impulses, a more pluralistic or democratic approach to form and language—have their counterpart in SF during the past twenty years. Is this an accident, or do these parallels have their source in larger cultural obsessions?

UL: These parallels are hardly accidental. SF of the last couple of decades has been quite central to these movements and directions of art. But please don't ask me to speculate as to why we artists are doing what we're doing. It's much more important to let us get on with doing it. Very often, the work itself is by far the clearest answer to the question, Why? To analyze the intellectual content of a work of art and talk about its "ideas" is probably a necessary exercise within the university, and quite harmless—until people begin to believe that art *is* ideas. Then the work of art has been impoverished radically. A work of art, whether a painting or a dance or a song or a poem or a novel, is a *thing*. It has the presence and irreducibility of a *thing*. It is an intellectual/emotional/material construct, an object. It may be an object made of words, a rather extraordinary kind of object; but there it is.

Q: In *Always Coming Home* you make a distinction between the "ordinary artist" and the "mysterious artist." To which do you aspire?

UL: The completely ordinary and completely mysterious.

An Interview with

Joanna Russ

It is surely no coincidence that so much important contemporary fiction has been written by women SF authors, such as Ursula Le Guin, Joanna Russ, Octavia Butler, Suzy Charnas, Kate Wilhelm, Suzette Elgin, and James Tiptree, Jr. (Alice Sheldon), and Vonda McIntyre; or that a number of "mainstream" or postmodernist authors have written SF or quasi-SF works—for instance, Doris Lessing's Shikasta series, Margaret Atwood's *Handmaid's Tale,* Carol Hill's *Eleven Million Mile High Dancer,* Monique Wittig's *Guerilleres,* and Marge Piercy's *Woman on the Edge of Time.* There are of course, significant personal, intellectual, and aesthetic differences among all these authors, which account for their individual reasons for choosing to work within SF. But certain aspects of SF's broad appeal to women authors are obvious. Its elasticity as a genre allows women who are interested in gender issues (and those social, political, linguistic, and cultural issues that immediately arise from and attach themselves to gender issues) to invent alien worlds specifically tailored to highlight these issues; to peer into Earth's future and project likely developments of current attitudes; and to juxtapose alternate universes with our own for the purpose of examining contemporary gender roles—and their possible alternatives.

Joanna Russ has probably been the most consistently successful in taking full advantage of the possibilities offered by SF to develop feminist themes. Only Ursula Le Guin rivals Russ in wedding stylistic virtuosity to thematic relevance, but not even she has challenged our gender assumptions—and the fictional norms through which these assumptions are usually reinforced—so often and so radically. An ardent feminist and lesbian, Russ has been a disruptive and controversial figure within the SF community ever since her novel *Picnic on Paradise* (1968; later incorporated into *The Adventures of Alyx* [1976]) was nominated for the Hugo Award. Complex differences underlie the nature of and intent behind the experimental tendencies evident in Russ's work, but they are united by her unwavering attention to freeing her work from the restrictive, male-dominated patterns underlying most SF—and most realistic fiction.

Why Women Can't Write, Russ's important critical study, examines the problems and pressures that have faced all women fiction writers since the rise of the novel—insights she expands and relates to her own work in the conversation that follows. Her critical position and the assumptions guiding much of her best fiction derive from her conviction that women authors who aim at portraying the most salient features of women's lives often write fiction that is typically misunderstood and undervalued by readers whose responses are guided by the assumptions of most realistic fiction—a "realism," Russ argues, that is phallocentrically oriented. What is needed in feminist fiction, she insists, is for female authors to create narrative strategies and develop patterns of heroic action that are appropriate to feminine experience, rather than merely to recycle male models. Her early Alyx stories demonstrate exactly what she has in mind, for Alyx is an utterly independent, fiery, and self-sufficient figure whose aggressiveness, passion, anger, and unwillingness to compromise her own needs and desires set her far outside the norms of the heroines in most SF.

Russ remains best known for *The Female Man* (1975), a complex, witty, thought-provoking study of the multiple selves that exist within every woman. Already acknowledged within and outside SF as a key feminist novel, *The Female Man* contains unusual formal features—its impulse to collage; its blend of ordinary realism, myth, and fantasy; its metafictional devices, including an ongoing dialogue between Russ, her various fictional alter egos, and the reader; and its self-conscious flaunting of literary devices in order to examine the provisional nature of all societal and literary "meanings"—-that are strikingly similar to those found in the postmodernist works of Donald Barthelme, Robert Coover, and John Barth. *The Female Man* deals with a woman (who bears a certain resemblance to Russ herself) who encounters three alternative selves from other universes: a woman from the feminist utopia Whileaway (which Russ first presented in "When It Changed"); a woman from a brutal, radically patriarchal world; and a woman from a world in which gender conflicts have escalated into armed violence. The interactions and juxtapositions produced by these alien encounters with our own culture create contexts that are moving, surreal, troubling, and frequently bitterly funny—and provide a remarkably rich, revealing commentary on sexual politics.

In *The Female Man,* Russ broke new ground for SF with her frank, sensuous descriptions of erotic scenes between women (quite shocking at the time) and her even more controversial depiction, in the figure of Jael, of the murderous, violently aggressive—but usually unacknowledged—responses that the war of the sexes engenders within women. Her intricate, multilayered employment of the familiar "alternate world premise" also demonstrated the way recent SF authors have re-employed some of the genre's stock metaphors for their own purposes. (Other examples of sophisticated uses of the alternate-world premise include William S. Burroughs's *Cities of the Red Night* [1980] and Philip K. Dick's *Man in the High Castle* [1962].)

The Female Man remains Russ's greatest critical and commercial success to date (over 500,000 copies sold in paperback after being rejected as "unreadable" by dozens of mainstream publishers); and this success has tended to obscure the broader range of her accomplishments in short story forms and novels, in criticism and reviewing, in fantasy and SF. Her early experimental novels, *And Chaos Died* (1970) and *We Who Are About To* (1968), for example, employ a lyrical stream-of-consciousness narrative technique to express the perspectives of two alienated castaways; in both cases, Russ's gifts for poetic, sensuous prose and for undercutting genre expectations are impressive. Another ambitious novel is the unduly neglected *The Two of Them* (1976), in which a female agent is sent to rescue a girl whose life in a harem on a quasi-Islamic planet bears close resemblance (metaphorically) to the repressive white-male cultural situation Russ experienced as a youth during the '50s.

In two recent collections of stories, *The Zanzibar Cat* (1984) and *Extra(Ordinary) People* (1984), Russ exhibits mastery of strikingly different moods, modes, and textures. Ranging from brief, Borgesian metaphysical fables, to gothic and fantasy tales (and pastiches of such tales), to reflexive, self-ruminating stories about the limitations of human power and knowledge, these pieces reveal Russ's eye for satiric detail and emotional nuance. They also display a sense of humor and an intellectual balance that her detractors often overlook. *Extra(Ordinary) People,* a series of tightly interwoven tales of interlocking metafictional and feminist concerns, is a particularly good example of the high degree of intellectual sophistication and self-consciousness that characterize the work of the new breed of SF's best authors.

Perhaps because Russ has frequently been portrayed by unsympathetic critics as being "hard-edged," "angry," even "anti-male," I was more anxious than usual when I knocked on her office door at the University of Washington on a wondrous August afternoon in 1986. My fears, however, were unwarranted. It was not Jael, the murderous, ball-busting warrior, who greeted me but a warm, sensitive woman who made me feel instantly at home. Her short hair beginning to gray, and possessed of delicate features, Russ initially impressed me as being physically frail—an impression that was quickly dispelled by her piercing eyes and a sense of inner strength that emerged whenever she talked about those issues that arouse her passion.

Larry McCaffery: Rather than inventing idealized female protagonists who are loving, nurturing, and noncontroversial figures, you tend to create women whose complex, probably more controversial character-istics—including aggressive, even violent personalities—defy the usual gender stereotypes. Are you criticized by feminists for not creating "more positive" role models?

Joanna Russ: Not much. As a literary figure, I'm pretty isolated; I'm not a person anyone is going to attack or defend wildly. What *has* happened is that even before I get criticism, *I've* become aware of problems or faults in my writing. For instance, I knew people were going to criticize the Arabic world in *The Two of Them* as being very racist—the Arab men are always sexist, the women are submissive, and so on. Actually, the world portrayed there is our own world of the '50s, with a kind of window dressing. No reviewer or letter writer saw that—but they should have.

LM: How did that novel get started?

JR: Suzette Elgin's story "The State of Grace" was the most direct source of inspiration. When I finished it, I said to myself, Oh, no, this is just beginning! I wrote to her and asked if I could use that situation as a jumping-off point for my novel. Another important inspiration was a copy of *The 1001 Nights* that I got at a garage sale. It was a very old edition, translated I think by Edward Lane in the '20s, but it absolutely floored me because it was so fascinating. I only got about halfway through it—it's over 1,300 pages long—but I was tremendously impressed. It was a white/Anglo version of a medieval culture, but not the medieval *European* culture I was familiar with; even the language, which was very flowery nineteeth-century English and rather evasive, seemed wonderful. Large blocks of *The 1001 Nights* were formulaic oral storytelling, which very vividly evoked this other time and place, and when I started work on *The Two of Them,* a lot of what I had subliminally absorbed came out. I'm not sure exactly what I would do with the same materials if I were rewriting the book now, but I realize that I need to be careful about falling into the same sexual or racial stereotypes I criticize—the "All Arabs are terrible" kind of thing. The actual medieval Islamic world was quite different from what most Westerners associate with the Arab world today—far more civilized than its European counterpart, for instance.

LM: Don't some of our stereotypes about Islamic cultural attitudes toward sexism, religion, and violence have a grounding in reality?

JR: As much as their stereotypes about *our* violence, sexism, et cetera do. One thing you can see happening there (and it's apparently happening in India as well) is in response to the destruction of their cultures by Western imperialism. Tribal social structures were deliberately shattered, and what emerged was a lot worse. Some of what emerged was very European—like the British attitude about women: "Oh, our women are so much better, they never have to do any work." Recent Arab women writers have pointed out that one of the things of a *genuinely sexually segregated society*—"vertically segregated" is the technical term—is that women spend most of their time with women and men spend most of their time with men. For women, there are genuine advantages to that situation: they're not facing sexist putdowns all the time. Anyway, *The Two of Them* has nothing to do with reality, so in some ways it's a very ignorant, bigoted book.

LM: Yet weren't you partly using this world, conjured up by our own stereotypes and by the world that emerged from *The 1001 Nights,* as a mirror of America?

JR: I hope it's obvious that the world depicted there is transparently America. I do, however, apologize for the mirror. As Marge Piercy points out, women really *are* kept on tranquilizers: ladies really *are* kept as decorative ornaments. A lot of what I transpose to the SF world is simply commonplace in our own society.

LM: By the usual SF "treadmill" standards, you haven't written a lot, at least during the last decade. Does this have to do mostly with publishing difficulties or simply with your need for time to produce something you're satisfied with?

JR: Actually, a fair amount of stuff did come out a couple of years ago: the stories collected in *The Zanzibar Cat,* for instance, the series of pieces in *Extra(Ordinary) People,* and some other things. But for quite a while I had serious trouble with my back and eventually had to have an operation, in 1978; that changed my work habits, since I had to do all my writing (and reading!) standing up. I also had to relearn how to write by hand, which wasn't as easy as you'd think. Those problems, not to mention the pain, made it hard to concentrate for long stretches, so I wrote a lot of reviews, letters, and short stories. I was OK physically for a while, but recently it's been one goddamn thing after another. I've had trouble with my back again, and I now have tendonitis from swimming, which makes its difficult to type. I don't know what it is—maybe I'm just getting old.

But it's also true that my books take a long time to incubate; since I have the luxury of not having to earn my living from my writing, I can allow them to incubate for as long as they need to. They just don't flow effortlessly off my typewriter (or whatever writing instrument I'm using at the time), as they seem to for some authors. For one thing, I revise a lot as I go along, mostly making sure that every paragraph, every sentence, seems right before I move on to the next one; I wind up redoing places, over and over, until I'm satisfied enough to push on. This isn't something I feel the need to apologize for. The idea that every year or two years you're supposed to turn out these new books that are all going to be wonderful and commercially popular is a misguided notion that commerce has foisted upon us. The writing process has a rhythm all its own, and at least for me the rhythm is absolutely different for every book.

LM: Let's talk about *Extra(Ordinary) People,* in which you use an interlocking narrative structure. What interests you about this form?

JR: Part of my fascination has to do with it being, as far as I know, generic to SF. In a sense, furture history stories aren't *really* part of a series—they're both diachronic and synchronic because their elements change from story to story, a kind of variation-on-a-theme approach. Asimov's Robot stories, starting with the ones in *I, Robot,* are a good example of how this works. When you think about it, just about every one of the big SF people have worked with the form at one point or another: Blish's *Cities in Flight* and his trilogy that ended with *Black Easter* and *The Day after Judgment;* Asimov's Foundation trilogy; the many stories that comprise Heinlein's elaborate Future History series. You don't find anything really comparable to these in other literary genres.

LM: When I talked to Samuel Delany about his work with this form—in his Neveryon series—he said one of the attractions was that he could make changes as he went along; he could build on what he'd already done but also *improve* it.

JR: There's always a kind of double play at work as the separate parts unfold, the literal line of the future and the changes the author makes as she goes along. It's a little like the standard verse lines in poetry and the nonstandard breath line, where one is always playing against the other; or like the treble and bass interacting. They're wonderful to work on, intriguing in all sorts of ways, but as it turns out no one has ever done them the way I would like to do them—of course!

That was very much on my mind when I was working on *Ex-tra(Ordinary) People*.

LM: So early on you had in mind a series of interlocking stories?

JR: From the very beginning. When I started, I wasn't sure what my physical condition was going to be (I was afraid I would end up in bed again, unable to finish a novel), so I thought that if I wrote a series of stories, I would at least have the individual stories, even if I couldn't complete the series. But almost immediately I realized that wasn't the point, that the approach could be fascinating. And despite what some people have said, these stories do hang together. Oh, they're still individual stories, and they work perfectly well that way—except maybe the last one, "Everyday Depressions," which functions more or less as a thematic summing up. But all five stories are very strongly related thematically, and they're further connected in that they are all conceived as takeoffs on prior SF motifs and narrative conventions. Of course, comment on fiction (via metafiction) is comment on ideas, which is comment on economics, politics, history—in short, on society.

LM: This sort of self-conscious, metafictional approach is likely to emerge only at a certain point in a genre's development—namely, after enough traditions and conventions have been established so the author can take certain readerly expectations for granted in order to undermine these expectations, to play with them. Your ability to establish a running dialogue with prior SF texts—and the analogous ways people like Delany and Tom Disch and Ursula Le Guin have recently been doing this—suggests that SF has reached this "threshold."

JR: You have to have conventions and rigid symbols and patterns before you can upset them. That I and the others you're talking about do upset things is one of the ways my generation of SF authors is doing something different from what was done before us. It seems to me that this has to do with a leap in subtlety. Indeed, in our work we comment a lot on the rest of the SF field, but to an extent this has been going on for some time—and is bound to happen within any field as closely knit as the SF community has been. What's different about my work, and that of Delany and Le Guin and Disch and some others, is that I'm not doing this in the crude or obvious ways earlier writers did. And the *way* we do it, and the degree of interest we express in it, varies a lot. Disch really has abandoned the meta-approach, for example, and seems interested in other things. Delany says, "Well, suppose all this stuff in the Golden Age—the stuff someone like Doc Smith writes about—really happened. What would it *really* be like?" I think I go a step further, or maybe it's just a step in another direction, by suggesting that what's different about these most common SF structures, from what the earlier SF writers said they'd be, is that they are dramatically *opposed* because literature *is* social mythology, among other things. And that's inextricably involved with all sorts of social forces.

LM: The process seems to have a lot in common with what Robert Coover, John Barth, and other postmodernists have been doing: going back to certain popular myths and metaphors and re-examining what they really mean. Typically, such authors discover that these situations no longer seem relevant to our experience, so they turn them upside down, reformulate them as new shapes with new meanings.

JR: Revision, self-criticism, change—all these are essential for any art form to maintain a sense of vitality. Take the hidden-telepathic-community storyline, which has been done by Zenna Henderson and dozens of other people I can't even remember. An offshoot is the story about a mutated being who searches out similar mutated beings— Olaf Stapledon's *Odd John* or Theodore Sturgeon's *More Than Human* grow naturally out of the same motif. What would these people really be like? In "The Mystery of the Young Gentleman," I twist the strands of the story into the hardest knots possible. It was Coleridge who said of John Donne that he twisted iron pokers into knots. The idea that artists should be willing to push something as far as it will go, until they watch it *crack,* has always appealed to me. One reviewer called my technique "piezoelectric," which is exactly right. Just about anything will change shape under that kind of pressure, literary structures being no exception. What I found myself doing in *Extra(Ordinary) People* was seeking out *very* commonplace ideas, *very* ordinary story lines and assumptions, and doing something else with them. The only one that remains in any way banal is "Souls," the opening story, which I use as a science fictional introduction to the series. After that they get hard.

LM: The brief exchanges at the end of each story seem to act almost as glosses—comments that turn everything upside down, that reverse our expectations.

JR: In effect, I use the ending to state the central premise and then undercut it. Again, this is a musical device: establish a central, familiar melody, and then create something that plays off it. If you look carefully, you can see that I've always done this kind of thing, at least in my novels. I'm nearly always aware that there's counterpoint between what I'm presenting and what "should be" happening, based on the established confines of the premise I'm working with. If I weren't aware of this kind of tension, what would be the point? People accept all sorts of attitudes—about racism, sexism, and class—simply because they don't have the time or the energy to think these things through. It's easier to accept the status quo, especially if you're part of a privileged group and want to think well of yourself. So one way to make people aware of how morally atrocious and even downright *stupid* many of their assumptions are is to confront them with a pattern whose meaning they *think* they're comfortable with—and then to undermine the whole thing, forcing them to see how arbitrary and wrong they've been.

LM: "What Did You Do during the Revolution, Grandma?" seems to use reflexivity and the fiction-within-fiction device in much the same way as Jorge Luis Borges, Vladimir Nabokov, and John Barth—to force readers to question the "reality" of our own world.

JR: I don't do what Borges or Barth (perhaps) does—that is, call into question anything about the reality of real life—and I don't really think Nabokov has done that either. His themes are exile, loneliness, and isolation, from which art is an escape and to which he usually returns the reader at the end of the book, as in *Pale Fire.* I'm certain— often painfully certain—that real experiences *are* real. They're far too refractory not to be. The reality I call into question is not that of life but that of fiction, and I do it (as Nabokov sometimes does) to emphasize that fiction is fictive, artifactual, a communication between persons. For instance, it should be more obvious in "What Did You Do during the Revolution, Grandma?" than in the other stories that this is directly about SF—it's also about fantasy and cultural mythology, of course— in fact, you'd have to be pretty dumb not to notice that it's not really a medieval world; among other things, it's today's America. But emphasizing the story's status as fiction doesn't render reality unreal; rather, it emphasizes that life/actuality *is* real and that stories aren't.

LM: Still, there's the troubling sense in America that people are often engaged with the "realities" of images, computer graphics, abstractions, the convenient fictions of politicians, economists, historians. How "real" is the "real America" we live in, what with an actor-president?

JR: America is perfectly real. It's our social controls, human ideas, our way of explaining and justifying situations to ourselves that are not true or not complete or fake or made up.

LM: In "Everyday Depressions," the last story in the collection, you project yourself into the work fairly directly.

JR: I intended that story to more or less wrap up the collection, to bring the reader back to the present, just as I had done with the Alyx stories, where I put things into a closed, four-dimensional form I described as a "Klein Bottle." I implied that the heroine was going to grow up and write all these other stories, or think up all these other stories, which playfully introduced the issue of reality's fictional basis (and vice versa!). "Everyday Depressions" does much the same thing. It emphasizes the artifactuality of the fiction—and hence its communicativeness, its status as idea, thought, significance. In *The Second Inquisition,* emphasizing the fictionality of the rest emphasized the tragedy of the last story in the series—the timeworn shift from laughter to tears.

LM: That's a shift Nabokov makes at the end of *Invitation to a Beheading* and *Bend Sinister:* by suddenly seeing the author confront the fiction he or she has created, we see the world around us differently.

JR: Right. When Nabokov turns up in the last sentence of *Pale Fire,* we see the author—a bigger phenomenon than any character in the book—awaiting mortality, that "bigger Gradus." The changes in tone that accompany such shifts of attention or such dissolution of fiction are almost always from comedy to tragedy, laughter to tears, a sudden deepening, saddening, made more serious by the shift to a tone that corresponds to actuality. It's putting things back into the reader's lap. All serious fiction, in the sense of something that wishes to be more than escapism or vicarious whatnot, does this. I'll never understand the kind of writer who genuinely advances the proposition that life is a dream or a fiction. To me that's the voice of privilege, whether it's money, class, sex, color, or what have you. Most of us can't find refuge in anything so false.

LM: Did "Everyday Depressions" really evolve from your thinking about writing a gothic lesbian novel?

JR: Yes. I had all these things lying around that I was going to write, and this story was what I wrote when I realized I wanted to use the materials I had, but not for a novel. I had seen a gay male gothic novel called *Gaywyck* with this striking gothic cover—you know, the mansion in the background with the lit window, the two people in the foreground, one of them dark and brusque and male, the other one delicate, blonde, petite—and male! I thought, This is the ultimate comment on clichéd commercial covers and the expectations they set up. I loved it; it was one of the funniest things I'd ever seen. And I immediately decided I'd write a lesbian gothic piece that would use clichés and undercut them in much the same way. The first thing I thought of was *Lady Sappho* "in curly gold letters"—just the way "Everyday Depressions" opens. I spent three or four weeks playing with the plot until I got to the point where I realized that I didn't like what I was doing, that I was going to die of boredom! It was too much work; there were too many schlock elements that had to be worked in; it just wasn't interesting to me. Then it occurred to me that I should leave it in the shorthand form I had in front of me, since that was the form it obviously wished to be in.

LM: That sounds like Borges or Stanislaw Lem: save time by summarizing the novel you could have written.

JR: Exactly. Why drag it out? Writers do it all the time. It's like painting cereal boxes—you get this gleeful feeling of "Let's take this object and do a representation of it, not try for an identity."

LM: This "representation quality" is reinforced throughout *Extra(Ordinary) People* by the framing devices you use. There's very little direct action being reported.

JR: In fact, all the pieces in *Extra(Ordinary) People* are told to some other character directly or in a letter. Since these stories explore the way SF stories have been told, it seemed appropriate to have them framed by these literary conventions. The message is: Think about what I'm saying. "Souls" begins, "I tell it not as it was told to me but as I saw it, for I was a child then. . . ." And the second story, "The Mystery of the Gentlemen," is a letter. I think there are some interesting formal issues in these framing devices. For instance, using the epistolary convention immediately brings up the question, What do people *not say* when they're writing a letter to a friend? Well, you certainly don't say that you're female or male; and you don't say your age or any number of other things about yourself and about the person you're writing to—like "I'm telepathic, as you know, because you are too"—because these sorts of things are taken for granted when people write to each other. Which leads to questions about what people take for granted in general, what they think about, what they don't notice.

LM: Your narrator in "Bodies" says, "Goddamn it, writing isn't talking."

JR: And it's not. But *how* isn't it? That's why there's that admission, "Look, James, this isn't going to be an easy letter to write." I was aiming to cue readers in from the outset that the form was going to be part of the drama—a letter to a specific person that would be difficult to write because of the relationship between two people, because of what was going to be said, and because what was going to be said would be conveyed through the conventions of letter writing. By the time I started "Everyday Depressions," I was very conscious of this format and chose to write the story as a letter to a real person, a very good friend of mine, a feminist scholar named Susan Koppelman. So it began, "Dear Susanillamilla," because I use nicknames for friends. And I just wrote the thing out as if I really were writing a letter.

LM: That reminds me of the way Delany plays with epistolary forms in his Neveryon series—you know, where he includes in his appendixes letters from real people to the characters in his books (or was it vice versa?).

JR: Sure, and that device—creating a fictional letter addressed to a real person, a letter that possesses all the formal features of a real letter—shows how very flexible this form can be in terms of what you're going to put in and leave out. Really, being able to play around with this form let me finish the book. I can't imagine writing that kind of fiction straight; it would kill me with its falsity and its simplemindedness. That's why, near the end of the last story, I wrote what became a comment on the whole utopian theme: "Oh, teacher, what will save the world?" My conclusion in the book is: Nothing. Save the world from what? I don't know. What is life in the first place? Is it anything? Who invented it, and when? Why does it always turn green in the wash? *Does life exist?* Well, yes, it does. Life is—it's like this and that and nothing and everything. What makes anyone think the world has ever been saved? The situation I describe is very sad, even though the living in the stories is, I think, entertaining and exciting; these people have a lot of pleasure and satisfaction, a lot of joy, but that doesn't mean their world has been "saved." Maybe you just can't *do* that. Life is life. Life is mixed and sometimes horrible—but sometimes wonderful.

LM: This self-conscious pointing to the limitations of certain specific literary genres and conventions—say, the misguided assumptions of utopian fiction—is a good example of how metafictional approaches often force readers to re-examine the way they relate to the world outside the page—a point that often gets lost when critics discuss metafiction.

JR: Absolutely. It becomes a way to return the reader to the world. That's very much what I wanted to do at the end of *Extra(Ordinary) People,* to put everything in the reader's lap: This is the way of the world—and what are *you* going to do about it? Years ago I did an analysis of literary propaganda, what I called "polemical fiction," works like *Rubyfruit Jungle* and *Invisible Man.* I don't know if it had to do with the nature of the medium itself, but I found that plays by Shaw or Brecht and movies like Eisenstein's *Battleship Potemkin* could deal more easily with propaganda than fiction could. At any rate, all political propaganda generally ends the same way: it's yours now; this thing isn't over; I can't tell you what finally happened because it hasn't finally happened yet! This is always a problem when you write anything with real social or political consciousness—what you're describing *hasn't ended.* I suppose this is true, in a way, of all fiction. Some nineteenth-century fiction, like Thackeray's, used to do this by having the work conclude, "And so, children, the play is played out. The puppets are placed back in the box." Even "They all lived happily ever after" is an acknowledgment that somehow everything is moving away from the reader into that imaginary space. This sense of fading, of going away— the cowboy riding off into the eye of the sunset—suggests that something is pulling the fiction away from the merely illusionary—which isn't the case so much at the end of a short story but is often true with a book. Recognizing this and using it is very important for the artist. We need to force the reader always to come back to where we all are. Otherwise, it's pure game playing, escapism. And you fall out with an awful shock.

LM: In a number of your works you've teased readers about the relationship between the "real" Joanna Russ and your various fictional incarnations. I sense that you do this to remind readers that there are real associations between your literary texts and reality—that your works are not conceived as "pure entertainment."

JR: Exactly. I'm not saying that everything I write evolves out of didactic intentions; in fact, the distinction between didacticism and pure entertainment is nonexistent. What matters is how hard you have to think or feel and how anti–status quo those thoughts and feelings are. I usually have only a vague idea about a plot, sometimes accompanied by a notion of how I might do something interesting with forms. In most cases, though, I don't really know where I'm going until I get there; I don't work from outlines and in fact I structure things beforehand only generally—for example, I might know in advance that I want to create a confrontation between two characters. Still, I'm aware when I'm writing that I want to bring the readers in line with my feelings and thoughts—that's one reason why I sometimes let down my authorial disguises (or pretend to). All fiction, I think, is very much *of* the world. In the '50s, when I was in college, there was this absolute opposition between life and art, and that's utter nonsense.

LM: In your essay "The Aesthetics of SF," you say that SF is a didactic form *by definition*. Doesn't your claim that you don't sit down with didactic intentions clash with the didactic demands of SF?

JR: Not at all. A good writer, no matter how intent on making a point, never simply sits down and says, "This is my theme. Now how am I going to illustrate it?" Good writing, even the most heavily message-laden writing of Shaw or Brecht or whomever, doesn't come that way. My writing comes to me first of all *as fiction*, as an art form with aesthetic demands. As Eric Bentley said of Shaw, there's an art to preaching: the preacher doesn't sympathize with the audience but chides them. Part of the whole form of didactic writing involves aesthetic decisions: knowing how to use the formal means at your disposal to make your point in the way most likely to convince the reader. These are not trivial considerations. The realistic novel has its own assumptions, its own positions vis-à-vis the reader. Historically, it's quite different from, say, the Greek epic or medieval romance. There are many forms of fiction, and each utilizes different conventions, different metaphors (and deforming metaphors!) and motifs for its own purposes. Look at *Star Wars:* "pure entertainment" that ends up saying very reactionary things precisely because it wants to avoid saying anything serious!

LM: In many ways, SF has more in common with the forms that spawned it—the epic, the fable or allegory, the Renaissance travel/ adventure story, the gothic romance, and so on—than it does with the realistic novel.

JR: The novel was *not* developed to deal with collective concerns or even typical concerns. It can deal with these indirectly, of course, but the novel was developed specifically to portray individual histories—

LM: —while SF's strength is in presenting group concerns, collective myths and fears that critically reflect the world around us.

JR: Absolutely. SF was born didactic! It originated as a teaching medium—which is why its potential to actually effect some changes in people's attitudes is infinitely greater. It's got representative protagonists, for example—at least it starts like this in the works of H. G. Wells, Jules Verne, and other proto-SF writers. If you look at, say, *The War of the Worlds,* the human beings there may represent certain attitudes or types, but they are obviously *not* "individuals" in the sense that characters in the great realistic novels are. You see the same thing in horror stories, because the attitude or position they're trying to present is typical of human psychology or experience, not of individual history.

LM: You dedicated *And Chaos Died* to S. J. Perelman and Valdimir Nabokov, who was at Cornell when you were. Was Nabokov an early influence?

JR: I liked (and like) his playfulness, his wit, his sense of pain, his fear of and astonishment at life. His influence is there in my work, then and now—his views about literature and reality, for example. But when I'm asked influence questions today, I'm almost embarrassed by how brainwashed I used to be about which authors I could acknowledge as having affected my work. So I dedicated *And Chaos Died,* which was my second book, to the two males who were my "real influences." What I had difficulty admitting, even to myself, was that the books that profoundly shaped my literary sensibility—the novels of the Brontës, which I ritualistically read and reread all through my teen years, or of Virginia Woolf, which I devoured guiltily (they were "too feminine")— had influenced me as much as they had. As for Nabokov's views about literature and reality, I can agree with what he said about how unhappy living can be and how imagining and thinking can be a refuge. Nabokov always made the point (which some litterateurs seem to forget) that literature *is* real life, as real as anything else; it's part of living and it provides a commentary upon the world, a metaphorical model of what goes on around us. I love the idea of literature-as-model because life is full of pictures, blueprints, representative designs of different experiences and things. Horror stories are full of images of that sort.

LM: Even some of your earliest works, like the Alyx stories, *And*

Chaos Died, and *We Who Are About To,* proved to be nontraditional SF, manipulating familiar SF motifs. For instance, did you choose the castaways motif in *We Who Are About To* in order to expose how ludicrously it's usually handled?

JR: I was poking fun at that tradition, sure. I didn't think about the connection when I wrote the book, but the whole Robinson-Crusoe-and-the-desert-island business is, at bottom, an imperialist myth: you find a place "out there" and you make it *yours,* whether the people who already live there want you to or not. This goes on in SF all the time—you can see it in Marion Zimmer Bradley's Darkover series, for instance. I'm not interested in that notion. It's been obvious for at least twenty or thirty years now—certainly since the '60s to us white folks—that it's simply not a good attitude for people to take. And, of course, if you were really put in that situation, I'd think you'd do amazingly well just to stay alive.

LM: In *We Who Are About To,* one of the main ways you subvert convention is by showing that things aren't likely to go easily.

JR: These are ordinary, urban, well-to-do, very specialized people. It follows that they'd have a hard time in those circumstances. Reviewers called me a pessimist and didn't like what I had done, but I thought my intent was perfectly obvious. A lot of reviewers froth at the mouth whenever someone takes a hallowed situation and refuses to reinforce all the usual capitalist, imperialist, Americans-can-do-anything attitudes associated with it.

LM: Certainly, the basic impulse of several of your works—*We Who Are About To, And Chaos Died, Picnic on Paradise*—seems anti-utopian.

JR: I'm not anti-utopian in spirit. I'm just not so naive as to think that people can discard who they are. My point isn't that utopia is impossible—I think "Bodies" presents a real utopia—but that creating it isn't as simple as most SF implies. The whole premise of finding a virgin land in which people can leave behind the past and start all over again just isn't workable. In "Bodies," the people are much better off in utopia than they were in the twentieth century, and they know it; but that doesn't mean all people will be satisfied living in utopia. In a way, the woman writing that letter is filled with anger, even as she loves where she is. I made the man carry the weight of gay oppression and I gave the woman the burden of mortality. What I was driving at is that people will never be totally at home, spiritually, in *any* environment. The very things that make you wretched in your own society are also the things that are inextricably part of you, that you are most comfortable with—the things that make you *happy.* So the jump into utopia in most SF *is* impossible.

LM: You seem to be very critical of this world—and of utopian assumptions produced by SF writers—so why not propose your own version of a perfect society? Is it because a perfectly harmonious world might be boring from an aesthetic standpoint?

JR: I think most SF writers today would agree that describing that kind of world isn't very interesting, though it's a natural for lyric poetry. How could you generate any tension, or create the conflicts that usually move a narrative forward? Maybe this is why, in the last twenty years or so, writers have shifted their emphasis away from the "perfect society" to the "somewhat better society"—I think someone has coined the word "optitopia." This shift has to be for the good because it suggests that we're trying to write something that's closer, more intimately related to actual human possibilities. Of course, we have the advantage today of having witnessed the failure of some of these attempts to put utopian theory into practice. And the aims of those earlier fictions were not the same—works like Bellamy's *Looking Backward* usually concentrated on the effects of change in a single area. What has happened with Disch and Le Guin and Delany and me and some of the other people you've been talking to is that our education and training are not in a single area; that is, even though we've been trained in science or social theory or whatever, we're writers first.

LM: You apparently decided from the beginning to write SF and fantasy rather than, to use Delany's phrase, "mundane fiction." What was it about SF that appealed to you?

JR: First of all, I loved SF when I discovered it—I was about thirteen at the time. I read everything I could get my hands on—books, magazines, everything. I also liked horror fiction when I was in my teens, and I've written a good deal of that. But SF potentially has a freedom that most other fiction doesn't have. When I started writing, I was convinced that I didn't know much about "real life." In college I got a very good education in literature—at least from a technical standpoint—but it was completely male-oriented (there wasn't a single woman permanently in Cornell's English department at the time). I was constantly reading these stories about fucking in bars and fistfights and war, and my reaction, quite naturally, was that I didn't know anything about those things so I couldn't possibly write about them. And the stuff I *could* write about was considered trivial—writing about a fishing trip was considered "deep" and "raw," while a description of a high school dance was unimportant. There really was a profound bias about what was proper material for "Great Writing." So I decided to write about something nobody knew anything about—to transform the realism of my life into SF and fantasy. I was also drawn to the way SF writers' minds seemed to work. Current fiction bored me stiff, but not SF, where the *conceivable* was far larger than the personally observable. It's interesting to note that so-called mainstream fiction seems finally to be catching up to SF in this regard; it's becoming increasingly unrealistic, surrealistic, fantastic, "postrealistic." I feel justified.

LM: You said that one of your attractions to SF was the aesthetic freedom it offered. Why have you stuck more with SF than with fantasy forms? Wouldn't fantasy offer even more freedom?

JR: Fantasy forms offer less freedom, not more, because they are strictly regulated by the conventions from which they emerge. At least this is true in the kind of fantasy I like and the kind I write: vampires, werewolves, Dracula, elves, gremlins, haunted houses. The point is that you're continually caught up in all sorts of restrictions. You're immediately working with a fictional landscape that is very familiar—and hence very restrictive. Even the symbols you'll want to employ are going to be very familiar.

LM: What about fantasy writers who ignore the rules, like Franz Kafka or, a more extreme example, Raymond Roussel? Isn't it possible for a fantasy writer to make up his or her own symbols and narrative logic?

JR: Then they're doing Borges's trick: a kind of surrealism. It's precisely that commonality of echoes or resonances around a central figure or symbol that really makes fantasy work. Take it away and you're left with a bunch of strange events and strange people—and no unified effect. For example, it's now known that Kafka, who used to be considered such an absolutely anomalous artist, was working out of a clearly defined tradition of Yiddish fantasists; in fact, he used culturally central material, but in subtle and sophisticated ways. A lot of the current fantasy does try to invent its own rules on the spot, but I don't like it, don't understand it, and for the most part don't pay any attention to it. Most of Stephen King, for example, seems to be what I call "gore stories"—they're not fantasy or horror stories; they're not like the good old-fashioned nineteenth-century stories of Poe, Lovecraft, and others who used horror and fantasy as a means of projecting psychology outward. (Some people have called them "inner spacemen," which is a nice phrase.) But even with this inner-space fantasy, the rules you must observe are far more rigorous than they are in SF. I'd characterize horror fiction as "narrow but deep," whereas SF, which cannot be so psychologically focused, tends to be expansive, allowing authors more room to play.

LM: Marge Piercy points out in her introduction to *The Zanzibar Cat* that your short fiction relies more often on fantasy premises than on SF per se. Is that because fantasy forms are more economical in allowing you to get right into the story without having to support the action realistically?

JR: I wasn't conscious of this distinction at the time, but what I've just said helps explain why I might use fantasy more often—but only in my short fiction. Precisely because SF does tend to be so wide and expansive, it takes, technically, a great deal of deftness to create real SF in a very short form, at least nowadays. Until recently SF did exist in short forms. Even the novels written from the Golden Age up until the '50s were very short. My novels, you'll notice, are short: I just don't find it possible to write the long SF works that other people in the field seem to turn out effortlessly. Such novels are very difficult to do right—most of these long novels, of course, are bad—and usually the premise or story line just wears out. One of the demands of any good SF novel is to continually invent new details, which is a strain, since you can't just look outside your window or thumb through a history book when you need details. Heinlein writes short novels and is able to do so inventively. A lot of contemporary writers will set everything up in chapter one and then after that it turns into a banal adventure story. In a short story I can't usually put in everything that ought to be there to satisfy my own feeling for interrelationship and complexity. By the time I got to *Extra(Ordinary) People,* I was consciously compressing everything just as much as I could. Part of this had to do with shifting from typing to writing by hand because of my back pain. One of the things that standing up and writing by hand forced me to think about was *compression*—making every word say something. I had to stop looking at what I was writing and start hearing it in my mind. It was good discipline for me to pare everything down, to put new information into every single word.

LM: This approach requires readers to adjust their reading habits. Has this been a problem?

JR: I've heard complaints from readers, sure. They have to be on their toes every single second, otherwise they'll get lost, and most SF readers come to a book expecting to read it as fast as they would, say, a Harlequin Romance or an ad, where everything is said and said and said and said. Well, I only say it *once.* I'd been moving in this direction long before my back troubles. Fifteen years ago I very consciously decided that, except for musical or structural reasons, my principle would be: Say it only once. Don't repeat!

LM: Despite the freedom offered by the form of the genre, doesn't the fact that SF is such a commercial field produce a lot of pressures not to take chances? I'm thinking of the difficulties a really adventurous figure like Philip K. Dick had in gaining an audience.

JR: I'm very aware of how lucky I've been. A lot of things have allowed me to be adventurous in my work, and certainly the fact that I haven't had to rely on my writing to earn a living has helped me take more chances. It takes a special type of person, like Philip K. Dick, to be artistically adventurous in the face of economic precariousness, starvation. It's interesting, for example, that until recently so many European writers seemed to get better and better as they grew older. Some of this must have to do with the fact that they had a public all along, or could make a living from writing or didn't have to. George Eliot, Dickens, Tolstoy—one can see their development. But American writers always seem to be facing that pressure of commercialism, which actively prevents them from getting better. So our writers' careers tend to be the reverse of what you find in Europe. You see a lot of examples like Melville, where someone starts out achieving popular success with relatively conventional stuff and then develops more daring, sophisticated stuff; but once they create these innovative works, they stop selling and eventually stop writing. The realization that they can't make a living from their best writing destroys them as writers (or, as in Fitzgerald's case, they destroy themselves physically). They're like lyric poets are supposed to be: someone once said that lyric poets sing the songs of their youth out of tune or they fall silent. Novelists haven't tended to do that in Europe; they're like painters in that they've been genuine technicians as well as artists.

Being such a late bloomer—I was almost thirty when I wrote my first novel, *Picnic on Paradise*—was another thing that made it easier for me to take chances artistically. A lot of women writers tend to get started late, and this may help put things in perspective. Carol Emshwiller is a good case in point. She says she learned early on that writing was not for her, and that after she was out of school she spent ten years consciously *not* writing. I know that when I started writing, at first I was mainly just playing with this stuff that I had loved as a kid. Gradually, though, I got to the point of saying, Yes, I do love this stuff but now I've *done* it and it's starting to seem too dull, too safe. Luckily I was in a position where I didn't have to be afraid to go ahead and try out some of these other approaches. It's a lot harder if you know your livelihood for the next few months or years is going to depend on how many copies the book you're working on sells.

LM: Has the relative popular success of, say, Delany and Le Guin made it easier to publish serious SF these days?

JR: Oh, my God, *no!* If anything, it's harder to get my books published today, and it's been getting harder all along. Look at the economics of the big conglomerates. I suspect part of my personal "problem," if you want to call it that, is the feminist political orientation in my books—and the lesbian overtones haven't helped, either. But the so-called difficulty of my books is still a major obstacle. One editor wrote me and said, "I just don't *understand* this book!" so I lost my temper and wrote back—I'd never done this before—"All right, I'll explain it to you! I'm *tired* of this!" My anger in this instance was an accumulated response to all the letters I'd gotten from editors for a long time saying, "Send us your next book. We thought your last one was wonderful." So I'd send them my next book and they'd write back, "Oh, unfortunately we found this book to be a little too weird, we don't understand it, so we've decided we don't want it." Eventually this weird book would find a publisher, it would be praised to the skies by reviewers—and the reviews would prompt new letters saying, "Send us your next book, we thought your last one was wonderful!" After a while, you get sick of that crap!

LM: It's ironic that two of the most "difficult" and controversial SF novels ever published in this country—your book *The Female Man* and Delany's *Dhalgren*—have been two of the biggest sellers. Once these books were allowed to cultivate an audience, they seem to have acquired an ongoing readership, much the way other "difficult" books by Faulkner or Pynchon or Virginia Woolf have. SF publishers don't seem to let that happen very often.

JR: I don't think publishers really know what they're doing. You can't treat books like tomatoes. The difficulties I've had in placing my books has occurred despite the fact that they are selling better and better—they've never bankrupted anyone. I've heard that in the series of SF books Fred Pohl edited for Bantam, the only two that ever made any money were the two you just mentioned.

LM: Didn't *The Female Man* sit around for several years before Pohl accepted it?

JR: Yes, although that wasn't Pohl's doing. I'll give him credit: the minute he saw *The Female Man,* he bought it. The problem there wasn't the SF publishers—my agent was trying to place it with a commercial house for a few years. I remember the answers we kept getting from these idiotic people, usually along the lines of "We've already published our feminist novel this year, so we don't want another." One editor even wrote back saying, "I'm sick and tired of these kinds of women's novels that are just one long whiney complaint!" It's also important that women writers who have already established a reputation outside SF—I'm thinking of people like Marge Piercy, Doris Lessing, Margaret Atwood—can get their SF novels published by commercial houses, whereas those of us who have been branded as "SF authors" find it difficult to get our books looked at seriously.

LM: Aren't there enough women in editorial power these days to assure you of getting a sympathetic reading with some regularity?

JR: Women remain pretty low in the editorial hierarchy. And since most of them don't wield the *real power* in book publishing any more than they do in most other power structures, you find that, quite ironically, most women shy away from making controversial decisions. That's why it's not too surprising that it's been a man—David Hartwell, a very good editor—who's been most adventurous about buying feminist SF. The bottom line is that editors are encouraged to make judgments based mainly on whether or not they think something will make money. Most of these editors, unwisely I think, assume that readers don't want to be challenged.

LM: My experience is that a lot of people not familiar with SF— say, the editors at most commercial houses—have a difficult time evaluating *any* SF work because they quite literally don't know how to read it.

JR: This is often just as true of a professionally trained book editor as with college-age students encountering literature for the first time. You usually have to teach people how to read SF. Readers have unconsciously assimilated prejudices and assumptions about how fiction is "supposed" to work. If they encounter a text that starts off, "So when I came down from the North Pole to my communal family home, and then hopped over to a hut in Queensland," they will inevitably say, *"What?"* Delaney is right in his argument that SF texts *are* different from straight fiction: the language in SF functions differently, the conventions are different, the sorts of expectations you bring to these texts are different, the kinds of inferences readers have to make are different. SF provides a wonderful, open-ended possibility to authors in the way they can use language, but most people literally don't know how to read this language. For example, in the past, some academics misread "Heavy Planet," a Jovian story, as a nightmare; they were unaware of the accuracy of the background and the delight in this as the story's point.

The same thing can be said about ignorance concerning SF's history and conventions, which has led even well-intentioned academics to try to bring SF works into "respectablity" by claiming that they deal with the same subjects as mainstream fiction and use many of the same techniques. That's not true, and encouraging readers and scholars to read SF and make evaluations about it, based on this other set of values, is as self-defeating as trying to evaluate the work of Blake or Melville or Woolf or Anaïs Nin on the basis of Egyptian papyri. Women's writing has suffered from this sort of reading all along, since so often it's taken certain shapes and used certain techniques the critics—most of them male—aren't used to. Thus, the visionary strain you see in Emily Dickinson or Charlotte Brontë or Woolf or even Louisa May Alcott is often seen as failed realism.

LM: In one of your essays you say that you don't see SF ever becoming a major literary genre. Is this partly because so much background is required before readers can be expected to appreciate what's happening?

JR: Most serious SF is too intellectual a form for most readers to be able to respond to. It's a highly analytic, critical, intellectual form. Readers approaching SF have to read with a dual vision, a split consciousness of the writing's action and critical stance, and most readers simply don't want or don't know how to do that. Even educated readers in our culture certainly aren't trained to read that way. They could be, of course; but culturally, most people are encouraged to think of fiction as something you read with your mouth open and your eyes and ears closed, while somebody pours it down your throat.

LM: How do you explain the mass popularity of movies like *Star Wars* and *Star Trek?*

JR: They're both basically adventure stories with SF frills. They have a lot in common with the SF pulps of the '30s, true, but just as much with Westerns and other adventure formulas. *Star Wars,* to my mind, is *revolting.* If you look beneath the frills—which are nice frills—there are many disturbing (and clichéd) implications of the worst sort. The first thirty-five minutes of the movie are interesting, but then you see that this teenage white Christian middle-class male with buckteeth and no parents is the darling of the cosmos. And the whole setup is sort of like the Roman Empire—there are slaves, and this monarchy is supposedly better than democracy. Who needs that kind of reinforcement? Even the issues themselves are boring.

LM: I just saw another enormously popular SF movie—*Aliens,* the sequel to Ridley Scott's *Alien.* But whereas *Alien* strikes me as a perfect example of how materials from a pop formula can be turned into a multilayered work of art, the new movie seemed to recycle the central elements of the original into easily marketable images. You must have faced this temptation—to go back and rework materials that have a proven acceptability.

JR: I'm *very* familiar with what you're talking about; it's the we-want-more syndrome, which has been around for a long time now. Some writer back in the '30s or '40s said, "You write a story in which you have a nice idea, and your hero saves the world; but then everyone wants another world to be saved and then another and then another, until there are literally no worlds left to save—you've run out of material." Any material, no matter how potentially rich, can be mined until it's exhausted. The problem is that so often the publisher or producer doesn't *care* if it's exhausted; their attitude is, "You had this wonderfully engrossing book or movie, so do another one—the name alone will bring people in." That isn't always bad. Some of those SF television shows are good because in a series you have some flexibility. But once you're involved with a blockbuster film, you lose this freedom because even the good parts eventually become clichés.

LM: How did you avoid this trap when you were developing your Alyx stories?

JR: It was never a trap for me because it was a commerical temptation and I'm not a commercial writer. The main thing I did was to keep changing the premise from story to story. I found that there were so many different aspects of the Alyx mythos, or whatever you want to call it, that I could keep things fresh for quite a while before I sensed I was getting repetitive. Remember, those stories were a breakthrough for me: up until that point I had pretty much been following the usual cultural scenario by writing action stories with men as main characters and love stories with women protagonists; naturally, in the action stories the men usually won, while in the love stories the women lost. When I got to Alyx, for the first time I realized I had stumbled upon the chance to create a *new story*—really a whole series of stories—that could counter those gender stereotypes. One of the most exciting things about working in SF for me, a woman, is that SF is so open-ended—it's perfectly possible to imagine a world where sexism doesn't exist, or in which women can be presented in the context of new myths that women can admire or learn from.

LM: The figure of the adolescent girl who feels alienated, unhappy, and generally out of it appears so often in your fiction—in *The Female Man* and *The Two of Them,* for example—that readers are bound to feel you're conjuring up something of your own background. Maybe these suspicions would be heightened if they knew you started college at age fifteen and must have already been undergoing some identity problems because of being a lesbian.

JR: Oh, yes! But remember, you're also talking about the backgrounds of a whole lot of writers, maybe especially SF writers. It really is true that as kids most SF writers were geeky or shy or talkative in a nerdy way; they were the kind of kids who got together and swapped stories. In terms of my own youth, I owed much of my sense of alienation and unhappiness to being a baby lesbian. I also know that a lot of it had to do with being a baby intellectual, bookish. These qualities were gauaranteed to make *any* kid feel out of place in America, but especially a girl growing up in the '50s. Eventually, I was lucky enough to meet people like myself—SF people—and suddenly that part of what I was seemed great! In many ways my sense of alienation was also an artificial attitude created by my special circumstances. I was just too young when I was thrust into certain situations that require some emotional maturity. I skipped three grades in elementary school and got into high school when I was twelve, which is much too young to cope, to socialize. The other kids didn't know what to do with me. I was too young when I got to college as well. When I was teaching at Cornell, I met some of these kids who were the age I had been and I realized for the first time what *babies* they were! The difference between fifteen and eighteen is enormous. That was tough too.

LM: You loved science as a young girl. What made you decide to major in English in college?

JR: My love of science was basically aesthetic in orientation. As a kid, I remember coming across something called *The New World of Physics,* which talked about things like relativity and quantum mechanics, and I was immediately fascinated. I developed this awe of, this love of, astronomy, evolution, physics—which has found an outlet in what I write. But even though I had some practical abilities in science—I was one of ten finalists in the Westinghouse Science Talent Search in 1953—mainly I was interested in science in a detached, aesthetic way—the SF-ish sense of wonder and marvel that still guides my response to science. I remember my Philosophy 101 professor saying to me, helplessly, "But these are all tautologies you've written!" and me responding, "Yes, but aren't they *beautiful?"*

LM: What made you go on to Yale Drama School rather than pursue a graduate career in English?

JR: Part of it was that I felt I wanted to live outside academe. I found literary criticism in the '50s, which was mainly over-age, trendy New Criticism, to be horrible, lifeless, poisonous to anybody who wanted to write. And I was crazy about the theater. What I found out, though, was that I was a lousy playwright. Maybe I could have been a decent playwright, but I would have had to totally immerse myself in the theater— which I didn't want to do then and don't want to do now.

LM: Did your theatrical experience have any practical effect on your fiction?

JR: It taught me an enormous amount, but most of what I got out of it was on my own, pretty much catch-as-catch-can. The drama school then was not good—it was before Robert Brustein, and the place didn't seem to have much direction except toward commercialism. But I studied plays, plot lines, and dramatic structure until it was coming out of my ears, until I could do dramatic constructions backward, forward, and blindfolded.

LM: When I read your work I often get the sense that you'd begun to create a dramatic situation and then decided, "Nah, I've teased them with this, now let's try something else."

JR: Right. My work is haunted by the banal plots that are not there. People get upset because they recognize the cues and think they're going to get a nice old adventure story. When that doesn't happen, they wonder what the hell is going on. I do this metafictional commentary a lot. I had gotten to the point early on where I could watch the first two minutes of any TV show and know everything that would follow. The patterns become so predictable and so false that after a while you want to *play* with them, be sacrilegious. Again, you have to be aware of these structures in order to resist them and allow your texts to create a dialogue or dialectic with them.

LM: What were your plans when you left Yale Drama School?

JR: I was still interested in plays, but I'd about decided I just couldn't do them. What fascinated me about the theater then was that you could project a *private reality* onto actual material things: people, sets, voices, scenes. It gradually dawned on me that I could do this in words, too.

LM: Your SF apprenticeship coincided roughly with the rise of the New Wave. Were you aware of the direction that New Wave authors were taking?

JR: Heavens, yes! Delany and I began corresponding during that period—Chip was a whirlwind of critical influences in those days—and I read everybody I could get my hands on. Those were heady times. I felt the New Wave was pretty much nonsense—critical nonsense—and I still believe that about most of it. On the other hand, it seemed obvious that a lot of things were changing by the '60s. The paperback revolution had produced some of these changes, but mostly it was the presence of a generation of writers who had grown up taking SF for granted and who were also trained in literature. Unlike so many of the Golden Age writers, who were basically unself-conscious about the literary devices they were using, we were consciously aware of the distinction between what we were saying and the devices we were using to say it.

LM: It seems significant that in Europe there is a long tradition of serious writers doing SF—Wells, Huxley, Stapledon, Capek, and so on—whereas in the United States we tend to have SF writers with none of that training.

JR: Or who were self-trained—that's a key distinction, because some of them are marvelous writers and approach their craft with as much dedication, discipline, and skill as any other writers. Someone like Damon Knight at his best is simply wonderful. Or Avram Davidson. But these people didn't have the formal education in literature that Delany (who majored in symbolist poetry) had, or that I had, or that a fine poet like Tom Disch had. Ursula Le Guin was writing stories at the age of eleven or something. I don't know Gene Wolfe that well, but based on his writing I suspect his background is similar.

LM: Were you aware of the kinds of innovations going on at this same time in mainstream fiction? *The Female Man* shares thematic and formal concerns with some of the work being done by people like Donald Barthelme, Robert Coover, Kurt Vonnegut, and Ronald Sukenick.

JR: I was aware of what was happening, although I don't believe the analogies are as great as you're suggesting. I knew Sukenick in the '60s and I was reading a lot of Barthelme, for example, and other works by these "postrealists" (or whatever you call them). Those innovations were going on all over the place, they were somehow in the air, but my approach in *The Female Man* wasn't "influenced" by these other writers, wasn't governed by the same premises they were operating under. Actually, when I began work on *The Female Man* it was a fairly straightforward SF novel. But it didn't seem to want to "move" until I began fragmenting it.

LM: You've said that most of what goes on in the novel evolves from what was already present in the story "When It Changed."

JR: That's misleading. I wrote that story after an intersession colloquium at Cornell the year I started teaching there, which must have been 1969. The whole wave of late '60s and early '70s feminism was moving across the country, and it happened to hit us at that period. Kate Millett was there, Betty Friedan and a lot of other people whose names I've sadly forgotten—and suddenly the whole place seemed to explode. A few weeks after that colloquium I wrote "When It Changed," and people started coming up to me saying, "Why don't you write a novel based on what you've set up there?" A few months after that, the book started taking shape. But even though some of the same names are used, the world that began appearing in the book is really very different from the world I had suggested in the story. That was certainly one book I discovered as I wrote it—I had no idea what was going to happen next. It seemed to start making itself, finding its own structure, weaving different things in and out. The main complaint I got from feminist (and other) critics has to do with the structure—"Yes, we love it, but it's not really a *novel*." That goes back to what we were saying earlier about people's notions about what a novel is or should be. The realistic bourgeois novel. They're not aware that other writers have done this sort of thing long before; they've never read *Tristram Shandy* or anything like that.

LM: How did the different plot strands evolve? Did you start out with one basic plot that eventually began to split apart?

JR: I was aware of all four strands very early on—at least in the sense that I had all the characters and plot situations spelled out in my mind almost from the outset. The multiplot structure came from the idea of the world as infinite possibility, which is an old SF chestnut lots of writers have used (I think A. E. Van Vogt was the first). It's an ideal structure to express the notion of potentiality, difference, change. "What Did You Do during the Revolution, Grandma?" takes off from it. A lot of women have asked me, "How did you come up with that amazing idea for organizing your book?" I have to keep saying, "I didn't. It's commonplace in SF." That's a good example of the way SF writers have been borrowing from each other for years. We've been very generous in that way. It seems as if these ideas float around in a huge swimming pool, like minnows, and we dive in after them.

LM: One commonly recycled motif is the alien encounter. You've used that repeatedly, from the Alyx stories to *And Chaos Died* to most of the stories in *Extra(Ordinary) People*. I'm reminded of Sandra M. Gilbert and Susan Gubar's discussion in *The Madwoman in the Attic* about *Frankenstein* as one of the first alien encounter books—they point out that this motif is especially useful to women writers, since they so often feel like aliens.

JR: Women SF writers have created a series of alien disguises for themselves. James Tiptree's "The Women Men Don't See" displays probably the most consciously sophisticated, subtle, and really gorgeous use of this disguise motif. Gubar wrote an essay about C. L. Moore's work in which she said that Moore often does self-portraits disguised as alien encounter stories. The other women in her works are all stereotypes, but the self-portraits are of aliens. It's undeniable that Moore did this, the best examples being "No Woman Born" and the story about the woman from Callisto. Women only occasionally disguise themselves as men, but more often they write about themselves as hermaphroditic ambisexuals—the sort of thing you see in Le Guin's Gethen in *The Left Hand of Darkness* or in Suzy Charnas's *Vampire Tapestry,* where at first the vampire seems to be a male but turns out to be a nonhuman imitation male, another alien. You can see this in the telepathic alien in *Extra(Ordinary) People* or the alien who is the abbess. This kind of thing pops up all over the place in SF by women, when they're not busy doing that standard male-hero thing.

LM: Is the need for women to deal indirectly with these things changing?

JR: I don't know what the new generation of women SF writers is doing in this regard—I just don't keep up—but I suspect women still aren't comfortable being direct. I know most of the women in my generation who were doing groundbreaking work usually felt the need to find a way to distance a lot of personal, controversial issues. And while some awareness on some questions has gone up among the general public, so that it may be possible to say things out loud now that in 1965 or 1970 were certainly very tough to say out loud, in many ways they're getting tough to say again. Back in the early '70s, I shocked myself in writing parts of *The Female Man.* It scared the dickens out of me. I doubt that women are ever going to feel comfortable being direct, at least not until our society's undergone some changes of its own. When women try to speak totally directly, we lack the social forms or the cultural images or the permission to do so. These things just aren't in our vocabulary yet, so we still have to get at things in a roundabout manner.

LM: There's a mystical or religious strain running through your work that I've also found in several other writers—for example, Wolfe, Delany, Le Guin, Benford. What's the source of SF's ability to speculate so widely?

JR: I think this spiritual bent—which I agree is very strong in SF, especially in very good writers—has to do with the broad cultural surroundings, the way social attitudes have evolved since the nineteenth century. Science has taken on much of the public prestige and mystery and hope that religion previously had. During the '60s, science started to lose some of this aura, but among ordinary people it still has an enormous cachet. The whole Darwin controversy was between religion and science over who's going to control people's minds. Science won that battle, especially in the United States, at least up through the '30s and '40s. Even though the popular acceptance of its creed has been tottering lately, science still gives people what they want: the reassurance of this big overarching, superprestigious explanation.

LM: Do I detect a personal skepticism that isn't always present in your work?

JR: Not at all. Just as spirituality isn't organized religion, belief in the intelligibility of the material world isn't scien*tism.* Keep in mind that I was brought up in a family that really knew popular science. I remember my father assigning each of us parts to show me how the Earth went around the Sun and the Moon went around the Earth— he was the Sun, my mother was the Earth, and I was Moon—which may have been symptomatic of who was who in the family! I remember being awakened to watch an eclipse of the Moon. My dad was so excited about astronomy that he took a class in lens grinding and made his own twelve-inch telescope, which we used to see the moons of Jupiter and the rings of Saturn. This was absolutely wonderful, superduper, marvelous stuff to a wide-eyed kid like me. I was totally caught up in the wonder of it all.

LM: Have you lost that?

JR: I've never lost the feeling of transcendental beauty and awe that attached itself to the physical world. Lucretius has a line in *De Rerum Naturae* that says something about how everything in nature fits together and gives a joy beyond expression. It's a feeling people have surely always had about the way the seasons or planets change, the way plants grow, a sense of joy or awe about what's around us. For a lot of people, including most SF writers, these feelings have attached themselves to science and have been manifested in odd ways in the fiction itself. For a while, we had a rush of heroes who were turning into the Messiah — a literary hazard, I suppose — but even these dime-store messiahs were being produced by this sense of cosmic awe and wonder that everybody has experienced. Fans call it "sensawunda."

LM: It's an interesting aesthetic issue — how one goes about producing this sense of wonder in the work of fiction. Obviously, most SF authors *want* to convey this feeling in their works, but only a few writers really succeed. I'll never forget that paragraph at the end of Olaf Stapledon's *The Last and First Men* —

JR: — "and this whole first book is only a few moments in the history of what now rolls before us." Stapledon is the master of supplying his readers with this raw, astronomical feeling. In a very different way, Doc Smith could evoke some of that sense of sheer distance, of lots and lots of space and time, of the whole great drama of cosmic evolution — which really isn't like the popular view of evolution at all; it's really much nicer, much more complicated and beautiful. Evelyn Fox Keller has written a book called *Reflections on Gender and Science* in which she notes that reality is much more plentiful than any description we can possibly give of it. Same difference. It's partially this recognition of the wonder of it all, and of the need to find new ways of talking about our relationship to all this stuff, that gets people into reading (and writing) SF. The people who see *Star Wars* don't want this, or don't get it, or don't really respond to what SF authors consider the real core.

LM: Are any contemporary SF authors doing significant work along these lines? Gene Wolfe's Book of the New Sun series seems to me to rank up there with C. S. Lewis's *Space Trilogy.*

JR: Wolfe writes theology when he writes SF (he's Catholic, you know). I find some of his stories very restrictive because of this, but he does convey this sense of wonder beautifully. Delany, obviously, does the same thing. One way of finding an objective correlative for this is the old cliché about looking at the star-filled heavens and wishing we could travel out there. I think inventing an objective correlative is crucial. Clearly, Wells was one writer able to do this. Jack London did, too. I remember teaching Wells's story "The Star," which ends with the exact perspective shift we've been talking about: the Martian astronomer who was observing this was amazed at how little damage had been done (I paraphrase). The point is to show how small the greatest of disasters can appear when seen from a distance of several billion miles or years.

LM: The perspective shifts you use in *Extra(Ordinary) People* have much the same effect.

JR: I've wanted to keep that sense in my work, even though it's more subtle, more sophisticated. What I'm aiming for is more a sense of how complex and fascinating and absolutely *rich* everything is. One of the things that happened in the '60s, with all the emphasis on social issues and human behavior, was that we discovered we could convey this richness without using the starry heavens or the billion-mile perspective. When I was twelve, I used to say things like, "If the sun was the size of an orange and each planet was the size of a pea, how big would the whole system be?" Well, what writer can match the sheer magnificence of that stuff!

LM: That brings us back to what we were saying earlier about how important these recent meta-SF approaches are. They help critique the simplistic attitudes in some of the earlier conventions that "normalized" this magnificence.

JR: Initially, of course, the conventions had to be simplistic. Delany has pointed out that any genre begins with broad, bold strokes; it has to delimit itself. Once you establish the territory, as it were—the parameters, the attitudes, the basic paradigms of the field—only *then* can you write subtle and sophisticated literature. I couldn't have used the approaches I do today in 1915; nobody else could either. In a way, Stapledon took SF to its supreme heights, and there are times when I absolutely wish I could *kill* him because he has made so much SF instantly obsolete. He's unconcerned with, or plain bigoted about, a great deal; but what he does, he does very, very well.

LM: The essay about your work in the *Dictionary of Literary Biography* argues that a lot of your books are allegories about people's relationship with God.

JR: That's nonsense. It makes me very angry because there is no God in any of my stories or in my beliefs. In fact, if there's one thread running throughout my fiction it's precisely the *lack* of that kind of authority. My books, I would say, are designed to undermine that notion, to force readers to question the authorities governing their lives, be they literary, sexual, political, religious, whatever. Cosmic awe isn't religion. I'm an atheist, and I loathe having religion imported into my work. If you believe in religion, do it, but don't assume or insist that I do.

LM: The forms you employ in *The Female Man, The Two of Them,* and *Extra(Ordinary) People* undermine any privileged way of reading (or living). They're open-ended and anti-authoritarian, both thematically and structurally.

JR: You're basically right, but that doesn't mean dissolving all standards. "Authority" can mean several different things, not all of which are bad. The "authority" of a text or a person—what *is* it? "Authority" is related to "author." Judy Grahn talks about the difference between creating something and owning it. An apple tree can make an apple, whereas an apple-tree magnate can buy the tree, cut it down, sell the apples—but there's no way he can make the apple. What this suggests is that an "author" needs "authenticity" to make something—the authority of the real thing, the real ability. People recognize real authority in each other, so they sense who has the kind of authority that's real, immanent. Shaw makes this same distinction between real authority and conventional authority, which must always be *enforced* because it's not rational, not real, not based on any substantive source of power. When I say I'm not anti-authority, I'm referring to that real authority whose source is the real world, the sunlight, the trees, the nitty-gritty, the ability, the authentic.

LM: This openness to real sources of power and wisdom, combined with a parallel condemnation of fake sources of dogma and convention, is almost a signature of writers who emerged in the '60s.

JR: The key for me wasn't the '60s but the early '70s and the feminist movement. Gloria Steinem once said that women get more radical as they get older because things start to pile up—the alienation, the out-sideness. We don't age as men do; there's no reward. We get out or go under. Radicalism for any oppressed group isn't youthful; it's lifelong.

LM: You develop this opposition between the inside and outside in several of your works—"My Emily," for example.

JR: Simply being a female so often has the effect of placing women so far out, so far on the margin, so far from being central or important, that when women go radical, they tend to jump a long way. Radicalism partly derives from the basic question, How much have I really got to lose? I'm not sure you can generalize about this, but it seems clear to me, from my recent researches, that black women are frequently more radical than white feminists and black lesbian feminists are more radical still, because just to stay alive they've had to become radical. Like Barbara Smith, Gloria Anzaldua, Cherrie Moraga. Audre Lorde has a collection of essays called *Sister Outsider* that is magnificent on this topic. There is a tradition of women on the Left being overlooked that I myself just found out about quite recently. I discovered that in the most amazing ways it's always been *women* who were the most radical figures on the Left. Suppressed radicals, punished radicals. Not only has this happened before, but it's happened and happened and happened and happened. There have been something like two to four feminist movements in the last three hundred years. Dale Spender's book, *Women of Ideas,* has some evidence of this. We've buried the slave revolts, and we constantly bury radical events like the labor wars.

LM: Since women's experiences as outsiders are usually more extreme than most men's, you'd expect there to be some differences in the way women SF writers develop the alien encounter motif. Are there?

JR: I think so. In a lot of the fiction you could characterize this way—stuff by me, Tiptree, Le Guin, Octavia Butler, and so on—there's no lead-in to this other world, with its different values or different conditions—you just start off there. Of course, that's modern, too. All those things Chip Delany has described as being absolutely paradigmatic in alien encounter SF stories are missing. *The Dispossessed* doesn't start off on Earth; nor does *The Left Hand of Darkness* begin, as you'd expect, with Genly Ai being briefed for his mission. By and large, with the works women have written, at least until recently, either you start off in a strange world—and you're already kind of at home there, really—or, as with Tiptree (and Vonnegut, who's not as invested in imperialism and sexism), you go off into space and find low comedy, pointless heroics, and death. If you look at Tiptree's stories, you'll see that when anybody goes out into space it's always an utter catastrophe, unless the women get away from the men, as in "The Women Men Don't See."

LM: A far cry from the familiar story line about leaving the restrictive values of Earth behind and finding a new Eden.

JR: For women, there's simply no easy way of finding some kind of fulfillment. The whole idea of going from your own world to an alien world makes sense only if you're not an alien in your own world. It's very hard to feel at home here when you're not. So women either don't go into space—you're either there or here but without much traveling in between—or you came from there and now you're here, but what the hell are you *doing* here?

LM: A lot of women SF authors seem interested in telepathy. Does this express a disguised longing for full communion with others?

JR: I don't think so. Maybe secondarily. I believe it's primarily an attempt to find a way of describing our actual experience. Women traditionally do an enormous amount of interpersonal work, but there's no public vocabulary for this sort of activity—just as there's no public vocabulary for what mothers do raising children, or what housewives do. Anne Wilson Schaef has pointed out that there is this public male reality and anything that isn't in it is either crazy or trivial or nonexistent. There's no consensual way of talking about what makes up the daily lives of most women, so it's not surprising that women have been exploring telepathy, ESP, magic, and alternative forms of communication. Marion Zimmer Bradley does, Le Guin does, I do, even Suzy Charnas—really, just about every contemporary woman SF author I can think of has worked in these areas. Vonda McIntyre, no . . . maybe—

but she creates alien or altered characters with nonhuman sensoriums.
But men don't, or when they do it's handled differently. Typically, the
magic in men's SF is ritual, technical, rule-following magic, not the
personal out-of-your-guts stuff. Zenna Henderson has a story in which
a woman holds back a forest fire: she gets the kids behind her and then
throws up her arms and lighting comes from her fingers, crackling down
from the sky, and the fire disappears—at which point she faints dead
away. What's happening there, and in a lot of similar works, is that
we're trying to find a suitable objective correlative for something in our
own experience. I know I am when I'm working in these areas. How
do we express what happens to our characters, what matters? The usual
public language—designed by males for male experience—isn't available to us, nor are the usual literary metaphors.

LM: Who are some of the SF writers you admire or feel affinities
with?

JR: Disch—real affinities, technical and emotional. I admire Delany,
even though I feel he's operating in such different areas that I'm usually
a stranger in his books. I'm very ambivalent about Le Guin; obviously,
she's a wonderfully inventive writer, but her lack of awareness about a
lot of political and historical issues just exasperates me. If I read her
fiction I usually have to forget a lot I know about people and the
dynamics of behavior. And sometimes her moralizing about everything
strikes me as not humanist at all. But I'm jealous of her, so all of this
is suspect.

LM: Given your respective political stances, it's ironic you and Le
Guin are so often linked.

JR: No—women get put in the "woman" box. Q.E.D. I'm sure it
annoys both of us. She's a charming person, incredibly witty and very
brilliant. But there are times I'd like to shake her down to her toes until
the loose change comes out. I don't think she really knows how political,
communal, people processes actually work. Delany, on the other hand,
clearly does, and he's applied this awareness to his public criticisms of
The Dispossessed.

LM: I take it you feel that you know how these processes work.

JR: I've had so much goddamn experience with feminism and wom-
en's studies courses and departmental politics and that kind of thing
that, yes, I know a whole lot about how they work. And I know how
a lot of people work. But it's clear from what Le Guin writes that she
isn't in touch with a lot of political realities, which causes her fiction
to fall apart. It's obviously a conscientious thing on her part—no one
can doubt her sincerity or genuine concern—but I wish she'd just let
go of it and write selfishly about things she enjoys. Because when she
does that, she's absolutely splendid. The darkness box, animal languages,

and so on. Superb. She has such a remarkable feel for the little details—the stories, the buildings, the language, the histories, the clothing and food, the fiction, the proverbs, the whole self-reflection of cultures.

I should emphasize that I've really read so damn little SF in the past ten years that my judgments are very suspect. Back in the '60s, I used to read every SF magazine that came out, with passionate abandon. Of course, most of it is awfully dull, and today when I do look at the magazines it seems like I've seen all this before. Nearly all of it is adolescent fantasy, which is very big commercially, so most of it is absolutely godawful, unbelievably bad. Even the people seriously involved in this sort of fantasy writing find it hard to do something interesting because the form is just so restrictive and thin. Delany eventually did something interesting with his Neveryon books, but only by getting rid of the three things absolutely crucial to all fantasy: magic, religion, and the feudal belief in hierarchy. The result is a mutation of the sword-and-sorcery genre, not an example of it. In fact, they are a form of metacritical text.

LM: One of the female characters in *The Two of Them* says, "I will be murdered by my own rage." Do you worry about having your creativity murdered by your own outrage—or is this anger necessary for your artistic life?

JR: Anger is a necessity. It's part of all radicalism. When Marxism isn't second-generation, academic, and establishment-theoretical, its motive is sheer fury. What else? When groups get past a certain point of oppression, it's a revelation to be angry. Prior to that you'd go through a stage of feeling you have to be so moral, so good, that anger seems inappropriate; you think you shouldn't get angry. Eventually you get to a place where you can more honestly express that anger, and that's fine. Mother Jones said, "Farmers in this state are raising too much corn and not enough hell!" There's a point where it's essential to get in touch with anger in situations where people or structures are dumping on you. You need this anger to resist looking at the structure and saying, "It's us, it's our fault"; or "What they're saying is true, we must be wrong." If you lose touch with this outrage, you wind up forgetting what you were mad about in the first place; you start feeling that you'd really rather not get involved, that you can't change things, that it's no use. Oppression is always mystifying and confusing. Lying, really.

LM: I asked about the necessity of anger because that sense of rage (often combined with a certain dark sense of humor) informs your best writing.

JR: A sense of outrage and a sense of humor aren't incompatible. One of the things I agree with Freud about is wit and the unconscious. He claimed that wit is a kind of rage, a form of hostility. Of course, things are funny for different reasons—there's a difference between humor and wit. But the kind of pointed-tendency wit—Jewish jokes, for example—isn't a wit that hides hostility, it's a way of emphasizing it. Irony is another way of emphasizing hostility. Joking says not only are you a pigheaded, destructive ass, but you're ludicrous, too. It adds insult to injury. And it adds enjoyment. It's a disguise. It's anger plus freedom. Or maybe that's just the difference between wit that avoids and radical wit that clarifies and inspires. Look at what Mother Jones said.

An Interview with

Bruce Sterling

For those readers whose main image of Bruce Sterling is that of an angry young man in a black leather jacket and mirrored shades, jacked into a Walkman that blares forth speed-metal rock, it will come as a surprise to learn that the picture of Sterling that most vividly stays with Brooks Landon and me is one of a new father patiently following his toddling daughter up and down the halls of the Hershey Hotel in Corpus Christi, Texas. We watched this teetering promenade for several days in July 1988, from inside conference rooms where Science Fiction Research Association members were engaged in panels that frequently discussed Sterling's work. Clearly, our image defies what most SF fans and critics expect of the controversial Sterling. Yet above his black leather tennis shoes looms the ayatollah of cyberpunk, the spokesman to whom other movement members defer, even as they heatedly insist there is no movement.

If William Gibson was the first star of cyberpunk, Bruce Sterling has been the movement's polemical center, adding to its seminal fiction with his early novel, *The Artificial Kid* (1980), his series of Shaper/ Mechanist stories and especially his radicalized antinovel *Schismatrix* (1986), and theorizing its paradigms with criticism as energized and provocative as it is lucid. With the introduction to *Mirrorshades* (1986)— the first anthology of cyberpunk fiction, which he edited—Sterling codifies this newest wave of SF first by acutely assessing its roots within SF. He notes that cyberpunk shares a number of themes and stylistic impulses with earlier SF authors—especially the New Wave authors of the late '60s, including "the street edginess of Harlan Ellison . . . the freewheeling zaniness of Norman Spinrad and the rock aesthetic of Michael Moorcock"—and exhibits the influences of Philip K. Dick, Alfred Bester, John Varley, and Samuel R. Delany. Sterling establishes not just congruences but also distinctions between cyberpunk and earlier SF, his most crucial arguments centering on his insistence that cyberbunk authors are "perhaps the first SF generation to grow up not only within the literary tradition of SF but in a truly science-fiction world. For them, the techniques of classical 'hard SF'—extrapolation, technological literacy—are not just literary tools but an aid to daily life. They are a means of understanding, and highly valued."

This insistence on the interaction of the literary programs of cyberpunk and the computer-generated, genetically engineered operations of contemporary daily life squarely aligns cyberpunk with the broader cultural concerns of postmodernism, of which it should most properly be seen as a subset. It's no accident, for instance, that seminal figures in postmoderism—William S. Burroughs, J. G. Ballard, Andy Warhol, Thomas Pynchon, the Velvet Underground and '70s punk musicians, filmmakers such as David Cronenberg and Ridley Scott, performance artists like Laurie Anderson and the Survival Research Lab—are all frequently cited by cyberpunk authors as having affinities with their own work. In this regard, perhaps the most telling remark in Sterling's introduction to *Mirrorshades* involves the "new kind of integration" he saw at work in cyberpunk: "The overlapping of worlds that were formerly separate: the realm of high tech and the modern pop underground."

"Visionary lunacy is what SF is all about," Sterling likes to say, giving equal emphasis to both the vision and the lunacy. While his own novels have brandished their share of appealingly lunatic notions—*Moby-Dick* recast on Nullaqua, a planet where the oceans are made of dust; flying islands composed of huge balloonlike creatures filled with tons of mud, vegetation, and animal life; human bodies merged first with rooms, then with entire cities—they have consistently depicted visions of a future that has more to do with pragmatic historical and sociopolitical speculations, with the steely-eyed extrapolations of Larry Niven and Robert Heinlein, than they do with lunacy per se.

The epic sweep and space-opera scale of Sterling's first major work, *Schismatrix,* does not disguise the fact that its central concerns are clearly grounded in postmodern culture—for instance, the denaturing of time, of the human body, and of language, and the fantastic political and technological evolutions that are currently being produced by the massive, unnerving collision of scientific advances with such very human qualities as love, hatred, and (always) the fear of death. The media-driven, drug-enabled combat artistry of *The Artificial Kid,* whose "kid" is 299 years old, seems inevitable in a culture that feeds on the exploits of Mike Tyson, Ben Johnson, and Hulk Hogan while making drug testing a standard feature of every sport. Even the fantastic dustworld conceit of Sterling's first novel, *Involution Ocean* (1978), is pragmatically tempered by the drug dependency, sexual frustration, and general anomie of its protagonist, as well as by the systematic rigor of Sterling's imagined Nullaquan ecology. Indeed, one of the hallmarks of Sterling's fiction has been the balancing of ideological goals against technological and biological realities, a scrupulously pragmatic attention to detail, whatever its toll on narrative.

In many ways, Sterling's intricately detailed fourth novel, *Islands in the Net* (1988), seems to have gotten him where he was headed from the beginning: to a future that's not only credible but also workable. Part international espionage potboiler, part feminist investigation, part cyberpunk, part hard-edged extrapolation of cultural and political realities that are shaping today's world, *Islands* is above all the product of an imagination seeking to understand and illuminate that future. Since *Islands* had been published only a few weeks before we met in Corpus Christi, it provided a loose focus for the conversation that follows, allowing Sterling to articulate how he had arrived at the edge of the future he had just conjured.

Larry McCaffery: One thing that drew me to your work and to William Gibson's work is its extremity, its intensity. I suspect that the cyberpunk phenomenon arose mainly among people who have grown up with a certain appreciation for intensity and the grotesqueness that we've seen in rock music, from the Velvet Underground and David Bowie's Spiders from Mars up through the punk scene. People who have been aware of that are going to have a different sensibility than people who haven't.

Bruce Sterling: It is a different aesthetic. To read *Schismatrix* hurts in a peculiar way, in the same way, that really harsh feedback hurts. It lacks melody. There's nothing there to ease you into the structure and boot you up if you lose your grip. When there is a seventy-year jump in *Schismatrix,* there's nothing under there to hold you. You've got to grab for the raveling end of the next stream of information or your comprehension falls into a crevasse. Each section in *Schismatrix* begins with a dateline and a geographical location. That's not what you call a standard literary device, but if you didn't have that, you'd really be adrift.

LM: Your handling of time in *Schismatrix* produces in the reader a sense of a world that is totally strange, a world of massive future shock.

BS: And future shock hurts. People can die from it. You can die from culture shock as well. It happens all the time: a woman gets off the airplane at Karachi, goes to her hotel, has an anxiety attack, and falls down and dies. Yet people pay billions of dollars to go to strange cities and wander around saying, "Oh, this is Madrid, isn't it darling. Can we get Elmer's glue here?" I don't want to make a career of being on the edge because, being an SF person, in some sense society forced me out there. It has taken me a long time to come to terms with that. Essentially, I was put on the edge because I was powerless. SF writers are usually people who were strongly shocked or misshapen in their formative years and have never recovered completely.

LM: When I was in school there was another group of alienated people: the guys with the slicked-back hair who were into rock music.

BS: Yeah, but the guys who had ducktails in the '50s are presidents of banks now, or dead. There's not that much left of their old bohemian order. Plus there's a reverse snobbishness to being hip that bothers me, because there's no commitment. If you're a professional outsider you can carp, but you never have to take responsibility for your own actions. If you're an anarchist you have no hostages to fortune. I mean, fuck the ozone layer. What did posterity ever do for you? I've regretted some of the "professional outsider" business that the whole cyberpunk thing has associated me with. I catch criticism now from all directions, and I think that's going to happen a lot with *Islands in the Net,* which is "not really cyberpunk" and in many ways *refutes* some of the unconscious tenets of cyberpunk, or turns them on their heads, or plays tricks with them, or pretends to refute them and then brings them up unexpectedly and slips them in. Every review the book gets will be along the lines of the two I've seen already: "Here's Bruce Sterling, a cyberpunk, who is attempting to bring cyberbunk to this new such-and-such." No one is going to say, "Here is this novel about the future," and then discuss it on those terms.

Brooks Landon: Why do you think Japan and France seem to be the two places where cyberpunk is all the rage?

BS: You'd have to ask Gibson about France. He's been there a couple of times recently. I haven't been to France, at least not as an author, but I was in Tokyo recently, where they treat cyberpunk as a pop culture rather than a genre phenomenon. It's really strange over there because there's this one-way culture clash between us and the Japanese. They know everything about us and we know almost nothing about them. They know the names of the most obscure bands from Athens, Georgia. They have an attitude toward American pop culture that reminds me of fanatic baseball card collectors: they don't only have the big guys, they have the rare ones, like the rookie who washed out. You know somebody's got those cards, and you've got to have them all to complete your set. There's a voracious appetite for American popular culture in Japan; they feed on it. They've got an entire scene there that's hip, intellectually alive with what Americans are doing, but for some reason it just doesn't flow the other way. Or only in very small ways.

LM: Is this notion of individual artistic and cultural identities—those tied to a specific national, geographical entity—something that we may have to get rid of anyway?

BS: I guess it is a Luddite reaction, but I recognize the great power of that. Look at someplace like Iran. Iranians want to be an Islamic republic. They're besieged by the images and ideas and ideologies of the West, and when they look inside themselves to see what they can combat that with, all they have is Islam. So they embrace Islam; they've got this enormous reservoir of familiar cultural artifacts that possess great power and energy. I don't think cultural homogenization or cross-fertilization is inevitable. People who are pushed by this stuff will push back. But, for me, it's more a matter of aesthetics. As a Texan, I've felt these kinds of cultural stresses too, especially in the early '80s when there was massive migration into the state during our economic boom. Suddenly, you could buy a knish in Austin, or get actual French bread (as opposed to what Texans *thought* French bread was). That cultural plurality is very convenient and seductive—and at the same time it produces cultural shock. Now that we Texans are broke, these guys are packing up all the French bread and German sausages and leaving. The dyed-in-the-wool Texas native feels some relief to get out from under all the semiotic pressure. But as far as my aesthetic tastes go, I prefer the stuff that comes from interzones. I just don't seem to get any kick out of the stuff that's supposedly ethnically pure—folk music played with real antique instruments, that sort of thing.

Down here we get a lot of *conjunto* stations—it's not really Mexican music, it's American music, Hispanic music. The other day on my car radio I heard these guys—I think they were called La Mafia—playing this type of music. They've got a traditional lineup—polka, accordion music, guitar—and they're playing accordion riffs on synthesizers. As I was listening, I was thinking, Man, this is *hot!* and I turned it up full throttle. I'm sure there are guys who are *norteño* purists who say, "This is disgusting, crap. When are these guys going to play real *conjunto* music? This is just rock 'n' roll with a synthesizer. What are they doing to the cultural validity of the form?" Well, I'm sorry, I just don't respond that way. Give me the fucked-up, hybrid-weird monstrous stuff. I feed on that. Other people may find it ugly or frightening or even a profaning of some supposed cultural purity, but that's where my aesthetics are.

BL: Maybe you ought to move to Houston, which reeks of that weird monstrous stuff.

BS: The thing is, even though I like to *look* at this stuff, basically I enjoy being a hick. That's why I like Japanese pop music, with its obvious imposition of a form onto a substratum. I live this peculiar gutter intellectual's life in a Texas city that doesn't really have a literary culture and doesn't really have a set-up role.

LM: What does it mean to be a Texas SF writer?

BS: There's still discovery in it, which is part of the kick. It's a feeling of openness, space to do whatever you want—I don't underrate the regional influence of Texas on cyberpunk. Austin is the only city with more than one cyberpunk in it—me and Lew Shiner—and because it's far from the commercial centers in publishing, there are no unconscious guidelines for what you can and cannot do. A guy like Howard Waldrop is obviously influenced by this because his work is so extremely eclectic. My work, too. Because Austin has no baggage it's very lively. The energy is there and the opportunity is there but the traditions aren't.

BL: One SF writer from Austin is Chad Oliver. Did you have any contact with him?

BS: Oliver is our gray eminence. Actually, it's not like Texans are completely without role models. There's Robert E. Howard, the patron saint of Texas SF writers. And there's Oliver, encouraging young writers and making it clear that it's not a physical impossibility to live here and write SF. Oliver is not an ideologue. He's not here to say, "All right, all you kids, get your ducks in a row and follow my example." His work has always been quite eclectic, based in soft science rather than nuts-and-bolts *Analog*-type stuff. He's not what you would call a mainstream SF cultural figure. His work is certainly well respected and influential in its way, but he has never been an editor or a big wheel in the SFWA. His influence is vivifying without being restrictive.

BL: I think I read that you lived in India for a while.

BS: I lived in India from the time I was fifteen until I was eighteen (my dad is an engineer). A lot of SF writers either had a serious illness, had parents in the service, or lived in a foreign country—the situations are the same. It's a period of being pulled out of your cultural matrix. When you come back to the reality, it's never the same because you see it with bigger eyes. The experience of alienation is really crucial to the evolution of the sensibilities of many SF writers.

LM: Did your immersion in SF begin while you were in India?

BS: I was pretty heavily into it in India. It's possible to get books there, but they're mostly British, so I was able to read a lot of British

SF—Ballard, Moorcock, Aldiss, and guys who didn't get published in the States, like Vincent King, a *New Worlds* writer who wrote a book called *Light a Last Candle.*

LM: Were you writing anything at that point?

BS: I had a notebook and I would write stuff, but I burned all of it. Yeah, I was ambitious to write. When I came back to the States, I started going to school in Austin and hanging out with the local SF subculture, the would-be literati, all those who were soon to be greats— like Waldrop. A lot of them were briefly well known but never really made careers in SF.

BL: When I attended the University of Texas, I was aware of the Salamander Weekly, a kind of odd Duck's Breath or Monty Python group that was into outrage with a definite SF cast to it. The group had this absolute fascination with televangelists—wild fantasies.

BS: Remember the Church of the Subgenius guys? I used to hang out with those Arts and Sausages party absurdists. I was involved in their campaign for the student council presidency at Texas when they nominated a juggler candidate who actually won. He wanted to replace the slogan "You shall know the truth and the truth shall make you free" with "Money talks." And there was Paul Spragens, who was a quadriplegic absurdist—I still keep in touch with him; he's been heavily involved in what you might call the marginal way of writing. Have you ever read Bob Black's *Abolition of Work and Other Essays,* which is one of the seminal underground documents of the '80s? There's a lot of that book in *Islands.* The antilabor party run by Dr. Bob Razak— it's all lifted from Bob Black. He's an antilabor activist, a brilliant, troubled soul.

LM: A lot of cyberbunk artists seem to be feeding into this network of counterculture absurdists. There's an interrelationship among the people interested in technology and the pop underground that those on the outside—like Gregory Benford—aren't in touch with.

BS: John Shirley pinned Benford when he said that Benford was not "culturally on-line." That sounds like a bizarre, pretentious slur, but it's an objective fact. There *is* a line there. It's very weird, but it's definitely there.

BL: Have you met any of the people connected with the Survival Research Labs or any of the industrial culture artists?

BS: I've spoken to them, but I don't really travel all that much and I haven't been to California in ages. It really makes me uneasy out there. I've talked to Andrea Juno and corresponded with the people at *RE/Search* magazine, which is one of the great cultural publications of our era; and I know Arbright & Barg, and Arbright & Barg know Mark Pauline and the SRL people, and so forth. There are definite connections there. Pauline has described himself as a cyberpunk—in *Vogue,* of all places!

BL: When we spoke last summer, the disdain with which you referred to movie deals was pretty thick. But it strikes me that someone writing the way you're writing is going to be a prime target. Are you still determined not to have anything to do with film and TV?

BS: Working in film and TV seems to me like shoveling air.

LM: Every time I hear from Bill Gibson he's working on yet another draft of *Aliens III.*

BS: Or had another imperious call from Hollywood that he had to answer at a moment's notice. You know, they fly you there first-class and feed you candied prawns, but nothing is accomplished because nothing is published or put into permanent form. People hunger for what cyberpunk represents, but it's necessary to get the message out in a way that's direct and tangible, not half-assed or passed by committee.

LM: Isn't that the trouble with the whole cinema situation? Brooks has written that film or TV images are where cyberpunk would naturally lead, but there must be something attractive about working in a medium like fiction that allows you to control the results.

BS: Max Headroom becoming a spokesman for Coca-Cola was an obvious object lesson. Anyone who could watch something like that and not realize the cultural vandalism that was going on there has to be blind—especially if you know anything about Rocky Morton and Annabel Jankel, the people who got Max Headroom up. They're what I would consider to be classic nongenre cyberpunks: '80s underground rock figures who are also computer graphics experts, moving seamlessly from the realm of the technological to the realm of the pop cultural. But they sold Max Headroom; he was like a trademark. They didn't control him in the way, say, I control the Artificial Kid, who's a copyrighted character. If I had been asked to make up the Artificial Kid as a commercial promotion for somebody else, then I'd be helpless, people could do with that property what they would. There's an arsenal of persuasion that these people use—they claim, "We can get you to a wider audience."

LM: Doesn't every artist want that?

BS: The wider-audience business is just a come-on, because you don't have any creative control. Writers tell me, "Well, you know, I'm working on this screenplay or that video thing, and, yeah, it's going to be sixty minutes long, but it's OK because I can get my two minutes of message in there." Give me a break.

BL: In your writing, there's no love lost on multinationals or on Big Science. But in *Islands in the Net,* you depict a future of mainly corporate structures that admittedly are tough but that keep social organization going. Is this a sign of cynical faith in the power of corporations?

BS: I'm not in favor of Big Science, but I'm not opposed to the scientific method. I'm not in favor of commodification of every aspect of human existence, but I think the corporation is actually a rather sensible way to harness human energies. You can't allow yourself to be defeated by the spectre of institutions—they're what people make them. The thing that differentiates Rizome in *Islands* from a modern corporation is that it's an economic democracy: it's politically organized; it's more of a Japanese feudal organization based on social ties rather than on the bottom line.

BL: In the section where David tries to explain to Prentice that Rizome doesn't separate concepts of work from those of play, David sounds more than a little fatuous. Were you agreeing with David that Rizome is a pretty good corporate structure?

BS: *Islands* is not a standard SF utopia—and if I never read another utopia or another dystopia, I'll be happy. Why write about the future as if it were not going to exist as its own entity, when you know it will? In *Islands,* the nature of the universe isn't millennially changed, even though characters are always talking about the premillennium and claiming that they're in the postmillennium and this is the "new" twenty-first century and so forth. These people sound innocent and fatuous because we live in a cynical world and they don't. If you talk to an old Bolshevik, or to an American revolutionary from 1777 who's full of the ideas of Thomas Paine, he'd seem pretty fatuous too. The lives of the people of the *Islands* are by no means perfect, and their world isn't without skulduggery and various temptations and so forth, but they're ideologues. That's one of the things I suspect will be tough for the reader to take in this book. I've established all the dialectics, but I leave the synthesis up to the reader. One of my aims is to replace oppositions with ambiguities. I'm not doing everybody's thinking for them. That's a departure from most SF.

LM: Was *Schismatrix* more consciously designed as a series of dialectics?

BS: In *Schismatrix,* lines are always drawn because it's the logic of the place. Things drift farther apart and then the edges calcify; things fly apart into small pieces. In *Islands,* there's obviously a global polity that is being formed, so that all forms of opposition are constantly under pressure. The semiotics are everywhere; you can see Laura and David as agents of that synthesis. The logic of what they're attempting requires them to dissolve all boundaries whenever possible, so they'll seldom, if ever, tell somebody, "Well, you're wrong. No, that's evil." They always say, "We have some expertise in that too, so let's negotiate." These webs of interaction by their very logic eventually subsume people. *Islands* is based on the cultural logic of the '80s underground, or the '60s underground: a group of angry rejectionists are eventually won over by the mere logic of commodification, the logic of subsuming. Gresham represents the person who simply will not integrate, the militant rejectionist. And the reason Gresham is able to get away with it is that, unlike the Grenadians or the Singaporeans, he is simple not interested in what the Net has simply to offer—whereas Grenada and Singapore are criminal organizations, which parasitize the energy of the Net.

BL: What's your interest in the individuals in *Islands?* Laura and David survive, and each of them learns a lot about the world, but as individuals they're clearly not as happy at the end of the book as they were at the beginning. Their lives have been complicated in every way.

BS: This book, unlike, say, *The Artificial Kid,* is aimed deliberately at people who are like Laura and David Webster; it is a deliberately ambiguous political novel that is meant to disturb people, to force them to examine for themselves. This is opposed to, say, *Neuromancer,* where you're lost if you don't have a feeling for what it means to be a suicidal speed-freak thief. I'm as big a fan of Gibson's work as anyone, but in a way it fails to carry the war to the enemy. People like Laura and David Webster are the ones who make the decisions in society. They're the people with money to spend; the people who read the magazines and newspapers and actually vote in elections; the people who try to control their own lives and think in the long term. There are issues they don't like to confront, but I don't believe they're evil because they're bourgeois. The middle classes are stabilizing forces, and I'm glad to live in a stable society.

LM: Your focus on ordinary people like David and Laura is one of several departures from what we find in most cyberpunk novels.

BS: If *Islands* were a cyberpunk novel per se, the main characters would have been Sticky Thompson, the Grenadian third-world terrorist, and Carlotta, the hooker. Laura and David would then be slick corporate hustlers, mealy-mouthed manipulators with shadowy political connections. But I wanted these people portrayed as what they mean to our real society and—in a sense David and Laura are the enemies of terrorism and instability, the agents of integration. No matter what you feel about this integration—and I am ambivalent about it—it's coming, and it needs to be discussed and thought about.

BL: Marxism seems to have gone belly up in Laura and David's future, yet, you distributed an awful lot of Marxist style over the various movements. What do you think about Marxism and Marxist views of the future?

BS: Marxism is a nineteenth-century industrial ideology and this is a postindustrial world. Certain aspects of Marxism remain—like the vocabulary, the semiotic layer—but nothing like the dictatorship of the proletariat or the withering away of the state or the controlling of the means of production. People don't seize the means of production in *Islands,* but they often seize the means of information. The world government, or what passes for the world government (it's simply called Vienna), is constantly meddling with journalists, shutting down and putting lids on various scandals and atrocities. The climactic scene, when Laura seizes the means of information to spill the story of the Malian scandal over the world satellite net, can be construed as a Marxist revolutionary act. But I'm more interested in examining "economic democracy," a concept that is never codified in this book. If I really knew how to establish corporations that ran on democratic principles, I would be a multimillionaire—or an economic guru like Alvin Toffler or Peter Drucker—not an SF writer.

LM: What about the processes involved in writing *Islands?* For example, what was the initial motivation or idea that started the book, and how did it evolve?

BS: The motivation was essentially ideological, both politically and in terms of what I like to do with SF. I've developed further insight into the basic structures of the genre. *The Artificial Kid* and *Involution Ocean* are space operas. *Involution Ocean,* although it contains drug culture references and so forth, is essentially a standard SF novel about science and mysticism and drugs. *The Artificial Kid* is about violence and politics and media—and you can begin to see that the SF adventure form is being strained by what I want to use it for. *Schismatrix* is about the technological revolution, the limits of human form in posthumanity—the conventional structure of the space opera is entirely destroyed, and what's left is not a novel structure (which is a difficulty, but not an inescapable one) but a sort of Stapledonian schematic that might conceivably have been turned into six conventional SF novels, each covering a period of, say, twenty years.

LM: In *Schismatrix,* I felt a literary imagination trying to discover or invent a form that would apply or reinforce the abstractions you wanted to examine. And yet, the analogies you make between your own work and punk music suggest self-contained antiformalism.

BS: Form is left-handed work to me, because it's not where my natural gifts lie. Like most SF writers, I'm fixated more on the mental pyrotechnics. It's only as I've lost a bit of my youthful fire that I've gained the guile of age and taken a more formal interest in crafting this stuff. I've also tried to stretch in different ways. In *Islands,* for instance, I have a woman protagonist who is probably the most completely delineated character in any of my work. I felt that I needed to do that in order to teach myself. But it's not something that comes to me instantly. I can't pretend to have any particular gift of formal analysis, the sort of ability that would allow me to reinvent the novel structure for post-industrial literature. Ideally, I would like to create postindustrial literature that would be equally at home in an art gallery or a genetics lab. I can see that it needs to be done, but I don't know whether I have the formal ability to do it, though I think the way to do it is probably in structuralism. In any case, it will involve a radical reanalysis of the nature of literature and its social functions.

The people who have mainstream reputations in SF are generally those who have managed to paper over the crevices in their work—the logical flaws, the rational and imaginative lapses—with gaudy prose. Ray Bradbury is a great example, or Gene Wolfe. People who can lift you up into this mellifluous, purple atmosphere of vivid imagery and never let you down. But you can never punch through that surface layer to get at the underlying contradictions of the form. SF writers have been doing this for many years, and we've never ever been able to face down the difficulty—I don't know if it's faceable. It's part of a deeper cultural problem, a contradiction between what we've learned, what science has taught us, and how we react to our knowledge.

BL: *Schismatrix* strikes me as one of the few SF works to attempt to face these contradictions.

BS: As a radical attempt to reshape a literary convention it did OK; it's an all right book and has had an influence, but it isn't *Dune* or *Stranger in a Strange Land,* or one of those bombshell novels that quickly reshape the thinking of the genre. Its influence probably will not be felt for another twenty years, in the same way that the influence of Ballard's *Crystal World* or his condensed novels shows today because Bruce Sterling, who read them when he was a teenager, managed to assimilate them.

LM: *Islands* is a very different work (compared to *Schismatrix*) in terms of the way it unfolds.

BS: It was my deliberate attempt to portray a *plausible* version of a livable human future, whereas *Schismatrix* was intentionally quite jarring and alien. A lot of people aren't going to be able to detect any form in *Schismatrix,* partly because it's not a novelistic form but also because they just won't be able to get into the headspace that produced it. I couldn't have made the novel more accessible without completely changing it, blurring what it attempts to say. I wrote *Islands* in a way that makes it accessible to the standard citizenry of the '80s but nevertheless plants extremely subversive, difficult ideas they will not be able rid themselves of. It's a political novel that was meant to have an impact on my contemporaries, to say in a gentle but firm voice, "Look, this stuff is actually going to come. Let's quit this ridiculous obsession with the apocalypse and the millennium, both of which are just ways we of the later twentieth century escape the consequences of our own carelessness."

You can see this obsession in a movie like *Mad Max* or in any of the postapocalypse books and movies. In a way, Ballard has really got this down: he describes his disaster novels as "novels of psychic fulfillment," which is literally true. For us the apocalypse movie or document is a vehicle of psychic fulfillment in that its premise enables us to avoid confronting the complexities of our postindustrial existence. Everything is simplified when you've got to kill your neighbor for gasoline or a can of dogfood, plus you get to wear nifty black leather clothes and drive around real fast. High speed and hallucinogenic drugs— the two twentieth-century pleasures. I regard that as essentially morbid and decadent in the classic sense of indicating the collapse of the set of values. So I feel it's a moral and ideological necessity for SF writers to develop a portrait of a future we might actually be living. The many old people in *Islands in the Net* are our contemporaries. In the year 2023 I'll be almost seventy, and assuming that my chromosomes haven't been warped by a global thermonuclear holocaust, I'll probably be around, maybe even be in pretty good shape.

LM: A lot of what you've just been saying certainly refutes the usual criticism of cyberpunk—that it's all decadence, sleaze, and surfaces.

BS: That's the standard reaction of anyone whose value system is being questioned—they'll accuse you of being a nihilist because they can't envision any value system outside their own. Gibson says that a lot of people say to him, "Gosh, isn't *Neuromancer* morbid? I mean, all these people are criminals and they never seem to come out during daylight." His response is, "Well, if you're in a situation where you can punch deck and get youself a pair of jeans, that's pretty much OK." There's a lot in *Islands* about people's obsession with the apocalypse. I've lived in the Third World, and I know what misery looks like. I've seen lepers, people with elephantiasis, people drinking sewage and living in mud huts. When you see stuff like that, it destroys the romantic allure of "Boy, if only we could destroy the patriarchal control systems. . . ." That's the flip side of the *Mad Max* scenario: the supposed return of pastorality, where there are no TVs and everyone eats goat cheese. But this delusion doesn't have any more to do with the way things are going to be than the dystopian, apocalyptic view. Those are like psychic tumors, stress reactions, visions of powerlessness. What we really need is some way to make sense of our predicament and to empower people to control their own destiny. SF is nearly always a literature of and for people who are powerless. It's mostly an escapist fiction, but *it doesn't have to be.* Wells certainly didn't use it as such. SF is a tool that can be directed in many ways, and in *Islands in the Net* I felt it was necessary to carry the war to the enemy. People are wrong about technology. They talk about it in terms that are utterly, ideologically incorrect, as if it were a shiny silver box that beeps and gives you candy. That's absurd, immature. Technology is a state of mind. It's deeply embedded in our most profound social convictions, part of the wiring of our brains.

LM: When you say "our," are you talking about people *here,* in developed countries? What about the wiring of third-world peoples?

BS: I am talking about Westerners, the people who live in technological surroundings. There's a great book called *What a Blow That Phantom Gave Me,* by an American media theorist who went into the Third World with a video camera and a tape recorder. What he found was that if you present people in New Guinea with a tape recorder, it's a millennial advent. People rush up, crowd around—the potency of these things is enormous. Technology is like the air we breathe; it's all around us so we don't see it, we don't observe its deeper cultural roots. Even scientists don't understand their own cultural roots, but when people state this criticism it is always interpreted as Luddite nihilism. Scientists are passionless, rational, objective, right? So if you make a statement of fact like "Half of the physicists in America are employed by the Defense Department," which is true, that raises a host of unacknowledged contradictions. People immediately assume that you've got to be some sort of scientist-bashing Luddite, so the whole thing remains undiscussed, the ambiguities unconfronted.

LM: Gregory Benford argues that scientists have an allegiance to follow the truth and therefore have a moral force—which is why they are increasingly becoming an important sociopolitical force. Does it really follow that if you originally follow a scientific principle you are therefore moral?

BS: We're getting into territory now that is going to be covered by my next book—the one Gibson and I are working on, *The Difference Engine*—which is essentially about nineteenth-century social roots and the evolution of the scientific, technocratic, industrial complex that we all know and love. Benford is saying what Huxley said in his Darwinism debates with Bishop "Soapy Sam" Wilberforce. Remember the famous interchange in which Wilberforce inquired snidely whether Huxley's grandfather or grandmother had been an ape? When Huxley replied that there was no shame in having an ape for an ancestor—that it was better then being a lousy sneak like Wilberforce, who deliberately obscured the truth to protect his own position—woman fainted and men ran up and down the aisles shaking their Bibles and screaming, "The

Word, the Word!" It was a moment of deep sociocultural crisis, which Huxley won. His ideology was always that of "I am a scientist, and I will follow the truth wherever it leads, no matter how much social damage it creates or what the consequences are to the status quo of my own society." That was fine at the time, because Huxley didn't exist in the same social framework as a modern scientist does—the framework that has resulted in, say, genetic engineering and the Manhattan Project.

BL: What kinds of books do you read?

BS: Mostly nonfiction, although I try to keep up with fiction—I feel an obligation to do that. Unlike many writers, I don't emerge from an English lit background. I have a journalism degree, so I like to have facts to chew on. I read a lot of science journalism, even scientific reports, an endless amount of technical material (the deadliest prose on this planet). In fact, I thought of being a science journalist, and someday I would like to do a pop science book—it gives a certain éclat to the SF writer to have done pop science. But I'm not a very prolific writer, so it's necessary to work on fiction, at least for the time being.

LM: When you read fiction, do you read mainly SF?

BS: Right now I'm interested in something that really doesn't have a name—I suspect that when it does, it will carry considerable pent-up force, the same way the term "cyberpunk" did. I read novels that deal with the terminology and the tenets and the cultural territory of SF but aren't genre material. Pynchon is the obvious exemplar of that, a guy who has won literary awards when his books are actually about the military-industrial complex and the ideology of Werner Von Braun, who aimed at the stars and hit London. There are a surprising number of writers working in that whole complex of things that Pynchon discusses. Martin Amis, for instance, who wrote *Einstein's Monsters,* a collection of SF stories about nuclear war. I don't know how many copies it sold, probably not too many. Amis has no genre ID, so his book has had little effect on SF. The same thing happened to *Easy Travel to Other Planets* by Ted Mooney, another guy who works with an SF topic without any of the genre moves, like using traditional jargon—his jargon sounds better: "information sickness."

LM: How about Don DeLillo? He seems to fit into this category.

BS: I love *White Noise.* It's like an SF disaster novel; a great book that deals with the cultural roots I was referring to earlier—the airborne toxic event. It could have been a John Wyndham novel.

LM: Have you read many of the non-SF experimental writers—postmodernists like Robert Coover and Donald Barthelme?

BS: I've read some Barthelme, but in general, no. My tastes in the early years were nowhere near so suave as they are now. Essentially, I like to read stuff that's whacky, and I don't care if it's crude. A great many SF writers don't know how to structure a novel; they're hopeless primitives. Some of them can hardly write English. On the other hand, I find some of their work to be most refreshing. Conventional narrative bores me. But then try reading a Rudy Rucker novel. He's a writer of considerable gifts. You read one of his paragraphs and there's real authorial insight there. You're in the hands of somebody who notices things, who obviously has a great idiosyncratic mind. But his novels, *as* novels, are indescribable; they're not really novels but prose assemblages.

LM: Are there any other contemporary authors you admire or feel affinities with, within or outside SF?

BS: John Gardner. And John Updike—I liked *Roger's Version,* a strangely anti-cyberpunk novel with a character who has definite cyber-eighties affinities. I've also been reading Ian McEwan. I like British SF quite a bit. A great borderline writer is Iain Banks, whose *Wasp Factory* is an amazing book.

LM: What about more fantasy-oriented writers—people like Angela Carter or Steve Erickson?

BS: I've read some Carter, but I tend to take that left-handed magical realism in light doses. I couldn't get into Erickson. Something like *Rubicon Beach* lacks a rational spine, so I find it very difficult to develop the suspension of disbelief that's involved. Gibson loves Erickson, but I am too hardheaded. The journalist in me is always tearing at the structure, and when I do this to Erickson's books, they go to pieces. If something is too dreamlike or too obviously self-contradictory, that bothers me. On the other hand, there's a lot of magical realism I do read and enjoy. I'm a big fan of the South Americans, Borges, Márquez, Cortàzar, that whole crowd. I'm interested in all sorts of innately peculiar work because, as an SF writer, I work in a bastard field.

BL: Your work displays two tendencies: toward the sweeping, SF space-opera-oriented imaginative tradition, and toward the present. I get the idea, from hearing you talk today, that you're not much interested in doing that sweeping all-stops-out invention anymore—but can you ever see yourself going back to wild flights of imagination?

BS: Maybe, but in shorter forms. I've been so deeply radicalized by eight years of Reaganism that there are wells of rage I haven't begun to tap. When I wrote *The Artificial Kid* and *Involution Ocean,* I was a young man, a student, footloose and fancy free. Now I'm in my mid-thirties; I've been married for many years; I have a small child. I feel a different responsibility about what I'm doing. A book like *The Artificial Kid* is a pop commodity; there's no way you're going to read it and really have your life changed. You may be entertained, and you may have your mind expanded, and it may add something to your repository of daydream imagery, but that's about it.

BL: A corollary question: Once you've evolved the very rigorous and highly detailed near-future that you give us in *Islands,* are you limited to working within that world in future works?

BS: I'm not going to be limited by *Islands in the Net,* which will date very quickly—political novels always do. In a few years it's going to sound like Phil Ochs singing about ending the war in Vietnam. I don't think *Schismatrix* will date at all rapidly; I can easily see it being reprinted many years from now, in the same way that Stapledon's work is being reprinted today. But what you're really asking, I think, is, "How in the world can I go on working that hard with no obvious payoff?" *Islands* is no more rigorous and required no more brainwork than *Schismatrix.* If anything, there was less, because a great deal of the material in *Islands* is readymade, images lifted right off the surface of modern culture, whereas *Schismatrix* was built bit by bit from deep, basic principles to form societies that are really quite alien. People talk about the complexity in my work—maybe "fractal prose" captures what's involved in this complexity, because there are levels of material that I use to build my work from the ground up. I use details, as in the great cyberpunk tagline: "to carry extrapolation into the fabric of daily life." That slogan represents what is probably cyberpunk's most important conceptual breakthrough. Cyberpunk grabs you by the back of your neck and rubs your nose in the nitty-gritty.

LM: Is this embedding of cultural implications in specifics—the sort of thing you do in *Schismatrix*—something you've had to cultivate?

BS: It's blood and pain for me—though for Gibson, it happens as soon as he opens his eyes. He's a compulsive observer in the same way I'm a compulsive extrapolator. I think SF in my sleep—which is the way I order the "blooming, buzzing confusion" of sensory impressions. It's something that has come naturally to me, and I do it with great ease. People wonder how I can write *Schismatrix* and then write *Islands in the Net*—two books that are full of this vast complexity. But it comes as naturally to me as breathing. So I'm doing a book now, with Gibson, that will do for the nineteenth century what *Islands* does for the twenty-first.

LM: How did *Schismatrix* evolve out of the stories that you were working on in the Shaper/Mechanist series?

BS: I've always been interested in space opera, one of those standard SF genre traditions. I started working on the Shaper/Mechanist stories early in my career; "Swarm," for instance, was my first published short story. By that time I had a greater sense of my own ability, and I wanted to get in on this genre (subgenre, really) and turn up its amps. I knew I could, so I nibbled at the edges, first by doing short stories: "Swarm," "Spider Rose," "Cicada Queen," and so on. Once the series was well established, a novel was inevitable; I knew I didn't want to go on writing Shaper stories for the rest of my life. Nowadays, I don't have to worry about that sort of thing, because I'm well enough known that people will buy a Sterling book on its own merits. I didn't want to end up writing the same thing all my life, so I decided I would just burn it all with *Schismatrix,* remove any possible temptation to write ten novels about it. *Schismatrix* really is three books, at least. The three sections could be three different books: "Sundog Zones" (a cyberpunk SF novel), "Community and Anarchy" (a novel with social structures and political and economic manipulations), and "Moving in Clades" (a novel of Clarkean transcendence). But *Schismatrix* is bare bones, like a Ramones three-minute pop song: we're not going to have any pretentious lighter shades of pale guitar noodling here, it's going to be "Sheena Is a Punk Rocker," blam blam blam, let's move on. Those three sections of *Schismatrix* exemplify the classic modes of space opera. There's a pulp tradition of the action-adventure novel, and there's the sort of Georgette Heyer novel of social interaction, and there's the scientistic, Clarkean, mystic novel at the end. They're all there.

BL: The notion of fractal prose seems to apply to your early experimental pieces, like "Twenty Evocations."

BS: "Twenty Evocations" is a miniaturized schematic of *Schismatrix;* it's like a Ballard condensed novel. I love and respect those Ballard condensed novels because they seem to get at something that's very native and valuable in SF. People talk about SF as a branch of literature or a subgenre of fantasy, but I don't see it that way. That's like saying rock 'n' roll is a subgenre of the European tradition of symphonic music, whereas it's actually an alien, African-based tribal music that has some of the tropes of Western music laid on it. SF is a similar sort of thing. Real people who are actual litterateurs prefer their literature untroubled by visionary lunacy, whereas to me visionary lunacy is the entire point of SF. And if you've got that quill, you can do what you will to the structure.

The novel form was invented in eighteenth-century England and isn't equipped to deal with people who live for two hundred years and undergo extreme sociocultural change. Monographs are equipped to deal with that. Take Le Guin's *Always Coming Home,* which is like an anthropological monograph. You can say, "That isn't a real book," and you'd be right—it's not a "real book," it's a box of different sorts of materials that Le Guin assembled. The way to explain how to read this stuff is to have somebody say, "Look, I've discovered this interesting thing about this culture, and here are my notes, in this cardboard box. It's a little messed up, but I know that you, as a fellow academic, will be interested in this." That's the literary experience conveyed by *Always Coming Home*. I don't agree with Le Guin's politics—I find many of her attitudes kind of retro, and I'm sure she would have similar caveats about my work. But I do respect her a great deal for having done something like *Always Coming Home*. It's a much truer SF novel than anything that, say, a hard SF writer like Gregory Benford ever wrote, because it goes deeper and tackles a lot more of the actual potential of the genre.

BL: In many ways, *Schismatrix* is structured right down the line of the paradigms of postmodernism; it's postmodernism with a vengeance: writ-large disruptions in space, disruptions in time, disruptions of the human body, disruptions of the self. For example, Kitsune, the female character whose body dimensions expand until she becomes a city of flesh.

BS: But in a way, Kitsune is less postmodern than Lindsay, who has a severe case of postmodern "subjectivity fragmentation." He does have some kind of affect, but he's mutated by his psychotechnical diplomatic training. Someone refers to it as "hypocrisy as a second state of consciousness." Someone else asks, "Is it true that it changes so much that you have no capacity for sincerity?" And Lindsay replies, "Sincerity is a slippery concept."

BL: Obviously your decision to use a woman as your protagonist in *Islands* wasn't accidental.

BS: You can't get away from feminist rhetoric in modern SF, so there's a lot of commentary on feminism in *Islands*. Feminism is a tricky thing to get into because it's difficult to find the proper party line. I read a lot of feminist work before I wrote *Islands,* and I approach feminism in the book as a technological artifact, a product of postindustrialism based on breakthroughs in contraceptive technologies. Of course, there's a lot of stuff in *Islands* about the disintegration of the family and about old clan-based power structures and their replacement by new structures, either corporate or national or ideological.

LM: William S. Burroughs has talked about these issues from almost the beginning. He says that only by getting rid of the family can we get rid of political structures. But he never explains what's supposed to replace the family.

BS: Burroughs is an anarchist and doesn't believe the family should be replaced at all. The classic Burroughs character is the classic American fiction character: hard, isolated, stoic, a killer. But people like that don't make a society, and what you find in *Islands* is very definitely a society. As much as I find some anarchist ideas attractive, I don't see how we can have a population of six billion people living in anarchy. You could have some sort of anarchist system on, say, Samoa. Or here, if you had an underclass of mindless robots to do all the scut work. But the world in *Islands* is a very crowded world—and it's obviously far better ordered than our own.

LM: One thing that impressed me in *Islands* is that you don't simplify Laura's character. Your feminist portrayal confronts many of the stereotypes of feminism.

BS: SF's version of feminism is topheavy with overtones of West Coast hippiedom; it doesn't have that much to do directly with the political rights of women today and tomorrow. As I said, I read pretty widely in feminist theory before I started writing *Islands,* and I found enormous gaps and contradictions. Take, say, Betty Friedan, who is a liberal democratic feminist. I read her work and didn't find anything in it that I disagreed with. Her arguments are rational, logical, reasonable; and they make a devastating case for the liberation of women. Then you read something more radical and disturbing, like Susan Brownmiller's *Femininity,* which examines sex roles and the imagery of sexuality in a way that Friedan doesn't. Friedan says that women deserve this and that, whereas Brownmiller says that the very notion of femininity is a patriarchal tool. The images we associate with the feminine are actually hallmarks of oppression. Our notions of womanly beauty or grace are essentially tricks, to see to it that women can't repair their own cars or hook up their own stereos. Then there are the goddess feminists, theologians who go out and call down the moon on a midsummer's eve. Medieval lunacy writ large. A little of that found its way into *Islands* in the guise of the Church of Ishtar. The stuff that calls itself "feminism" has a very eclectic agenda. And in the same way, many things the Church of Ishtar does are hybridized. Again, oppositions are replaced with ambiguities.

LM: It strikes me that what you're doing goes against the whole novelistic tradition—that is, you're deliberately creating the kinds of ambiguities and complexities that novelists traditionally try to resolve.

BS: One of the marks of critical thinking, or at least of the intellectual life of the late '80s, is a willingness to confront complexity and chaos. In fact, chaos theory is intellectually sexy right now—I'm thinking of starting a magazine called *Chaos Theory.* We have computers now that can simulate very complex systems, and people are used to thinking in terms of multiple levels of complexity or multiple viewpoints. This ties in with postmodernism and relativism and the shattering of the self, which is our equivalent of alienation as a breakdown of the self. And of course multimedia presentations. Part of our *Zeitgeist* is not to be afraid of complexities.

LM: Timothy Leary and others allege that cyberpunk tends to deal with people who are manipulating, controlling, and *playing with* these machines.

BS: That's very much a part of the cyberpunk ethos. And it's also tied in with a collage aesthetic, which cyberpunk has embraced, that announces, "Look, I'm not going to reinvent all this stuff when I can just rip a big chunk of it from here and slap it down there and put it to my own uses." Classic twentieth-century motifs: collage and surrealism, Max Ernst, Semaine de Bonté. I'm a big fan of all that. There's a lot of collage material, what Ballard called "invisible literature," in *Islands,* and it carries with it so much freight. Some of the people in *Islands* even *speak* in collage forms—one moment what they're saying has Marxist overtones and then they switch to New Age or feminist or even a '60s slant.

LM: In *Schismatrix* you present the idea that systems inevitably evolve into things that are more complex. Even a hundred years ago, Huxley and his notion of evolution suggested the possibility of returning to something less complex—devolution, as Devo would say. How does the system of evolving into something more complex fit in with entropy, say?

BS: Right now we don't have the vocabulary to talk about this, but we're going to discover a lot about it very soon, and that excites me. In *Schismatrix* there is a great deal of talk about systems, but much of that is essentially theological-political rhetoric on the part of characters who are advancing it for their own self-interest, or because of ideological concerns. I had a lot of fun with that, really, because the "Prigoginic Levels of Complexity" are the religion of "Cicada Queen" and the driving politics of *Schismatrix.* Of course, if I knew what religion would *really* look like in the twenty-fifth century, I wouldn't be an SF novelist. It's sort of treated as a joke, but at the same time there are genuinely disturbing elements there. *Islands* and *Schismatrix* are opposite sides of the coin. In *Schismatrix* the dynamics of commodification are writ large. There's no such thing as a natural world in *Schismatrix.* Every landscape is man-made, and the human body is essentially a natural resource, like iron ore or a corn plant. Breed it to improve it, graft things onto it, it's a part of the landscape, no more sacred than a bulkhead or a rocket.

LM: Everything in *Schismatrix* is manipulated by people who are afraid of dying, who are trying to find in some really deep level a way to continue their existence.

BS: They *reject* death—there are no limits in *Schismatrix,* other than what is technically feasible. The Mechanists and the Shapers are fighting death in two different ways, so this leads to a schism. But they don't accept the inevitability of death: it's just a question of finding the proper techniques to maintain the body, or, if necessary, just scrapping the body and replacing it with something better. When you do that, you embed yourself very deeply into a maintenance system. You really are no longer an individual but a part of the system, an integral part. Ryumin, the wirehead in *Schismatrix,* says, "Think of us as angels on the wires." That carries the logic of technological development to a crisis pitch. The logic of apocalypse, the logic of commodification invades every aspect of the human mind and body. But *Islands* is a retort to that. When I wrote *Schismatrix* I felt, in a very late '70s or standard punk sort of way, that there was no way to resist the remorseless drive of technology (there should be a better term, the "techno-state of mind," perhaps). I felt there was no way to resist the logic implicit in the postindustrial milieu because there was no way to resist it on its own terms. When you accept those premises, you've got to follow them to the end. The only way to escape that system is via a political solution, and I have less faith in political systems than I do in industrial ones.

BL: One of the startling things in *Islands* happens when Laura is suddenly in prison, away from the interactions she is used to, and the reader is alone with Laura's language.

BS: Prison is the price the political activist pays—prison or death. If you look at anybody who has been involved in real social movements in the twentieth century, they've either been lined up and shot or else they've done time. Every major American social reformer has done time—King, Malcolm X, Thoreau. A lot of Laura's experience in *Islands* is taken from the Iranian hostage situation. I've never done time, and I hope I never do, but if they want me, they know where I live.

An Interview with

Gene Wolfe

Gene Wolfe's earliest stories began appearing in various SF magazines and anthologies, notably Damon Knight's *Orbit,* in the late '60s, and a generally undistinguished first novel, *Operation Ares,* was published in 1970. Then, the appearance of *The Fifth Head of Cerberus* in 1972 abruptly signaled an end to Wolfe's literary apprenticeship. Displaying a blend of intellectual and aesthetic sophistication, an eloquent and poetic prose style, and masterful storytelling instincts, *Cerberus* established Wolfe as an eccentric but important new figure in SF. Its prismatic manner of exposition, its sure control of a variety of imaginative narrative voices and of an intricate web of symbolism and literary allusion, its ingenious reworkings of familiar SF motifs, and its exploration of complex moral, social, and epistemological issues became central features of Wolfe's subsequent best work.

It is clear that Gene Wolfe has already produced a major body of SF, quasi-SF, fantasy, and unclassifiable fictions, displaying an equal facility with novelistic and short story forms. Particularly noteworthy has been Wolfe's striking integration of formal innovation and thematic concerns, and also his presentation of vividly imagined characters and symbolically charged actions that are placed within landscapes so rigorously drawn and rich in evocative details that they seem to rival reality itself in terms of their diversity and vitality. Wolfe has developed a series of grandly ambitious themes that include: the very nature and origin of the universe and of Life's role within cosmic evolution; the meaning of Good and Evil (and of acceptable versus unacceptable behavior) in a morally and epistemologically ambiguous universe (significantly, the main character in Wolfe's masterful Book of the New Sun tetralogy is a torturer by profession—a role perfectly suited for examining moral and psychological ambiguities); the nature of human memory and perception, and how this perception is transformed first into language and then into the larger structures of myth, fiction, science, history, and other cultural constructs.

It is Wolfe's remarkable gift as a prose stylist, as much as his formal ingenuity and the intelligence he brings to bear on issues large and small, that makes his fiction so distinctive. In his best works—*Peace* (1975; a much-neglected "mainstream" novel), *The Island of Dr. Death and Other Stories* (1980; a generous collection of stories), and his four-volume magnus opus (1980-82), comprised of *The Shadow of the Torturer, The Claw of the Conciliator, The Sword of the Lictor,* and *The Citadel of the Autarch*—Wolfe's prose charms, amazes, and seduces us with its lyricism, its eccentric lingoes and vocabularies (as often drawn from arcane and ancient sources as from modern science), and its surprising use of metaphor.

This eclecticism of taste is equally evident among the authors who have influenced Wolfe's literary sensibilities. Although his unusual methods of organizing his narratives are usually seen as evolving within the context of the experimental fervor of the '60s New Wave, the effort to situate his central formal and thematic concerns within a narrowly defined SF context is fundamentally misleading. William Faulkner, Jorge Luis Borges, G. K. Chesterton, Vladimir Nabokov, Charles Dickens, Marcel Proust, and numerous other non-SF authors have all exerted influences on Wolfe's prose mannerisms and approach to form/content issues. Equally significant in the case of Wolfe's conception of the Book of the New Sun are the examples of other masterworks of symbolic fantasy that similarly aim at presenting a justification of the ways of God to man: Dante's *Inferno,* Milton's *Paradise Lost,* C. S. Lewis's *Space Trilogy,* and probably closest in terms of its achievement, Tolkien's *Lord of the Rings* cycle.

Finally, however, such lists of comparisons and influences are only moderately useful, as is sifting through the details of Wolfe's life and professional career for clues about his work. At first glance, his life seems so *ordinary.* Born in Brooklyn in 1931, raised largely in Houston, Wolfe attended Texas A&M briefly, dropped out, and was drafted into the Korean War, where he saw limited combat duty. After his discharge from the army, he married, worked (until recently) as a mechanical engineer in Barrington, Illinois (where he still resides with his wife, Rosemary), and gradually began developing his career in SF. While his comments when we spoke in 1986 reveal that the "ordinariness" of his life is somewhat misleading, autobiographical details alone do little to account for his highly original artistic vision.

Classifying Wolfe's work with any taxonomical precision is further complicated by the allegorical cast of his imagination and his willingness to intermingle magic and fantasy with scientific principles. His sensitivity to the ambiguities and contradictions of human experience—and those of the physical universe as well—makes it similarly difficult to reduce his thematic preoccupations to simple polarities (optimistic/ pessimistic, liberal/conservative) or formulas. Like Joanna Russ, Samuel R. Delany, Stanislaw Lem, and Gregory Benford, Gene Wolfe frequently plays with—and eventually deconstructs—SF's stock paradigms in order to question their assumptions. In a certain basic sense, his works oppose the usual principle guiding most SF in their emphasis on the subjectivity of human perception rather than on the assurances of rational thought and scientific methodology. An even more radical departure from SF norms is his suggestion that religious faith, not science or any other system, provides our most profound insights into our relationship to the universe. His religious orientation—akin to cosmic mysticism but specifically associated with Catholicism—finds its most complete expression in the Book of the New Sun.

Undoubtedly, there will continue to be readers and critics within and without SF's boundaries who will be bothered or puzzled by the many paradoxical features of Gene Wolfe's literary imagination. But if it is true that a great individual is someone who never reminds us of anyone else, then Wolfe has the earmarks of greatness.

Larry McCaffery: Let's discuss what sorts of things have drawn you toward writing SF. Are there certain formal advantages in writing outside the realm of "mainstream" fiction, maybe a certain sense of freedom?

Gene Wolfe: It's not so much a matter of advantages as of SF appealing to my natural cast of mind, to my literary imagination. The only way I know to write is to write the kind of thing I would like to read myself, and when I do that it usually winds up being classified as SF or science fantasy, which is what I call most of my work. I'd argue that SF represents literature's real mainstream and that so-called realistic fiction—what we normally consider the mainstream—is a small literary genre, fairly recent in origin, that is likely to be relatively short-lived. When I look back at the foundations of literature, I see literary figures who, if they were alive today, would probably be members of the Science Fiction Writers of America. Homer? He would certainly belong to the SFWA. So would Dante, Milton, and Shakespeare. *That* tradition is literature's mainstream, and what has grown out of that tradition has been labeled science fiction or speculative fiction or whatever.

LM: That's why I wonder whether you were attracted to SF by the freedom it offers.

GW: It's a matter of whether you're content to focus on everyday events or whether you want to try to encompass the entire universe. If you go back to the literature written in ancient Greece or Rome, or during the Middle Ages and much of the Renaissance, you'll see writers trying to write not just about everything that exists but about everything that *could* exist. As soon as you open yourself to that possibility, you're going to find yourself talking about things like intelligent robots and monsters with Gorgon heads, because it's becoming increasingly obvious that such things could indeed exist. But what fascinates me is that the ancient Greeks realized these possibilities some five hundred years before Christ, when they didn't have the insights into the biological and physical sciences we have today, when there was no such thing as, say, cybernetics. Read the story of Jason and the Argonauts—you discover that Crete was guarded by a robot. Somehow the Greeks were alert to these possibilities despite the very primitive technology they had, and they put these ideas into their stories. Today, it's the SF writers who are exploring these things.

LM: Did you read a lot of SF as a kid?

GW: Every chance I could. I had a very nice grandmother named Alma Wolfe who used to save the Sunday comics for me; when I visited her, there would always be a huge stack to read, and I paid particular attention to "Buck Rodgers" and "Flash Gordon." I came across my first SF book as a kid in Houston. I had fallen off my bike and hurt my leg, badly enough that my mother had to drive me to and from school. On one of those drives, I noticed a paperback book on the front seat, and when I looked at the cover I saw a picture like the ones I had seen in the "Buck Rodgers" and "Flash Gordon" comics, a tremendous chrome tower and a rocket ship being launched. It was a paperback collection of SF stories edited by Don Wollheim, who was about twenty-two then; my mother had brought it to read while she waited for me after school (she was a big mystery fan but had bought this as a change of pace). I asked her if I could read it when she was finished, and she said I could have it right away since she didn't much care for it. That's how I came across "The Microcosmic God" by Theodore Sturgeon, which was my first real encounter with SF. At that point I realized these were not just stories I could enjoy—like those of Edgar Allan Poe, or the Oz books by L. Frank Baum, or the books by Ruth Plumly Thompson—but part of a genre. From the Wollheim anthology, which was the first American SF paperback anthology, I worked backward and discovered the SF pulps—*Planet Stories, Thrilling Wonder Stories, Weird Tales, Famous Fantastic Mysteries* (my favorite), and *Amazing Stories,* each of which could be bought for twenty or twenty-five cents. In junior high school, I used to walk six blocks or so up to the Richmond pharmacy, where I'd pick up one of those magazines, hide behind the candy case, and read until the pharmacist saw me and threw me out. Since I was usually interrupted in the middle of a story, I'd go away for a few days and then sneak back and take up where I'd left off.

LM: What kind of family atmosphere did you grow up in?

GW: One important thing was that I had a mother who read to me— a great blessing that I suppose just about everyone who writes has had. My father came from a small town in southern Ohio and was fairly adventurous as a young man, but eventually he became a regional sales manager in New York City. He met my mother—and married her— when he was assigned to Belhaven, North Carolina, for six months. My mother's family was right out of a Faulkner novel. Neither of my parents ever went to college—I suspect my mother never graduated from high school—but they were tremendous readers. And that world of literature was very important to me while I was growing up because I was an introverted kid, an only child who spent a lot of time in his imagination. I was constantly sick, beginning with infantile paralysis, and I was allergic to lots of things, like wheat and chocolate, that aren't much fun for a kid to be allergic to.

LM: Did all those stolen hours of reading behind the candy case help you decide to become a writer?

GW: No, I'm afraid it was more of a cold, practical decision. I wrote my first stories while I was at Texas A&M, studying engineering. My roommate was connected to the college magazine as an illustrator, and he thought it would be nice if I'd write some stories that he could illustrate. I wrote three or four forgettable pieces. Eventually, I dropped out of college—my grades were terrible—and was drafted into the army during the Korean War; later I went back to college on the GI Bill. By 1956 I had married Rosemary and was working as a mechanical engineer in research and development for Procter and Gamble. We were both making fairly good money, but we didn't have any reserves, so we were living in a furnished attic we didn't much like—two rooms, both with pointed ceilings so you could only stand up straight in the middle of them. It was then I decided that maybe I could write something, as I had in college, and sell it so we could get enough money to buy some furniture, move into a house, and live like real human beings. I tried to write a novel, but it was terrible—it never sold and it never will. But I was bitten by the bug. I discovered I liked writing; it had become a hobby. I kept on writing other stuff until finally, in 1965, I sold a

little ghost story called "The Dead Man" to *Sir,* which is one of those
skin magazines, a poor man's *Playboy.*

LM: Why did it take so long to sell your first piece? Was your work
really that bad, or were you already writing far enough outside the
accepted genre conventions that it was difficult to find a home for your
stories?

GW: It was a combination of everything. It wasn't just working outside
the SF conventions—I'm still doing that today, of course, but I'm doing
it better. Certainly, one of my problems was that I didn't know anything
about marketing when I was starting out. But mainly, I was simply
learning the art of writing. You don't go out, buy a violin, and then
immediately get a job with a symphony orchestra—first you've got to
learn how to play the damn thing. Writing is a lot like that. There are
cases like Truman Capote, who got his first five acceptances in one day
when he was seventeen, but he was a very unusual and precocious
writer. I remember vividly how afraid I was after I got that first acceptance that it was just blind luck, that I was never going to sell anything
else again.

LM: You dedicated *The Fifth Head of Cerberus* to Damon Knight,
"who one night in 1966 grew me from a bean." I suspect there's an
anecdote behind that dedication.

GW: The circumstances are a little complicated but probably worth
relating. I'll never be able to repay Damon Knight for his help and
support, although I've made some stabs at it in the past. I've received
a lot of help from other people since I've achieved some recognition,
but the only person who helped me with my writing when I really
needed help was Damon Knight. After I sold that story to the skin
magazine, I sent one called "The Mountains Are Mice" to *Galaxy.* I
didn't know who was editing what, but it turned out that *Galaxy* was
being edited by Fred Pohl. At any rate, I got back "The Mountains
Are Mice" with a simple rejection note, which was the way I got back
everything in those days. I was working from one of those lists of SF
markets published in *The Writer,* so when *Galaxy* rejected me I sent
the story to the next magazine on the list, which was *If.* I got an
acceptance from Pohl, who was also editing *If,* with a check. His letter
said, "I'm glad you let me see this again. The rewrite has really improved
it." Of course, there had been no rewrite. Once that story appeared I
received an invitation from Lloyd Biggle to join the SFWA, which had
a listing of markets that included *Orbit,* the anthology Damon Knight
was editing. I wrote a story called "Trip Trap" and sent it to *Orbit* and
got it back with a letter from Knight that said he liked the story a lot
but thought it needed to change here from viewpoint A to viewpoint
B—and this is why—and then to switch from B to C—with more

explanations—and a long list of very sensible suggestions. After I read that letter I lay on the bed for a long while before I suddenly realized, "By golly, I'm actually a *writer* now." I said something like that to Damon in my next letter to him, and he wrote back, "I didn't know I had grown you from a bean," which is the line I stole for my dedication to *The Fifth Head of Cerberus*. During the next few years Damon was buying my work, making a lot of useful observations about what I was doing, and basically giving me confidence in myself when no one else was.

LM: In looking back, are there any stories that you would point to as being "breakthrough" pieces?

GW: The real breakthroughs came before I started selling anything. I wrote a story called "In the Jungle," which was never published, about a kid who wanders into a hobo jungle, and at the time I thought it was a milestone in American literature. You know the way *Romancing the Stone* starts, with that woman writer staring at the typewriter and crying, "My God, I'm so good!"—well, I felt that way about "In the Jungle." I sent it out to about eighteen places and then watched the rejection slips pile up. Two or three years later, I pulled the story out, looked at it, and realized the story I'd had in my head had never gotten down on paper. What I learned to do in those apprentice years was make those really good stories run down my arm.

LM: Some of your works proceed in a relatively straightforward manner, while others unfold in a more complicated fashion, with the events being filtered through memory, dream, unreliable narrators, stories-within-stories, different points of view. What draws you to these "refracted" methods?

GW: First off, my intent in using these approaches is not to mystify the reader. My agent once said to me, "I know you thought no one would 'get' this in your story, but *I* understood what you were up to." I wrote back that if I had thought no one would get it, I wouldn't have put it in there. There's no reason for an author to deliberately make things obscure. What I try to do is show the way things really seem to me—and to find the most appropriate way to tell the particular story I have to tell. I certainly never sit down and say to myself, Gee, I think I'll tell a story in the first person or the third person. Some stories simply seem to need a first-person narrator; others are dream stories; still others require a third-person narrator. What I try to do is find the narrative approach that is most appropriate to the subject matter.

LM: And since a lot of your work seems to deal with the nature of human perception—the difficulties of understanding what's going on around us—a straightforward approach would be inappropriate.

GW: It's the hackneyed notion, "The medium is the message." As I work on a story, the subject matter often seems to become an appropriate means of telling it—the thing bites its tail, in a way—because subject and form aren't reducible to a simple this or that; the two are interacting through the story. That's what I meant when I said I try to show the way things really seem to me. My experience is that subjects and methods are always interacting in our daily lives. That's realism; that's the way things really are. It's the other thing—the matter-of-fact assumption found in most fiction that the author and characters perceive everything around them clearly and objectively—that's unreal. I mean, you sit there and you think you're seeing me and I sit here and I think I'm seeing you, but what we're really reacting to are light patterns that have stimulated certain nerve endings in the retinas of our eyes—light patterns that are reflected from us. It's this peculiar process of interaction between light waves, our retinas, and our brains that I call "seeing you" and you call "seeing me." But change the mechanism in my eyes, change the nature of the light, and "you" and "me" become entirely different as far as we're concerned. You think you're hearing me directly at this moment, but you're actually hearing everything a little bit after I've said it, because it requires a finite but measurable amount of time for my voice to reach you. Fiction that doesn't acknowledge these sorts of interactions simply isn't "realistic" in any sense in which I'd use that term.

   LM: Maybe because of your awareness of the interrelatedness of form and content, you seem to be among a relatively select group of SF authors (Samuel Delany and Ursula Le Guin come to mind) who pay as much attention to the language and other stylistic features of their work as to the plot development or content (in the gross sense). I assume you do a lot of rewriting, but what sorts of things do you focus on when you're making revisions?

   GW: I do a minimum of three "writes" for everything—an original and then at least two rewrites. A lot of stuff goes through four drafts, and some of it goes through fifteen or more drafts; basically, I'm willing to revise until I get it right. And what I focus on in these rewrites varies. It's certainly not all just trying to capture a specific atmosphere or a cultural attitude. I remember I completely rewrote the opening pages of "The Fifth Head of Cerberus" at least eight or ten times because it seemed essential to capture that certain flavor I wanted the story to have, the feeling of stagnation that affects a lot of what follows. I particularly remember struggling with that passage about the vine scrambling up the wall from the court below, nearly covering the window. But since character usually seems to be the single element in my works that I'm most interested in, a lot of the rewriting I do involves fine-tuning character. This is especially true when I'm working on a novel, where character has more time to predominate, rather than in stories, where often the idea or plot twist seems more important. It's always a problem for me when I have a character like Malrubius in the Book of the New Sun novels who shows up in widely separated places—I want to make sure he's the same person on page 300 that he was on page 10. Of course, sometimes I like the man on page 300 better than I did earlier on; then I have to go back and rewrite page 10 to make him match the way he appears later on.

LM: You exhibit not only a near-encyclopedic knowledge of words and their origins but you obviously have a great feel for language and for inventing contexts in which different lingoes can be presented. Yet one theme that recurs in many of your works—and throughout the Book of the New Sun—is the *limitations* of words, the way language distorts perception and is used to manipulate others. Is this a paradox— or an occupational hazard?

GW: Any writer who tries to press against the limits of prose, who tries to write something genuinely different from what's come before, is constantly aware of these paradoxes about language's power and its limitations. Because language is your medium, you become aware of the extent to which language controls and directs your thinking, the extent that you're manipulated by words—and yet the extent to which words necessarily *limit* your attention and hence misrepresent the world around you. In *1984* Orwell dealt with all this much better than I've been able to. He said, in effect: Let me control the language and I will control people's thoughts. Back in the '30s, the Japanese used to have "Thought Police" who would go around and say to people, "What do your think about our expedition to China?" or something like that. And if they didn't like what they heard in response, they'd arrest you. What Orwell was driving at, though, goes beyond that kind of obvious control mechanism. He was implying that if he could control the language, then he could make it so that you couldn't even *think* about anything he didn't want you to think about. My view is that this isn't wholly true. One of the dumber things you occasionally see in the comic books is where, say, Spiderman, as he falls off a building, looks down, sees a flagpole, and says to himself, If I can just grab that flagpole, I'll be OK. Now nobody in those circumstances would actually do that— if you're falling off a building, you don't put that kind of thought into *words,* even though you're somehow consciously aware of needing to grab that flagpole. Rather, you think below the threshold of language, which suggests a preverbal sublevel of thinking that takes place without words. Orwell didn't deal with this sublevel of thinking, but the accuracy of his insights about the way authorities can manipulate people through words is evident in the world around us.

LM: Your works often appear to rely on fantasy forms in order to find a means of dealing with these preverbal aspects of consciousness. For instance, several scenes in the Book of the New Sun series dramatize inner psychological struggles that aren't easily depicted in realistic forms. I'm thinking about, say, Severian's encounter with the Wellesian man-apes in *The Claw of the Conciliator,* or his later confrontation with the Alzabo. These scenes function very much like dreams or fairy tales in which our inner fears or obsessions—those nonrational aspects that seem out of place in the mundane world of most realists—are literalized, turned into psychic dramas.

GW: That's a good way to put it. One of the advantages of fantasy is that I don't have to waste a lot of time creating the kinds of logical or causal justifications required by the conventions of realism. I can have that Alzabo simply come in the front door of the cabin without having to justify his arrival. (Keep in mind that even in a standard SF novel I would have had to do something like have a spaceship land and then have the Alzabo emerge from the ship). That's one of the limitations of forms restricted to descriptions of everyday reality or of events that are scientifically plausible. Of course, I'd argue that while the Alzabo and those other creatures Severian meets may appear to be dreamlike, they very much exist within a continuum of human potential—they're not really fantastic at all but embodiments of things that lie within all of us. And it seems important for people to be able to occasionally confront these things—that's what dreams and fairy tales have always done for us. That Alzabo is a monster, sure, but it's something many people fear a great deal when they work for a major corporation: that they'll be swallowed up, become a cog in the corporation's innards or a voice coming out of its mouth. Its corporate beastliness is also what people don't like to recognize when they look in the mirror. If you're a human being, you probably realize that it's possible for you to degenerate into a beast; and people who *don't* acknowledge this have actually degenerated in a different way, have lost a certain amount of insight. You *can* regress into animality, if that's what you really want to do, by drinking, for example, which helps turn off the higher brain centers. People drink or use drugs to get rid of the *pain* of being human (maybe the pain of consciousness itself), to find ways of going back down the evolutionary ladder. Every once in a while in the *Tarzan* books, Tarzan gets sick of civilization and desperately wants to go back to being an ape. That desire may seem scary to most people, but it's inside all of us.

LM: Who were some of the writers you were reading back in the '50s and '60s who might have influenced the development of your work? I take it they weren't exclusively SF authors.

GW: Reading *anything* exclusively is dumb. Someone asked me once how long I could read SF before I would burn out. I replied that I never burn out on SF because I never read it exclusively. I always mix SF reading with ghost stories and mysteries and straight novels, what have you. At any rate, I recall that when Damon Knight asked me back in the '60s whom I was reading, I wrote back and said, "J. R. Tolkien, G. K. Chesterton, and *Mark's Engineer's Handbook*." Chesterton isn't very popular these days, but in my opinion he was a great writer who will come back into vogue. *The Man Who Was Thursday* is a tremendous novel, and *The Napoleon of Notting Hill* is a wonderful, forgotten fantasy work. I was reading other people in those days as well—Proust, Dickens, Borges, H. G. Wells. Proust, of course, was obsessed with some of the same things I deal with in the Book of the New Sun—memory and the way memory affects us—except that he wrote his remarkable works eighty years earlier.

LM: This issue of memory is central to a lot of your work—*Peace, The Fifth Head of Cerberus,* each book in the Book of the New Sun tetralogy, and a lot of your stories. Why do you return to it so often?

GW: Memory is all we have. The present is a knife's edge, and the future doesn't really exist—that's why SF writers can set all these strange stories there, because it's *no place,* it hasn't yet come into being. So memory's ability to reconnect us with the past, or some version of the past, is all we have. I include racial memory and instinct here ("instinct" is really just a form of racial memory). The baby bird holds onto the branch because of the racial memory of hundreds of generations of birds who have fallen off. Little kids always seem to know there are terrible things out there in the dark that might eat you, and that's undoubtedly because of hundreds and hundreds of little kids who were living in caves when there *were* terrible things lurking out there in the dark. This whole business about memory is very complicated, because we not only remember events but we can also recall earlier memories. I allude to this in the Book of the New Sun when I make the point that Severian not only remembers what's happened but remembers how he *used to remember*—so he can see the difference between the way he used to remember things and the way he remembers them now.

LM: You didn't cite as influences any of SF's New Wave writers who were emerging during the '60s while Michael Moorcock was editing *New Worlds*. Were you aware of those authors?

GW: I was not only aware of what they were doing, I even placed one story in *New Worlds*. What was happening with the New Wave was that a lot of SF authors with literary backgrounds, rather than scientific backgrounds, were applying what they knew in their works in the same way people with engineering and scientific backgrounds—Heinlein, for instance, or Asimov—had applied those backgrounds earlier. This approach didn't work fundamentally; at least it never became popular. As *art* it worked in some cases, while in others it didn't—which is true about everything, I guess.

LM: Why didn't these "literary" approaches catch on with SF audiences?

GW: Probably because a lot of experimentalism was handled in such a way that it alienated readers, many of whom were raised on the pulps and didn't give a damn about "literature" in any kind of elevated sense. I was personally sorry to see it not catch on, since some of what it was trying to do certainly struck a responsive chord in me. When Harlan Ellison put together his *Again, Dangerous Visions,* he included three stories by me, so I was associated with the New Wave. It was a time in which a lot of people were yelling at us for what we were doing, and we were yelling back at them. Actually, at various times I was put into both camps by different people, which was fine with me.

LM: In some ways, the three interlocking novellas of *The Fifth Head of Cerberus* operate like a Faulknerian novel, with each succeeding section revealing aspects of the larger puzzle, which only comes into focus when the book is completed. Did you realize when you started out that you were going to develop this kind of structure?

GW: Not at all. I wrote the title story for Damon Knight's *Orbit,* where it originally appeared. That same year I went to the Milford Conference and presented the story there. Norbert Slepyan of Scribner's was at that meeting and he really liked the story. He said that if I could write two other stories of roughly the same length, he'd publish them as a book. We agreed that I'd write one of the pieces and, if it was good, he'd offer me a contract. So I wrote "A Story by John V. Marsch," and Slepyan was sufficiently impressed that he issued me a contract. At any rate, the specific interrelations that you see were developed as I went along.

LM: The opening sentence of "The Fifth Head of Cerberus" echoes Proust; you set the story in a place called Frenchman's Landing; and you drew various other French elements into the story. What prompted all these references to France?

GW: It had struck me for some time that it's ludicrous to assume, the way practically every SF story does, that people who go to the stars and set up colonies there are necessarily going to be Americans. I saw I could counter this parochial notion by setting my story in a French colony. Frenchman's Landing is actually modeled on New Orleans. Somebody, I think it was John Brunner, did an SF book that opens with the words, "The Captain bore the good terrestrial name of Chang."

When the first space captains go into outer space, there'll be a lot of Changes out there.

LM: Presenting the sections of *Cerberus* out of chronological sequence forces the reader to re-evaluate information received earlier. Did you ever give any thought to rearranging the sections so that they would appear in sequence—that is, with the Sandwalker story first?

GW: No, because I didn't want to show what John Marsch had been researching—the material that makes up his "story" in the second novella—until I had actually introduced John Marsch the researcher in "The Fifth Head." I decided to present the Sandwalker story as a legend, as something Marsch had uncovered, rather than as straight reportage because I wanted to keep all three stories set in roughly the same time frame—the "present" of the opening novella. Since the period in which the Sandwalker scene was—in terms of the "present" found in the rest of the book—taking place in the distant past of the planet, it made more sense to say, "Here's a legend that has survived from that period" rather than simply jump into the past and present it directly. In the last piece, "V.R.T.," I show what had become of the Sandwalker's world (this is only hinted at in "The Fifth Head") and what eventually happened to Marsch.

LM: All this "showing" in "V.R.T." is made intriguingly ambiguous by the confusion about who Marsch really is.

GW: In the end, of course, it's important that the reader *not* be confused about this, although part of the fun is supposed to be figuring out what's happened. I leave a number of clues as to who the narrator actually is. For example, both V.R.T. and the narrator are shown to be very poor shots, whereas Marsch is a very good shot; and there are other hints like that. If you hire a Shapechanger as a guide, there's a definite possibility that he's going to change into *your* shape at some point. Which is what happens.

LM: Is there any consistent pattern to the way your stories or novels tend to get started?

GW: I usually have a bunch of different things knocking around in my head until something jars me into realizing that these things can come together in a story. Typically, I'll read something or see something or dream something and I'll think to myself, Gee, that would be interesting to put into a story. It's usually later on that I think up a character or a person who might fit into the context of that original "something" in an interesting way. Then at some point I recognize I could incorporate *all* this material—I could take *that* woman and *that* ship and *that* situation and put them all together in a story. There's a wonderful "Peanuts" cartoon that pretty much describes what I'm talking about: Snoopy is on top of his doghouse and he writes something like, "A frigate appeared on the edge of the horizon. The King's extravagances were bankrupting the people. A shot rang out. The dulcet voice of a guitar sounded at the window." Then he turns and looks at the reader and says, "In the last chapter I'm going to pull all this together!"

LM: I take it that you've usually pulled things together far enough in advance so that you know, once you actually begin the story, where it's heading?

GW: Absolutely. I wouldn't start a work unless I had at least a vague idea where it was going to end up. Of course, sometimes I have difficulty *getting* to where I'm heading. That's what happened, on a grand scale, when I began work on the Book of the New Sun—I knew roughly where I was going, but as I was trying to get there, I discovered a great deal more between "here" and "there" than I had anticipated.

LM: Where was it that you knew you were heading when you began the series?

GW: I knew I wanted Severian to be banished and then to return to the Guild in a position of such authority that the Guild would be forced to make him a Master. And I wanted to have Severian be forced to confront the problem of Thecla and the problem of torture and the role of human pain and misery. At that time I had not yet read *The Magus,* so the thought didn't come from there, but I was very conscious of the horror, not only of being tortured, but of being forced to *be* a torturer or executioner. I didn't want the reader to be able to dismiss violence and pain with platitudes. It's very easy to say how terrible it is to beat someone with a whip or lock someone up for thirty years or execute someone. These are indeed awful things. But when you are actually in authority, you find out that sometimes it's absolutely necessary for you to take certain distasteful actions.

LM: Severian makes the point somewhere that if he didn't execute some of these people, they would be out killing people themselves.

GW: And he's right. What are you going to do with someone like John Wayne Gacy—who used to live about eight miles from where we're sitting right now—if you're not willing to lock him up for the rest of his life? If you let him out, he's almost certain to start killing more innocent people. I wanted Severian to have to face at least the possibility that being an agency of pain and death is not necessarily an evil thing. That's one recognition he must come to grips with when he decides to leave a knife in Thecla's cell to help her commit suicide. He's partially responsible for the blood he sees seeping from under her cell door, just as every member of a society is responsible for the blood shed by people it decides to execute. Of course, when Severian later receives a letter from Thecla telling him the suicide was a trick that permitted her to be freed unobtrusively, that creates all sorts of other dilemmas for him—and for me as well. I had started out assuming I was writing a novella of about 40,000 words whose title was to have been "The Feast of Saint Catherine," but now I began to see this material had greater possibilities. The writer has a problem when ideas, characters, and so forth don't seem to come, or when they aren't good enough when they do come. But when they're too good and too numerous, that's another problem. By the time I finished *The Shadow of the Torturer,* I had completed an entire novel—but Severian was hardly started. Instead of winding up the plot, I had begun half a dozen others that needed to be worked out. Eventually, I decided I needed to write a trilogy to be able to develop everything sufficiently, and when the third book turned out to be almost twice as long as the first two combined, I finally expanded things into a tetralogy. When I was done I discovered that I had arrived at the place I had set out for—but the trip to that place was very different from what I had expected.

LM: What gave you the initial impulse to make Severian a torturer? Was it that abstract notion of wanting your hero to deal with the nature of pain and suffering?

GW: No, the possibility of having a character who was a torturer was one of those initial ideas that wasn't tied to anything for a while. It first came to me during some convention I was attending at which Bob Tucker was the guest of honor. For some reason Bob felt obliged to go to a panel discussion in costume, and since he wanted someone to accompany him, I went along. So I went and heard Sandra Miesel and several other people talk about how you do costumes—how you might do a cloak, whether or not it's good to use fire as part of your costume, and so forth. As I sat there being instructed, I was sulking because no one had ever done one of my characters at a masquerade. It seemed as though I had done a lot of things that people could do at a masquerade. But when I started to think this over more carefully, I realized there were few, if any, characters who would fit in with what Sandra and the others were saying. That led me to think about a character who *would* fit—someone who would wear simple but dramatic clothes. And the very first thing that came to mind was a torturer: bare chest (everybody has a chest; all you have to do is take your shirt off), black trousers, black boots (you can get those anywhere), black cloak, a mask, and a sword! Here was an ideal, easy SF masquerade citizen. All this stuck in my head somehow: I had this dark man, the personification of pain and death, but I didn't yet know what to do with him. Gradually, a lot of things began to come together. For instance, I read a book about body-snatchers that captured my fancy (body-snatchers were the people who used to dig up corpses and sell them to medical schools for the students to dissect). And I also had in mind that it would be interesting to be able to show a young man approaching war. So I began to put things together: I could have my young man witness the body-snatching scene that I was now itching to write; this same young man could be the guy who is pulled into the war; he could be a torturer, and so on.

LM: It was a bold stroke to make your hero into a man who's both a professional torturer and yet possessed of the capacity for passion, for love and tenderness. That reinforces your point about the multiplicity of selves existing within us all.

GW: And I was particularly interested in the way that multiplicity points out the potential within everyone for good and evil. Whether we like it or not, that potential is part of what makes us people. We tend to look at somebody like the death camp guards in Nazi Germany and thank God we're not like that. But those guards weren't "fiends," they were human beings who were pulled into a certain game whose rules said it was OK to be a death camp guard in Nazi Germany. Later on, we came along and changed the rules on them. It was important for me to be able to show the way evil expresses itself in people, because I think it's essential that we recognize the existence of this potential within us all. It's the only way we can safeguard ourselves from this sort of thing. If you're watching a man on his way to the scaffold and you can't realize "This could be me," then you've got no right to hang him. I dealt with a similar idea in "The Island of Dr. Death," where at the end of the story Dr. Death tells Tackie that if he starts the book again, "We'll all be back." If you don't have Dr. Death, then you can't have Captain Ransom. You can't have a knight unless you have the dragon, a positive charge without a negative charge.

LM: Once the scope of the Book of the New Sun became obvious, you must have developed some kind of detailed outline.

GW: Actually, I never use an outline when I work. Even with something like that, where there's an elaborate structure, the outline exists only in my head, not on paper. The only exception was with a book I did a while back called *Free Live Free* in which a lot of the action takes place in an old brick house on a city street. For that book I had to draw a floor plan of the house because otherwise I found myself getting tangled up in details. Could you see the street from this window? Could you see from this room to that room? When Ben Free is in his room, can he hear someone walking overhead in another room? I had to figure out where the bedrooms and bathrooms and stairs all were. But, of course, a floor plan isn't really an outline.

LM: In a sense, all four volumes in the Book of the New Sun form a single novel, just as the individual books that comprise Proust's *Re-*

membrance of Things Past form a single work. As you were working on the volumes individually, were you aiming at different formal effects that would be more appropriate to what you were talking about?

GW: I saw everything falling into four distinct segments: a presentation of Nessus, getting from Nessus to Thrax, Thrax, and the war. And despite some slopover, you'll find that I pretty much focus from book to book on those areas, each of which required me to develop a *way* of storytelling that would be appropriate for my focus. For instance, when I finished *The Shadow*—and keep in mind that I didn't have a final draft of the first volume until I had all four volumes in second draft—I was very conscious that in *The Claw* I was going to get outside of Nessus and show the atmosphere and surroundings of that world. In order to do that, I needed to show cultural elements of this world that would allow the reader to understand it: What kinds of clothes did people wear? What kinds of stories did they tell? What jokes did they make? That sort of thing. That required a slightly different approach and maybe gives the book a different texture from the others.

LM: I was constantly struck in all four volumes by the richness and variety of textural detail—not just physical details but meticulous attention to a wide range of cultural, anthropological, and linguistic elements.

GW: From the very outset, one of the things I had in mind was to show a vast civilization that I could make plausibly complex. I've always been irritated (and usually bored) by the Simple Simon civilizations presented in most SF novels—the galactic empire spread over umpteen light years that has a culture that's as uniform as, say, Milwaukee. Except for instances in which a culture's livable area is small—essentially one island, or something equally isolated—and those in which there's a small population possessing a high technology, this assumption of a uniform culture covering an entire world is simply incredible.

LM: You mentioned earlier that one of the first ideas you had for the Book of the New Sun was to present a young man approaching a war. Did your own experiences in Korea serve as inspiration for this?

GW: Very much so. I had gone through that rite of passage in which war at first seems impossibly remote and then you find yourself gradually pulled into the actual fighting. At the time I was drafted, I didn't think I would ever end up fighting, maybe partly because the war seemed so distant. Oh, my father was worried and wanted me to join the air force or something, but enlistment meant a six-year commitment, whereas the draft was only two years, which seemed a lot more attractive. Keep in mind that the Korean War was much more remote to the American people at the time than the Vietnam War was to the next generation. We didn't have the live TV coverage and the media barrage. Anyway,

I can vividly recall watching myself being slowly sucked into this vortex. I rode a train all day and all night up to the front lines, which gave me a lot of time to think about what was happening, and when I stepped off the train I could hear guns firing in the distance. At that moment it came to me: My God, I didn't miss it! Here it is! Here I am! You can find a similar progression in *The Red Badge of Courage,* but I wanted to develop mine within an SF setting.

LM: Despite the setting, while reading your battle scenes I was often reminded of the Civil War or World War I. Did you research these scenes?

GW: I didn't research anything specifically for them, but they probably came out of a lot of reading I've done about the Napoleonic wars, the Civil War, the two world wars, and so on. In presenting the war itself, I was trying to guess what war might be like for a decadent society in which there was still some high technology, though most of it was unavailable. Around 1960, you know, there was a civil war being fought in what used to be the Belgian Congo, in which tribesmen with spears were led into battle by European officers with submachine guns, supported by jet planes. I wanted to show what that kind of war might be like, so I had some people ride animals while others used laser cannons and assorted advanced weaponry.

LM: Did your war experiences have a permanent effect on your sensibility, as was the case for writers like Norman Mailer, Ernest Hemingway, and Kurt Vonnegut?

GW: I'm sure they did, but it's difficult to say exactly how. I only caught about the last four months of the war — I was there for the ceasefire and for quite some time afterward — but I saw enough action to realize what it was like. I got shot at a few times, shot at a few people, was shelled. You don't go through those experiences without gaining a different outlook on life. Just before you arrived this morning, I was talking on the phone with Harlan Ellison about a recent incident in which he wound up decking Charles Platt, and he mentioned how many of his friends had censured him for his violent reaction. Well, it would never occur to me to rebuke Harlan because I accept that if you're not violent at certain times you're going to wind up being the victim of violence. The fact that you stand there and let someone hit you in the face doesn't do anything to eliminate violence and may even contribute to further violence — which is one of the underlying themes in the Book of the New Sun.

LM: What kind of research was involved in the tetralogy?

GW: The main research was on Byzantium and the Byzantine Empire, which was a stagnant political entity that had outlived its time in much the same way that the Urth of the Commonwealth had. One of the things that bothered me about the reviews of the Book of the New Sun novels was how often my world was compared with that of medieval Europe. Insofar as I was trying to create any parallels with an actual historical period here on Earth—and obviously I wasn't aiming at developing an exact analogy—I was thinking of Byzantium. Incidentally, I also got into trouble with some reviewers over my presentation of the Ascians, who were my equivalent of the Turks. If you read the book carefully, it's clear that the action takes place in South America and that the invading Ascians are actually North Americans. What I didn't anticipate was that nine-tenths of the readers and reviewers would look at the word "Ascian" and say, "Oh, these guys are Asians!" I was accused of being anti-Asian, a racist—which I'm not. Actually, the word "ascian" literally means "people without shadows"; it was used in the classical world for people who lived near the equator, where the sun is dead overhead at noon and thus produces no shadow. I felt it would be an interesting touch to show that the ordinary men and women in the southern hemisphere weren't even conscious that their attackers would come from the northern hemisphere—in fact, they weren't even aware that there was another hemisphere.

LM: That kind of suggestive use for archaic or unfamiliar words is evident throughout the tetralogy, and I'm sure a lot of readers had the same mistaken impression I did that you were making up these wondrous, bizarre words—especially since the use of neologisms is so common in SF. Why did you choose to use mainly real words rather than inventing your own?

GW: I should clarify the fact that *all* the words in the Book of the New Sun are real (except for a couple of typographical errors). As you know, in most SF about unknown planets the author is forced to invent wonders and then to name them. But that didn't seem appropriate to what I was doing here. It occurred to me when I was starting out that Urth already had enough wonders—if only because it had inherited the wonders of Earth (or the alternate possibility that Earth's wonders had descended from Urth). Some SF fans, who seem to be able to tolerate any amount of gibberish so long as it's invented gibberish, have found it peculiar that I would bother relying on perfectly legitimate words. My sense was that when you want to know where you're going, it helps to know where you've been and how fast you've traveled. And a great deal of this knowledge can be intuited if you know something about the words people use. I'm not a philologist, but one thing I'm certain of is that you could write an entire book on almost any word in the English language. At any rate, anyone who bothers to go to a dictionary will find I'm not inventing anything: a "fulgurator" is a holy man capable of drawing omens from flashes of lightning; an "eidolon" is an apparition or phantom; "fuliginous" literally means soot-colored (a complete black without gloss), and so on. I also gave the people and other beings in the book real names, with the exception of the Ascian who appears in *The Citadel*—Loyal to the Group of Seventeen. Severian, Vodalus, and Agilus, for example, are all ordinary, if now uncommon, names for men. And if you'd like to call your daughter Valeria, Thecla, or Dorcas, she'll be receiving a genuine name many women in the past have had (and some in the present). As for the monsters' names, I simply named them for monsters. The original Erebus was the son of Chaos—he was the god of darkness and the husband of Nox, the goddess of night; furthermore, Mount Erebus is in Antarctica, the seat of Erebus's dark and chilly power.

LM: I noticed that you gave one of your creatures, Baldanders, a name used by Borges.

GW: Yes, I took the name of the giant who is still growing from *The Book of Imaginary Beings,* which may not be Borges's best work but which I felt free to steal from disgracefully because even second-rate Borges is very good indeed. Borges is capable of making up much better books and monsters and authors than anyone can find in libraries.

LM: Did you find working on your non-SF novel *Peace* to be different in any fundamental sense from your other works?

GW: Not at all, perhaps because the subjective nature of the book gave me so much freedom. It was the book I wrote after *The Fifth Head of Cerberus,* and there was enough continuity—*Peace* is also about memory and the meaning of stories, about "story" as a thing— that it seemed like the obvious next book for me to write. It remains my favorite of all the novels I've written.

LM: On what basis?

GW: By asking myself how close the book came to being what I wanted it to be when I started it, how close I came to my own goals, which have naturally been different in each case. You never reach those goals 100 percent, but some books wind up being closer to your ideal than others. So far, *Peace* is that book for me.

LM: Was *Peace*'s main character, Dennis Weer, someone you personally identified with?

GW: I identify with all my main characters, but certainly Weer is very much modeled on me, with his engineering and food industry background, his introversion, his sense of isolation. The house on the hill is basically modeled on my mother's father's house, which I visited when I was a child. My grandfather was an absolutely incredible man who made a tremendous impression on me—he was a Scottish seaman as a kid, jumped ship in Texas, fought Mexican bandits as a U.S. cavalryman in the 1880s, became a circus performer, and wound up as an old man with a wooden leg, a pit bull, and a lot of corn whiskey which he'd drink out of a jug. The grandfather in *Peace* who lights the candles on the Christmas tree is pretty much based on him, while the town in the novel is largely a fictive representation of Logan, Ohio, where my father was raised. So there's a lot more direct autobiographical material I'm drawing on here than in my other books.

LM: The Book of the New Sun, maybe especially *The Citadel of the Autarch,* deals with the nature of death and the afterlife, the role of human beings in the scheme of the cosmos, all sorts of grand issues. Are the basic insights Severian eventually achieves essentially those that you personally share?

GW: They're very close indeed, which is why *The Citadel* is my favorite of the four books. I tried to prepare the reader for some of these insights by earlier placing Severian within that immense backdrop of war. Severian is a soldier; and like any soldier in any war, he sees parts of the battlefield he's in as vitally important, essential, whereas he's really just a very small part of a very large picture. Having established Severian's relationship to the larger picture, in the latter part of the book I wanted to say, "Look, this is just a small backwater planet — one of many planets — and this isn't even a particularly interesting or pivotal period in its history. The solar system to which this planet belongs is part of a galaxy similar to quite a number of other spiral galaxies. And all this exists in a universe that is just one of a whole series of recurring universes. What any individual human being sees, no matter how broad the vista, is just a tiny corner of what's happening in creation."

There's a scene in C. S. Lewis's *Great Divorce* that made a lasting impression on me. The book is about a one-day bus excursion for people who are in Hell and want to visit Heaven to see what's there. Toward the end, everyone is saying, "Wow, everything here is so beautiful, look at these gorgeous trees and waterfalls and animals! But where is the infernal city we just left?" At this point the angel who's leading them around says, "It's right there in that crack between those two rocks — *that's* the infernal city you've come out of." At the end of *The Citadel,* I wanted my readers to experience a similar shock of recognition at their own insignificance.

LM: The outlook expressed at the conclusion seems fundamentally religious in orientation.

GW: I don't scoff at religion the way many people do when they look at anything that has to do with speculations about things we can't touch. I'm a practicing Catholic, although I don't think that designation would give people much of an idea about what my beliefs are. People tend to have a very limited, stereotyped view of what it means to be a

Catholic, images taken from movies or anti-Catholic pamphlets, but there's much more to it than that. I know perfectly well, for example, that priests can't walk on water, that they are merely human beings who are trying, often unsuccessfully, to live out a very difficult ideal. But I certainly don't dismiss religious or other mystical forms of speculation out of hand. I read it and try to make my own judgments about it. And in the Book of the New Sun, I tried to work out some of the implications of my own beliefs.

LM: Who are some of the contemporary writers you most admire?

GW: Among SF writers I'd include Algis Budrys, Joanna Russ, Ursula Le Guin, Damon Knight, Kate Wilhelm, Michael Bishop, Brian Aldiss, Nancy Kress, Michael Moorcock. And Theodore Sturgeon, Clark Ashton Smith, and Frederick Brown, who are dead now but not forgotten. One other SF writer I greatly admire is R. A. Lafferty, who writes very strange stuff that's hard to describe (the St. Brendan's story in *Peace* is my version of a Lafferty story); he's an old man who's developed a cult following, a much-neglected figure I think. Among the non-SF writers I most enjoy are Nabokov (*Pale Fire* is a truly amazing book) and Borges. Robert Coover's *Universal Baseball Association* is one of my favorite novels, and I love *The Tar Baby* by Jerome Charyn, a writer I know nothing else about. Of course, there are a great many earlier writers I'm fond of: Proust, Dickens, E. M. Forster (whom I'm just now reading), Chesterton, George MacDonald, Poe, Lovecraft (who is usually regarded as an SF writer, but to me he's the real successor—if that's possible—to Poe's line of horror). I've read a lot of Arthur Conan Doyle, and I grew up with Kipling, which is one reason I used his lines from "The Dawn Wind" as an epigraph to *The Citadel of the Autarch*.

LM: You grew up in an age that has seen the development of nuclear weapons and the landing of men on the moon. The use of science and technology seems to be leading us to two different futures, one unimaginably awful, the other filled with marvels and wonder. Which path do you think we'll take?

GW: Actually, there are more than two paths. I feel both optimistic and pessimistic about what we've been doing with technology. As you say, it has already been used to produce both wonderful and terrible things. The greatest ecological disaster to yet hit this planet has come from technology—the invention of plastics. (If I could go back into the past and repeal a single discovery it would be the discovery of plastics.) On the other hand, we're getting into space now and doing some amazing things with the life sciences, including cybernetics and robot development. Technology is like a punch or a gun: it's good or bad depending on what you *do* with it. The world is full of people who assume you can get rid of evil if you can just get rid of the punch or the gun.

LM: But if that gun is firing nuclear weapons or that punch in the jaw is going to destroy an entire nation . . .

GW: I don't believe we're heading for a nuclear holocaust. (If I did, I wouldn't be living this close to Chicago!) Using nuclear weapons is too clearly a no-win situation for both sides, so I don't think they'll be used in a war, at least not under the present circumstances. War usually starts when one side feels it can achieve a quick, clear-cut victory— Iraq invading Iran is a classic example of this, because Iraq thought it could simply march in and win an immediate victory. And Hitler had sold himself so completely on the idea that the Germans were strong and pure, while the rest of the world was weak and degenerate, that he was able to convince himself and a great many other people that Germany could achieve an easy victory in Europe. It's difficult for me to see how people in Russia or the United States could convince themselves they could use nuclear weapons to achieve that kind of easy victory. Of course, there's another scenario that's much more dangerous—the one where one side feels pushed against a wall and decides it must fight now or eventually be destroyed.

LM: Even assuming there is no nuclear holocaust, it seems essential for people to do some basic rethinking about the management of our resources; otherwise, the issue of how technology is going to evolve will simply become moot. Once we exhaust our resources, we'll be left in the kind of world you describe in the Book of the New Sun.

GW: That possibility was very much on my mind when I was creating the Urth. I was trying to come to grips with the end result of the do-nothing attitude so many people have about the future. They seem to feel that space exploration is a lot of bullshit ("There's nothing really out there we can use"), that undersea exploration is a lot of bullshit ("There's nothing down there for us"), that we should just go about our business the way we are and be "sensible." But what's going to happen if we keep on being "sensible" in the way they're suggesting, if we keep clinging to Earth, waiting for the money and the resources to run out? The Urth I invented is the world that follows that course, the world in which people are so limited in their vision of the future that they see no other option except what is immediately in front of them. They're practical and down-to-earth; they go on planting their cabbages. Well, there's nothing wrong with planting those cabbages, God knows, but when you ignore any possibilities *except* those cabbages, you wind up living in a world something like Urth, with its exhausted mines and exhausted farmlands. There may be a long period of relative peace and stability, but it's also a period of slow decay. I keep tropical fish, and I remember a fad among fish owners about trying to keep a perfectly balanced environment in the tanks—seal everything up to see how long it would take the fish to die. Sometimes it would take eighteen months or more, but eventually the last fish died and you were left with a tank full of scummy green water. That's what the Urth of the Commonwealth has become—and what we're headed for unless we look to the future more adventurously—a tank full of scummy water.

Index